OVID, *AMORES* (BOOK I)

Ovid, *Amores* (Book I)

William Turpin

*With contributions by Bart Huelsenbeck, Bret Mulligan,
Christopher Francese, and JoAnne Miller*

http://www.openbookpublishers.com

© 2016 William Turpin

The Manuscript Tradition of Ovid's *Amores* © 2016 Bart Huelsenbeck

This work is licensed under a Creative Commons Attribution 4.0 International license (CC BY 4.0). This license allows you to share, copy, distribute and transmit the text; to adapt the text and to make commercial use of the text providing attribution is made to the author (but not in any way that suggests that he endorses you or your use of the work). Attribution should include the following information:

Turpin, William, *Ovid, Amores (Book I)*. Cambridge, UK: Open Book Publishers, 2016. http://dx.doi.org/10.11647/OBP.0067

Further details about CC BY licenses are available at http://creativecommons.org/licenses/by/4.0

Recordings made for this volume by Aleksandra Szypowska, CC BY 4.0.

Please see the captions for attribution relating to individual images. For information about the rights of the Wikimedia Commons images, please refer to the Wikimedia website. Every effort has been made to identify and contact copyright holders and any omission or error will be corrected if notification is made to the publisher.

In order to access detailed and updated information on the license, please visit http://www.openbookpublishers.com/isbn/9781783741625#copyright

All external links were active on 4 May 2016 and have been archived via the Internet Archive Wayback Machine at https://archive.org/web

Updated digital material and resources associated with this volume are available at http://www.openbookpublishers.com/isbn/9781783741625#resources. Turpin's commentary is also available online at http://dcc.dickinson.edu/ovid-amores/preface

This is the second volume of our Dickinson College commentaries series:

ISSN (Print): 2059-5743
ISSN (Online): 2059-5751

ISBN Paperback: 978-1-78374-162-5
ISBN Hardback: 978-1-78374-163-2
ISBN Digital (PDF): 978-1-78374-164-9
ISBN Digital ebook (epub): 978-1-78374-165-6
ISBN Digital ebook (mobi): 978-1-78374-166-3
DOI: 10.11647/OBP.0067

Cover image: Sleeping Cupid, Royal Ontario Museum. Image from Wikimedia, https://commons.wikimedia.org/wiki/File:Sleeping_Cupid_-_Royal_Ontario_Museum_-_DSC09788.JPG

All paper used by Open Book Publishers is SFI (Sustainable Forestry Initiative), PEFC (Programme for the Endorsement of Forest Certification Schemes) and Forest Stewardship Council(r)(FSC(r) certified.

Printed in the United Kingdom, United States, and Australia
by Lightning Source for Open Book Publishers (Cambridge, UK).

Contents

Preface	ix
Abbreviations	x
1. The Life of Ovid	1
2. The *Amores*	3
3. The Manuscript Tradition of Ovid's *Amores*	7
by Bart Huelsenbeck, with the assistance of Dan Plekhov	
4. Select Bibliography	11
5. Scansion	13
Prosody	13
Elision	14
The elegiac couplet	15
Reading aloud	16
6. Epigram: preface from the author	19
Notes on the Epigram	19
7. *Amores* 1.1: Ovid finds his muse	21
Suggested reading	23
Amores 1.1	24
Notes	25
8. *Amores* 1.2: Conquered by Cupid	31
Suggested reading	34
Amores 1.2	35
Notes	37

9.	*Amores* 1.3: Just give me a chance	43
	Suggested reading	44
	Amores 1.3	45
	Notes	46
10.	*Amores* 1.4: Secret signs	49
	Appendix: the *vir*	52
	Suggested reading	53
	Amores 1.4	54
	Notes	56
11.	*Amores* 1.5: The siesta	63
	Suggested reading	65
	Amores 1.5	66
	Notes	67
12.	*Amores* 1.6: On the doorstep	71
	Suggested reading	74
	Amores 1.6	75
	Notes	78
13.	*Amores* 1.7: Violence and love	85
	Suggested reading	87
	Amores 1.7	88
	Notes	90
14.	*Amores* 1.8: The bad influence	99
	Suggested reading	103
	Amores 1.8	104
	Notes	108
15.	*Amores* 1.9: Love and war	121
	Suggested reading	123
	Amores 1.9	124
	Notes	126
16.	*Amores* 1.10: Love for sale	131
	Suggested reading	134
	Amores 1.10	135
	Notes	137

17. *Amores* 1.11: Sending a message	145
Suggested reading	147
Amores 1.11	148
Notes	149
18. *Amores* 1.12: Shooting messengers	153
Amores 1.12	155
Notes	156
19. *Amores* 1.13: Oh how I hate to get up in the morning	159
Suggested reading	160
Amores 1.13	161
Notes	163
20. *Amores* 1.14: Bad hair	171
Suggested reading	172
Amores 1.14	173
Notes	175
21. *Amores* 1.15: Poetic immortality	183
Suggested reading	185
Amores 1.15	186
Notes	187
Full vocabulary for Ovid's *Amores*, Book 1	193

Preface

This book contains a Latin text, recordings, notes, images, and vocabulary for Book I of Ovid's *Amores*. Much of the material published in this edition stems from the online critical apparatus prepared for the Dickinson College Commentaries and freely available online at http://dcc.dickinson.edu. I am the author of the notes, introductory matter, and essays on each poem. Bart Huelsenbeck, Postdoctoral Fellow in Digital Classics at Dickinson, contributed the essay on the manuscript tradition of Ovid's *Amores*. The vocabulary was prepared by Bret Mulligan, Associate Professor of Classics at Haverford College. Content for the original website on which this book is based was edited by Christopher Francese, Bart Huelsenbeck, and JoAnne Miller.

The notes owe a great deal to the editions of John Barsby, J. C. McKeown, and Maureen Ryan and Caroline Perkins; they have been improved by the comments of Robert Sklenar, Christopher Francese, and Rosaria Munson, who used earlier drafts in their classes. I am especially grateful to Nandini Pandey, Talitha Kearey, and Jen Faulkner, who all read the entire manuscript and have made valuable suggestions and corrections.

Note that vocabulary for each poem may be studied in the lists provided on the Dickinson College Commentaries website, divided into "core" and "non-core" words. The same lists can also be studied on "Brainscape," a free flashcard program that runs on all computers and on IOS portable devices; see https://www.brainscape.com/packs/6178202/invitation?referrer=61746

The Latin text is close to that of Kenney, E. J. *Ovidi Nasonis: Amores, Medicamina Faciei Femineae, Ars Amatoria, Remedia Amoris* (Oxford Classical Text, revised edn: Oxford: Oxford University Press, 1994). Further information on the grammatical concepts covered is provided throughout the text via links to the relevant sections from a revised and corrected version of *Allen and Greenough's New Latin Grammar*. Historical maps for the locations Ovid mentions are drawn from the Pleiades website. The excellent recordings of the Latin text are by Aleksandra Szypowska.

Abbreviations

AG *Allen and Greenough's New Latin Grammar for Schools and Colleges*, eds. J.B. Greenough, G.L. Kitteredge, A.A. Howard, and Benjamin L. D'Ooge. Boston: Ginn & Company, 1903, rpt. New Rochelle, 1983 (cited in text).

OLD *Oxford Latin Dictionary*, ed. P. G. W. Glare, Oxford: Oxford University Press, 1982.

sc. scilicet (literally "no doubt"), i.e. "understand."

† indicates corruption in the text for which the editor can see no convincing solution.

1. The life of Ovid

Publius Ovidius Naso was born in 43 BC, in Sulmo (modern Sulmona), in the rugged mountains of the Abruzzi about a hundred miles from Rome. His family, which must have been locally prominent and relatively wealthy, were Roman citizens of equestrian rank and seem to have intended Ovid for a political career in Rome. Ovid was a conspicuous success as a student of rhetoric at Rome, went on a tour of Greece, and held at least one minor magistracy in Rome before turning to poetry as a full-time occupation. He married at least three times, and had a daughter and two grandchildren.

Fig. 1 Statue of Ovid, in Constanta, Romania (ancient Tomis). Wikimedia, https://commons.wikimedia.org/wiki/File:Statue_of_Roman_poet_Ovid_in_Constanța,_Romania.jpg

© William Turpin, CC BY   http://dx.doi.org/10.11647/OBP.0067.01

In AD 8 he was banished by Augustus to the remote Greek city of Tomis (modern Constanta), on the Black Sea coast in what is now Romania. According to Ovid there were two reasons for his exile: his *Ars Amatoria* had given offense, and he had committed a mysterious error, perhaps connected with the imperial house (Augustus' granddaughter Julia was exiled for adultery in the same year). Despite much pleading Ovid was never allowed to return from Tomis, and died there in (probably) AD 17.

Ovid apparently began writing his *Amores* in 26 or 25 BC; he tells us that he wrote poems about the lover he calls Corinna as a young man of 17 or 18. These poems were originally published in five books, but were subsequently republished in the edition we now have, in three books, sometime after 16 BC. His other early works, all largely concerned with love affairs and/or women, are difficult to date precisely, and no doubt overlapped with the writing of the *Amores*: the *Heroides* is a collection of letters written by fictional heroines; the fragmentary *Medicamina Faciei Femineae* concerns female cosmetics; the *Ars Amatoria* is a didactic poem about how to conduct love affairs, and the *Remedia Amoris* is about how to end them.

Ovid's greatest work is the *Metamorphoses*, an epic poem on mythological transformations. He also wrote the *Fasti*, concerned with the religious calendar, and the *Ibis*, an invective against an unnamed enemy. During his years of exile he wrote the *Tristia* and *Epistulae ex Ponto*. Two lost works are a drama, the *Medea*, and a translation of Aratus' astronomical poem, the *Phaenomena*. All his surviving works except the *Metamorphoses* are in elegiac couplets.

2. The *Amores*

In writing poems in elegiac couplets about a love affair (or affairs) Ovid was firmly within an established tradition. The elegiac couplet (on which see the next section) was originally used, first by the Greeks and then by the Romans, for short epigrams, often on erotic subjects. Catullus (c. 84 to 54 BC), wrote not only epigrams, but longer poems in elegiac couplets; he also gave to many of his poems a unifying story, about a difficult love affair with the woman he called Lesbia.

He was followed by C. Cornelius Gallus (c. 70 to 27 or 26 BC), who seems to have written four books of love poetry exclusively in elegiac couplets, probably called *Amores*. Almost none of Gallus' verses survive, but they depicted his affair with a famous actress of the day named Cytheris, whom he calls Lycoris. Gallus seems to have done much to establish the conventional figure of the poet as the broken-hearted lover; the allusions in Vergil's *Eclogue* 10 suggest that in one poem he portrayed himself wandering in the woods and carving his and Lycoris' names onto tree-trunks.

Perhaps the most important of Ovid's immediate predecessors was Sextus Propertius (born between 54 and 47 BC; died before 2 AD). Propertius published four books of elegies, the first appearing around 28 BC, a few years before Ovid's first poems in the genre. Like his older contemporaries Vergil (born 70 BC) and Horace (born 65 BC), Propertius came to be a member of the circle of Maecenas, the political advisor of Augustus, but at least in his first three books he rebelled against Augustan values more than Vergil and Horace ever did. Most of Propertius' poems concern a romantic affair with a woman he calls Cynthia, and in many of them the poet is portrayed as desperately, even morbidly, uncertain of her affections. Propertius wrote with self-conscious artifice (he claimed to be a Roman Callimachus), deploying mythological examples that are often obscure.

A near contemporary of Propertius was Albius Tibullus (born between 55 and 48 BC; died in 19 BC), who wrote two books of elegies, the first at about the time of Ovid's first *Amores*. Tibullus wrote poems concerning three different love affairs, with women he calls Delia and Nemesis and with a young man he calls Marathus. Tibullus' poems are much less mythological than those of Propertius, and the emotions he depicts are much less tortured. A second poet associated with Tibullus was Sulpicia, the niece of Messalla Corvinus. Six of her elegies are preserved in the third book of the Tibullan corpus, and describe (without many details) an affair with a man she calls Cerinthus.

Ultimately, perhaps, evaluating Ovid's *Amores* requires a first-hand knowledge of the tradition in which he was working; it is a truism of Latin scholarship that Ovid plays with, even mocks, the conventions of his predecessors. But for practical reasons the *Amores* make a good introduction to the genre; Ovid's Latin is relatively straightforward, at least compared to that of Propertius, and he offers a livelier account of the traditional Latin elegist's difficult love-life than either Tibullus or Sulpicia. The figure of the poet-lover that Ovid presents in the *Amores* is also a new departure in the western literary tradition, worth attention in its own right: we get our first hapless, light-hearted, insensitive, and selfish womanizer.

The reader approaching the *Amores* for the first time should be alert to at least three features of the poetry. Most important, though most elusive, is the question of tone, though it is not easy to develop a sense for the essential flavor of the Latin poetic idiom. We are so accustomed to high-flown language and ponderous allusions in our Latin that it is not easy to see when a poet is playing with the traditional language and mythology, but Ovid is (in my view) the best place to start: when he writes of abandoning the epic tradition (1.1), of the lover as a warrior (1.9), or the myth of Aurora and Tithonus (1.13), we get a clear sense of the playfulness possible in Latin poetry.

The second thing to be aware of in each poem is the structure of the "argument." Ovid has traditionally been regarded as someone who wrote verse with such facility that he simply kept on going, making the same point over and over again with a kind of effusiveness that belies close analysis. But while it is certainly true that he does not write with the fanatical self-control of Vergil or Horace, it is also a mistake to ignore his careful attention to the construction of his poems. It is important to be aware of the way each poem develops: some thoughts lead naturally to others, and at some places the poet jumps to a new idea, but there is always a reasonable representation of coherent thinking. Moreover it is usually worth asking oneself how (or whether) the final couplet works as a satisfactory conclusion to each poem; there is often (perhaps always) a kind of punch-line at the end, and getting the point there is often the key to getting the poem as a whole.

Finally, it is worth remembering that poetry books in Ovid's day were published with careful attention to their overall shape. Each poem was meant to be read, at least in part, as an element in the broader narrative of the poetry book, so it can be illuminating to ask how each poem relates to the ones preceding it, and serves as an introduction to the ones that follow.

3. The manuscript tradition of Ovid's *Amores*

Bart Huelsenbeck, with the assistance of Dan Plekhov

R Paris, BnF lat. 7311. 9th century. (*Ars amatoria*; *Remedia amoris*; *Amores Epigr.*, 1.1.3–1.2.19, 1.2.25–50).[1]

P Paris, BnF lat. 8242. 9th century. (*Heroides* [incomplete], *Amores* 1.2.51–3.12.26, 3.14.3–3.15.8).[2]

S St. Gall, Stiftsbibliothek 864. 11th century (*Amores Epigr.* 1.6.45, 1.8.75–3.9.10).[3]

Y Berlin, Staatsbibliothek, Hamilton 471. 11th century (*Ars amatoria, Remedia amoris, Amores*).[4]

The manuscript witnesses to the *Amores* fall into two groups: the four earlier manuscripts (*vetustiores*) listed above, and an abundance of later manuscripts, referred to collectively as *recentiores* and dating to the 12th century and after. Franco Munari (1951) and E. J. Kenney (1961), who produced the first modern critical editions of the *Amores*, regarded these two groups of manuscripts (older and more recent) as representative of two independent lines of transmission. The dates of the manuscripts seemed to correspond closely with two separate pedigrees: the *vetustiores* were traced back to a now lost hyparchetype, called α, and the *recentiores* to a second lost hyparchetype, called β. (The independence of the β manuscripts is guaranteed by the presence of verses [1.13.11–14; 2.2.18–22, 25–27] that are absent from α manuscripts.)

---

1 See http://dcc.dickinson.edu/sites/all/files/Paris7311_0.jpg
2 See http://dcc.dickinson.edu/sites/all/files/Paris-8242-fols77v-78r.jpg
3 See http://dcc.dickinson.edu/sites/all/files/StGall-Stiftsbibliothek-864-p383.jpg
4 See http://dcc.dickinson.edu/sites/all/files/Berlin-Staatsbibliothek-Hamilton471.jpg

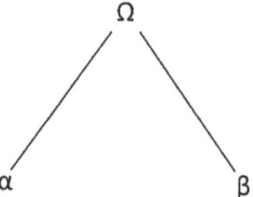

This view of the data, current at the time of the first edition of Kenney's Oxford Classical Text (1961), kept the textual transmission of the *Amores* relatively simple. The α branch was particularly straightforward since it consisted of only a few extant manuscripts. Making matters simpler still, within the α branch P was thought to be a copy of R. The perception that P descended directly from R could have eliminated its relevance in the eyes of textual critics, except for the fact that the portion of R (designated (R′)) containing the *Amores* is almost entirely lost. Consequently, P, which was believed to reflect α through the intermediary of R, needed to be used. S was, and still is, considered an inferior manuscript. It contains readings thought to be imported from the β branch, and, except for one passage (*Am.* 2.8.7), it does not offer good readings that cannot be found elsewhere. S, in the words of Kenney (1962:8), is "in an intermediate state of depravation" — textual critics frequently impute moral characteristics to manuscripts: the nature of its text shows that it belongs to the α family, but the later date of S (11th cent.) means that its text has "degenerated" and resembles in some particulars the text of β manuscripts.

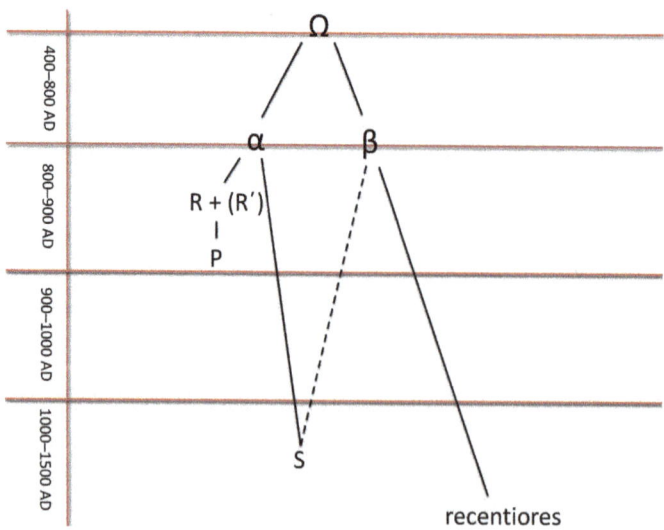

A discovery and further research were soon to complicate this rather simple reconstruction of the tradition. It was not long after the appearance of the first edition of Kenney's OCT that Munari (1965) first called attention to the Hamiltonensis (Y), which hitherto had been ignored. (Credit for the rediscovery belongs to Helmut Boese.) Because of a cataloguing error, which dated Y to the 14th century, neither Munari nor Kenney had taken Y into account in their editions.

The accession of Y to our knowledge about the tradition has had two important results. First, Y is a valuable independent textual witness—better than S and just as valuable as P. Second, and equally important, Y made obvious the "fog of unknowns" that still envelops a large mass of the tradition. With Y in the picture, there were now *two* manuscripts of the 11th century—but their texts were quite different from each other. Y was not a "depraved" representative of the α branch, as S was believed to be. Y had its own authority, offering readings now in agreement with α, now with β. It even had authoritative readings not found anywhere else (most notably, *Am.* 1.10.30, *licenda*).

The arrival of Y served as reminder of something else: the tradition is *not* bifid, though it has been represented as such. The division into two major branches of transmission (= a bifid stemma), corresponding to earlier and later groups of medieval manuscripts, is a convenient means to organize the tradition, but the reality is quite different. Y had shown that the dates of the manuscripts did not closely correspond with the nature of the texts that they offered. A good reading—a good reading attested nowhere else—could appear in a later manuscript. It had happened in the case of Y, and there was nothing to say it could not happen with a β manuscript. The β manuscripts vary widely in date and their relationships to each other have not been traced out, and for good reason: they are not a closely connected group. They are not one family, but amount to an intertanglement of many individual families. Kenney appreciated the complexity on the β side when he characterized β as a "convenient fiction" (1962:25). Later, he shrewdly observed (1974:134) that it would be more accurate to refer to the β branch as "non-α." The idea is that, whereas the α manuscripts are manifestly related, the β manuscripts do not derive from a single ancestor; their membership to the same group is solely by virtue of the fact that they do not derive from α.

Reconsideration of P's relationship to R has added a further wrinkle to the tradition's history. D. S. McKie (1986) forcefully argued that, contrary to what had been thought, P does not derive from R. Belief that P was copied from R came about through a tentative suggestion made by Tafel (1910) that eventually was taken over as fact; decades later Goold (1965) corroborated the idea. Because P's text of the *Amores* begins precisely where R's text goes missing it was assumed that the scribes of P must have taken this portion of R to serve as their exemplar (model). Furthermore, the date of P, which had been set as "late 9th or 10th" century, is earlier than often supposed. As was demonstrated by B. Bischoff (1961), P belongs to a group of manuscripts copied at the French monastery of Corbie in the period 850–880 (see Huelsenbeck 2013). R, P, S, and Y are all independent witnesses to α.

Therefore, recent developments in the study of the textual transmission of Ovid's *Amores* yield a more intricate, dynamic, and open-ended stemma. This stemma attempts to reflect the current state of our knowledge, showing what we know and do not know.

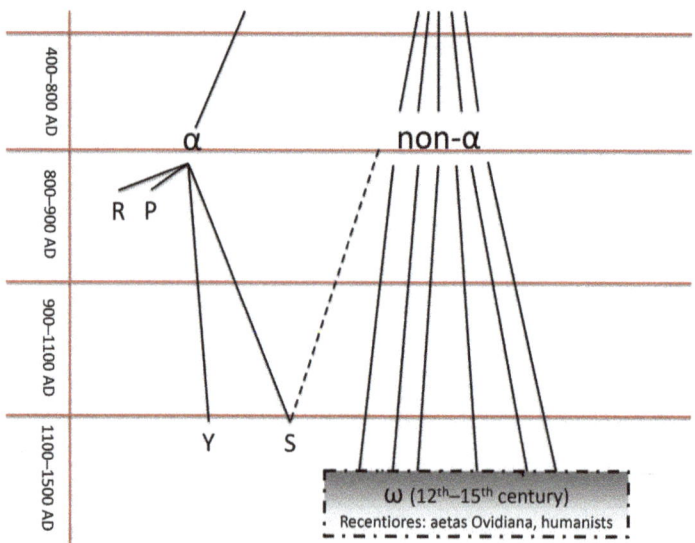

- Non-α (formerly β) is not a single textual family: the tradition is not bifid.
- In the stemma α and non-α are not shown to connect because non-α represents *multiple* families with intertangled connections. *How* and *when* α and non-α connect are unknowns.
- R, P, Y, and S are independent witnesses to α, though S draws some of its text from non-α.
- The copying dates of R and P are close.

4. Select bibliography

Adams, J. N. *The Latin Sexual Vocabulary*. Baltimore: The John Hopkins University Press, 1990.

Barsby, John A. *Ovid's* Amores: *Book I*. Oxford: Oxford University Press, 1973.

Booth, Joan. "The *Amores*: Ovid Making Love," in *A Companion to Ovid*, ed. Peter E. Knox, 61–77. Blackwell Companions to the Ancient World. Oxford: Blackwell, 2009. http://dx.doi.org/10.1002/9781444310627.ch5

Boyd, Barbara Weiden. *Ovid's Literary Loves: Influence and Innovation in the Amores*. Ann Arbor: University of Michigan Press, 1997.

Huelsenbeck, Bart. "A Nexus of Manuscripts Copied at Corbie, ca. 850–880: A Typology of Script-style and Copying Procedure," *Segno e testo* 11 (2013): 287-309.

Jestin, Charbra Adams and Phyllis B. Katz. *Ovid*: Amores/Metamorphoses, *selections*. Wauconda: Bolchazy-Carducci, 2000, 2nd edn.

Kenney, E. J. "The manuscript tradition of Ovid's *Amores, Ars amatoria*, and *Remedia Amoris*," *Classical Quarterly* 12 (1962): 1–31. http://dx.doi.org/10.1017/s0009838800011563

Kenney, E. J. *P. Ouidi Nasonis* Amores, Medicamina faciei femineae, Ars amatoria, Remedia amoris. Oxford: Oxford University Press, 1995 (orig. 1961), 2nd edn, reprinted with corrections.

McKeown, J. C. *Ovid*, Amores: *Text, Prolegomena, and Commentary in Four Volumes*. Liverpool and Wolfeboro: Francis Cairns. 1987–.

McKie, D. S. "Ovid's *Amores*: The Prime Sources for the Text," *Classical Quarterly* 36 (1986): 219–238. http://dx.doi.org/10.1017/s0009838800010673

Munari, Franco. *Il Codice Hamilton 471 di Ovidio*: Ars amatoria, Remedia amoris, Amores. Rome: Edizioni di storia e letteratura, 1965.

Pasco-Pranger, Molly Claire. "Duplicitous Simplicity in Ovid, *Amores* 1," *Classical Quarterly* 62 (2012): 721–730. http://dx.doi.org/10.1017/s0009838812000274

Raven, D. S. *Latin Metre*: An Introduction. London: Faber and Faber, 1965.

Ryan, Maureen B. and Caroline A. Perkins. *Ovid's* Amores *Book One, a Commentary*. Norman: University of Oklahoma Press, 2011.

Showerman, Grant. *Ovid,* Heroides, Amores. Revised by G. P. Gould. Loeb Classical Library. Cambridge, MA: Harvard University Press, 1977.

Stapleton, M. L. *Harmful Eloquence*: Ovid's Amores *from Antiquity to Shakespeare*. Ann Arbor: University of Michigan Press, 1996.

Tarrant, R. J. "Ovid, *Amores, Ars amatoria, Remedia amoris*," in *Texts and Transmission*, ed. L. D. Reynolds, 259–262. Oxford: Clarendon Press, 1983.

Volk, Katharina. *Ovid*. Malden and Chichester: Wiley-Blackwell, 2010. http://dx.doi.org/10.1002/9781444328127

West, David Alexander. "*Amores* 1.1-5," in *Ancient Historiography and its Contexts*: Studies in Honour of A. J. Woodman, eds. Christina S. Kraus, John Marincola, and Christopher Pelling, 139–154. Oxford: Oxford University Press, 2010. http://dx.doi.org/10.1093/acprof:oso/9780199558681.003.0009

Wilkinson, L. P. *Ovid Recalled*. Cambridge: Cambridge University Press, 1955.

5. Scansion

Since the *Amores* may well be among the first Latin poems a student encounters, it may be helpful to provide a brief introduction to the rules of Latin prosody (the quantity of individual syllables) and to the reading aloud of elegiac couplets. For fuller discussion see D. S. Raven, *Latin Metre: an Introduction* (London: Faber and Faber, 1965).

Prosody

Whereas English meters are based on a word's *accent* ("Múch have I trávelled in the reálms of góld"), Latin meters are based on *quantity*; what matters most is whether syllables are long or short.

For most of us the obstacle to reading Latin verse aloud is that we have not learned the quantities of Latin very well. All diphthongs are normally long by nature, but individual vowels can be either long or short, though a vowel followed by another vowel not in a diphthong is normally short. Ideally we would all know, say, that the first syllable of *miles* was long and the second one short, but in practice we are often uncertain, or even wrong, and it sometimes necessary to consult a dictionary solely to ascertain the quantities of a word.

An additional problem is that it is often necessary to know the meaning of a Latin word before one can know its prosody. Latin has a number of virtual homonyms, distinguished only by their quantity, such as *lĕvis* ("light") and *lēvis* ("smooth"). Much more common are the words whose *form* is identified only by their quantity: *puella* can be nominative singular or ablative singular, *cīvis* can be nominative or genitive singular or accusative plural, and *manus* can be nominative singular or nominative or accusative plural, etc. In such cases it is almost impossible to scan the line without also establishing its sense.

© William Turpin, CC BY http://dx.doi.org/10.11647/OBP.0067.04

On the other hand the endings of Latin words provide us with a large collection of easily learned quantities: with a review of the basic declensions and conjugations it is not difficult to learn that the *o* of *amō* is long, and that the *i* of *trādit* is short, or that the *ō* and *īs* of *puerō* and *puerīs* are long.

Other syllables with easily identifiable quantities are those which, though short by nature, become long by position because of the consonants that follow them. The most obvious instances are when vowels are followed by double consonants (*ll*, *mm*, *nn*, *pp*, *ss* etc.), and such words are also the easiest for a reader to speak correctly; in Latin there was a clear difference between the L-sounds in *malus* and *bellum*, and it is easy to make this distinction aloud once alerted to it (MAL-us vs. BEHL-Lum). More generally, a short syllable can be long by position when followed by *any* two (or more) consonants together (except h), or by *x* and *z*, which were each the equivalent of two consonants.

But before the following combinations of consonants the preceding short syllable *can* remain short:

- bl, br;
- cl, chl, cr, chr;
- dr;
- fl, fr;
- gl, gr;
- pl, pr;
- tr, thr.

However, a syllable *cannot* remain short when the two consonants following it belong to different parts of a compound *abrumpo*), or to different words (*et refer*).

Elision

A further complication in reading aloud is the fact that a vowel or a vowel + *m* at the end of a word is usually suppressed ("elided") when the next word begins with a vowel, or *h* + a vowel. This occurs even if the elided vowel would have been long.

āstĭtĭt īll(a) āmēns ālb(o) ēt sĭnĕ sānguĭnĕ vūltū (*Am.* 1.7.51)

nēc tē dēcĭpĭānt vĕtĕrēs cīrc(um) ātrĭă cērae (*Am.* 1.8.65)

A failure to elide (hiatus) is rare.

The elegiac couplet

The *Amores* are all written in elegiac couplets. This meter consists of a line of dactylic hexameter, the meter of epic poetry, i.e. six dactyls (— ⏑ ⏑) or spondees (— —), followed by a line of dactylic pentameter, i.e. five dactyls or spondees (with one of the spondees divided into two). The basic scheme is as follows:

$$-\smile\smile\,|-\smile\smile\,|-\smile\smile\,|-\smile\smile\,|-\smile\smile\,|\;-\;\mathrm{x}$$

$$-\smile\smile\,|-\smile\smile\,|-//-\smile\smile\,|-\smile\smile\,|\;-$$

In the hexameter line the fifth and sixth feet are almost always a dactyl and a spondee (the last syllable of each line is technically *anceps*, i.e. it can be either long or short, but for practical purposes the lines can all be read as if the last syllable is long); thus each line can be expected to end — ⏑ ⏑ / — —. The first four feet can be any combination of dactyls and spondees, and it is here that a knowledge of prosody becomes important.

In addition, the hexameter line almost always has a break between words in the third foot, most commonly after the first beat (whether of dactyl or spondee). This is called a strong caesura, e.g.

Iam super oceanum ‖ vēnit a seniore marito (*Am.* 1.13.1)

Sometimes the break occurs after the *second* beat of the third foot (which must be a dactyl), giving a kind of syncopated feel to the line. This is the so-called "weak" caesura, e.g.

quo properās, Aurōră? ‖ mănē: sic Memnŏnis umbris (*Am.* 1.13.3)

The first half of the pentameter line can be thought of as the first part of a hexameter line extending to a strong caesura. As in the hexameter line spondees can be substituted for dactyls in the first two feet. The second half of the pentameter essentially repeats the first, but here there are no spondees. As with the hexameter line, the last syllable of the pentameter is *anceps*, i.e. it can be either long or short, but for practical purposes each pentameter line can all be read as if the last syllable is long. (I cannot find this explicitly stated in the reference books).

Reading aloud

Despite the apparent complexities, elegiac couplets are reasonably easy to read aloud. The key, in my view, is to become thoroughly at home with the basic unit of — ᴗ ᴗ | — ᴗ ᴗ | —, which in its pure form provides the second half of the pentameter line, and which with spondaic variation provides the first half of the pentameter line and begins the vast majority of the hexameter lines. This, combined with the near certainty that the last two feet of the hexameter lines will be — ᴗ ᴗ | — —, makes it possible to guess how most of Ovid's couplets should be scanned, even if one's grasp of basic Latin prosody is weak. It is important, of course, to be alert to those quantities which can be known in advance, such as diphthongs, certain word endings, vowels followed by double consonants, and vowels followed by more than one consonant, while remaining alert to the exceptions mentioned above.

I suggest practicing by beginning with the easiest section to scan, reading the *second* halves of all the *pentameter* lines in a poem; here there are no variations from — ᴗ ᴗ | — ᴗ ᴗ | — and it is usually easy enough to see where the second halves of the lines begin. Follow this by reading the pentameter lines complete; the first two feet will offer some variation, but there are only four possible combinations for the first half of a pentameter:

$$— — \mid — — \mid —$$
$$— \smile \smile \mid — \smile \smile \mid —$$
$$— — \mid — \smile \smile \mid —$$
$$— \smile \smile \mid — — \mid —$$

Practicing the pentameter lines should make the hexameter lines much easier. Most lines will have a strong caesura, and will thus offer exactly the same four possibilities as the first half of the pentameter line. Following the strong caesura there will be either one long beat or two short ones to complete the third foot. The fourth foot will be either a dactyl or a spondee, and is thus usually the hardest foot to scan, but the fifth and sixth feet will almost certainly be a dactyl and a spondee. Lines with a weak caesura of course work slightly differently: the third foot will be a dactyl, with the caesura coming between the two short beats.

To introduce this approach to reading aloud, I print here a modified text of *Amores* 1.1. I have introduced gaps in the text to identify caesurae, all of which are strong caesurae. I have also put elided syllables in parentheses. In theory this should make it possible to follow the procedure suggested above with relative ease, so that unknown quantities can be deduced rather than looked up.

> Arma gravī numerō   violentaque bella parābam
>   ēdere, māteriā   conveniente modīs.
> pār erat inferior   versus; rīsisse Cupīdō
>   dīcitur atqu(e) ūnum   surripuisse pedem.
> "quis tibi, saeve puer,   dedit hōc in carmina iūris?   5
>   Pīeridum vātēs,   nōn tua, turba sumus.
> quid, sī praeripiat   flāvae Venus arma Minervae,
>   ventilet accensās   flāva Minerva facēs?
> quis probet in silvīs   Cererem regnāre iugōsīs,
>   lēge pharetrātae   virginis arva colī?   10
> crīnibus insignem   quis acūtā cuspide Phoebum
>   instruat, Āoniam   Marte movente lyram?
> sunt tibi magna, puer,   nimiumque potentia regna:
>   cūr opus adfectās   ambitiōse novum?
> an, quod ubīque, tuum (e)st?   tua sunt Helicōnia tempē?   15
>   vix etiam Phoebō   iam lyra tūta su(a) est?
> cum bene surrexit   versū nova pāgina prīmō,
>   attenuat nervōs   proximus ille meōs.

nec mihi māteri(a) est   numerīs leviōribus apta,
    aut puer aut longās   compta puella comās."   20
questus eram, pharetrā   cum prōtinus ille solūtā
    lēgit in exitium   spīcula facta meum
lūnāvitque genū   sinuōsum fortiter arcum
    "quod" que "canās, vātēs,   accipe" dixit "opus."
mē miserum! certās   habuit puer ille sagittās: 25
    ūror, et in vacuō   pectore regnat Amor.
sex mihi surgat opus   numerīs, in quinque resīdat;
    ferrea cum vestrīs   bella valēte modīs.
cingere lītoreā   flāventia tempora myrtō,
    Mūsa per undēnōs   ēmodulanda pedēs.

6. *Epigram*: preface from the author

The three books of the *Amores* speak on behalf of their author, named as Naso (in full, Publius Ovidius Naso), explaining that they used to be five. They make a joke at their own expense, in a bit of *captatio benevolentiae* (bid for good will).

> Quī modo Nāsōnis fuerāmus quinque libellī,
>> trēs sumus: hoc illī praetulit auctor opus.
> ut iam nulla tibī nōs sit lēgisse voluptās,
>> at levior demptīs poena duōbus erit.

Notes on the *Epigram*

1–2: **modo**: "only recently, just now." **Hoc illī ... opus** = *auctor praetulit hoc opus illī (operī)*; *praeferō* can mean "prefer" (OLD 6 and 7), with accusative and dative.

3–4: **ut iam**: "even if." *ut* can be used, especially with *tamen* or *iam*, to introduce a concessive clause (AG §527a); the author is here indulging in some mock modesty. **at**: "nevertheless"; here after a concessive clause, see OLD 14. **demptis ... duobus**: ablative absolute.

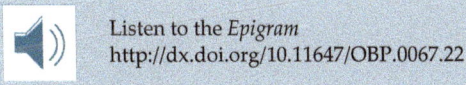

© William Turpin, CC BY   http://dx.doi.org/10.11647/OBP.0067.05

7. *Amores* 1.1: Ovid finds his muse

The first poem functions, as we might expect, as an introduction to the whole book: we are introduced to the aspiring poet, to the genre of his poems, and perhaps also to their subject. At one level the wit is easy to appreciate, but for me the poem gives the first example of a problem presented by many of the poems in this book: the question of coherence. Ovid's poems, in my opinion, are supposed to be *satisfying*: when we get to the end, we should feel that we have seen the point, and that the poem is a coherent whole. Often, as in this first poem, we do not at first have that sense of coherence, and my suggestion is that, when that happens, we take it as a challenge to read more closely.

The poem begins with a metrical and generic joke. The poet was preparing to write epic poetry: his first word is the same as the first word of the *Aeneid*, and he would have continued writing in dactylic hexameter, except that apparently Cupid "stole a foot" from every second line (lines 3–4), creating elegiac couplets instead, the metrical form particularly associated with love poetry. We thus have a witty variation of a *recusatio*, a standard poetic theme particularly appropriate for the first poem of a collection: poets typically explain why they have to refuse (*recusatio* means "refusal" or "excuse") to write the kind of patriotic poetry that their patrons or their public might be demanding.

The poet responds with a complaint, addressed to Cupid. Cupid has no right to interfere in the serious business of writing poetry: other gods stay within their appointed spheres, and Cupid should do so as well. Like the good rhetorician he is, Ovid offers a few *exempla* to drive home his protest (lines 5–16). He then adds that he doesn't *like* it when every second line is kind of feeble (lines 17–18), and on top of that adds that he doesn't have anyone (boy or girl) to write love poetry *about* (lines 19–20).

© William Turpin, CC BY   http://dx.doi.org/10.11647/OBP.0067.06

But Cupid responds to these objections by shooting the poet with one of his famous arrows; the poet is now a stereotypical wretched lover, and love reigns in his "empty heart" (line 26). Some scholars have taken this empty heart (*in vacuo pectore*) at face value: the poet is in love, but his heart is empty, so he must simply be in love with love itself. Others have argued, I think correctly, that this empty heart is one that *had* been empty, but is empty no longer; previously the poet had no one to write love poetry about, as we saw, but thanks to Cupid's arrow he has now fallen in love.

Fig. 2 Eros with the bow, Roman copy after Greek original by Lysippos. Rome, Musei Capitolini. Wikimedia, https://commons.wikimedia.org/wiki/File:Eros_bow_Musei_Capitolini_MC410_n2.jpg

On most readings the last four lines are a little disappointing. Having become a lover, of whatever kind, the poet returns to his own poetry: he is now going to write elegiac couplets, with lines of six feet, the hexameters, followed by lines of five feet, the pentameters (lines 27–28). He concludes by invoking the muse of elegy, first in the poetic language we might expect, with talk of her golden hair and myrtle wreath (line 29), but then in language that is ironically pedestrian, emphasizing the mere numerical fact that an elegiac couplet has eleven feet (line 30).

I would argue that in fact the poet never loses sight of his new lover: thanks to Cupid's arrow, as we saw, he is miserably in love, and with someone in particular. It is this new lover who is responsible for his change to elegiac couplets, the meter for lovers (lines 27–28). And it is this new lover who emerges triumphantly at the end: it is *she* who is the poet's new muse, wearing a myrtle garland on her golden hair, and inspiring the poetry that is to come, written of course in elegiac couplets.

Suggested reading

Moles, J. "The Dramatic Coherence of Ovid, *Amores* 1.1 and 1.2," *Classical Quarterly* 41 (1991): 551–554. http://dx.doi.org/10.1017/s0009838800004766

Turpin, W. "Ovid's New Muse: *Amores* 1.1," *Classical Quarterly* 64 (2014): 419–421. http://dx.doi.org/10.1017/s0009838813000876

Amores 1.1

Arma gravī numerō violentaque bella parābam
    ēdere, māteriā conveniente modīs.
pār erat inferior versus; rīsisse Cupīdō
    dīcitur atque ūnum surripuisse pedem.
"quis tibi, saeve puer, dedit hōc in carmina iūris?   5
    Pīeridum vātēs, nōn tua, turba sumus.
quid, sī praeripiat flāvae Venus arma Minervae,
    ventilet accensās flāva Minerva facēs?
quis probet in silvīs Cererem regnāre iugōsīs,
    lēge pharetrātae virginis arva colī?   10
crīnibus insignem quis acūtā cuspide Phoebum
    instruat, Āoniam Marte movente lyram?
sunt tibi magna, puer, nimiumque potentia regna:
    cūr opus adfectās ambitiōse novum?
an, quod ubīque, tuum est? tua sunt Helicōnia tempē?   15
    vix etiam Phoebō iam lyra tūta sua est?
cum bene surrexit versū nova pāgina prīmō,
    attenuat nervōs proximus ille meōs.
nec mihi māteria est numerīs leviōribus apta,
    aut puer aut longās compta puella comās."   20
questus eram, pharetrā cum prōtinus ille solūtā
    lēgit in exitium spīcula facta meum
lūnāvitque genū sinuōsum fortiter arcum
    "quod"que "canās, vātēs, accipe" dixit "opus."
mē miserum! certās habuit puer ille sagittās: 25
    ūror, et in vacuō pectore regnat Amor.

sex mihi surgat opus numerīs, in quinque resīdat;

ferrea cum vestrīs bella valēte modīs.

cingere lītoreā flāventia tempora myrtō,

Mūsa per undēnōs ēmodulanda pedēs. 30

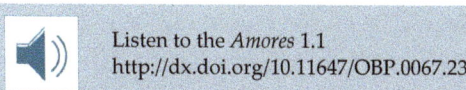 Listen to the *Amores* 1.1
http://dx.doi.org/10.11647/OBP.0067.23

Notes on *Amores* 1.1

1–2: Arma: a weighty and tradition-laden first word, given Vergil's famous *Arma virumque canō* (*Aeneid* 1.1). **gravī numerō**: *numerus* here means "meter" (of verse). The meter in question was dactylic hexameter, which as the meter for Greek and Latin epic poetry was considered the most serious of the meters. **ēdere** < *ēdō -ere -idī -itum*, "to emit, bring forth, produce"; also "publish." Barsby observes that it is unlikely that Ovid was really planning to write an epic, even though he elsewhere talks about his subject, the battle of the gods and giants (*Amores* 2.1.11–16); his claim about epic owes more to the traditions of the *recusatio* poem, in which poets of "lighter" verses explain their reasons for avoiding epic. **māteriā**: scansion reveals that the final *a* is long, and that the word is therefore ablative; it frequently happens that scansion is essential to establishing the meaning of a line. **modīs**: *modus* can mean "rhythm" or "meter"; dative, with *conveniente*.

3–4: par ... versus = *inferior versus erat pār*. **inferior**: here the "lower" verse; Ovid had been writing dactylic hexameters, so that his second line was equal (metrically) to his first. **dīcitur**: "is said" + infin. *rīsisse*. **ūnum ... pedem**: *pes* here means "foot" in its metrical sense; in elegiac verse the second line of each couplet is a dactylic pentameter: it is similar to the dactylic hexameter of epic poetry, but shorter by a foot.

5–6: in carmina: "over songs"; for *in* + the accusative with words expressing power or control, see OLD 11b. **hōc**: the o of hoc is actually short, but can be treated as long for purposes of scansion, since it was originally spelled *hocc*. **iūris**: partitive genitive, with *hōc* (AG §346.4). **Pīeridum ... sumus**: the emphasis here is on *Pīeridum* and *tua*: "we poets are the *Muses*' entourage, not yours." **Pīeridum** < *Pīeris -idos* f. "daughter of Pierus," i.e. a Muse. **vātēs** < *vātēs -is*, m. "a prophet"; "a poet" (here plural). A *vātēs* was a more formal and religious kind of poet than a mere *poēta*.

7–8: **quid**: interrogative; understand *dīcās* or something similar; *quid* thus provides the apodosis of the condition introduced by *sī praeripiat*. **flāvae ... Minervae**: dative with *praeripiat*, indicating the person forestalled. Minerva (Athena) is called "golden" (*flāvus, a, um*) because she was proud of her golden hair; she had turned Medusa's hair into snakes for boasting about hers. **arma**: Minerva/Athena was often depicted wearing breastplate and helmet and carrying a spear. **ventilet**: a second protasis, connected to *praeripiat* by an adversative asyndeton (i.e. the absence of a connecting word), indicating high excitement and/or a strong contrast. **facēs** < *fax, facis*, f. "torch"; a symbol of Venus.

Fig. 3 The "Minerva Farnese." 2nd century AD. Naples, National Archaeological Museum. Wikimedia, https://commons.wikimedia.org/wiki/File:Minerva_Farnese_02.JPG

9–10: **probet**: potential subjunctive (AG §447.3). **Cererem** < *Cerēs, -eris*, f. Ceres, the goddess of grain and agriculture in general. **lēge** < *lex, lēgis*, f. "law," but here perhaps "jurisdiction"; notice that (as in line 8) the clause is in asyndeton, to express excitement. **pharētrātae**: the reference is to Diana (Artemis), the goddess of the hunt. **colī** < *colō colere coluī cultum*, "to cultivate, till, farm."

Fig. 4 The "Diana of Versailles" (Artemis with a doe). 1st–2nd century AD, perhaps after a 4th century BC original by Leochares. Paris, The Louvre. Wikimedia, https://commons.wikimedia.org/wiki/File:Diana_of_Versailles,_Louvre_1_August_2013.jpg

11–12: **crīnibus**: ablative of respect, with *insignem*; Apollo was famous for his flowing locks. **acūtā**: "sharp" in two senses; Apollo is often said to sing *acūtā vōce*, but the adjective is transferred to Mars' spear. **instruat**: *instruō* can mean "equip" (+ abl.); potential subjunctive, AG §447.3. **Āoniam** < *Āonius -a -um* "of Aonia, Boeotian"; Aonia was a region of Boeotia, in which was situated **Mt. Helicon**,[1] home of the Muses. **movente**: another double meaning, since *moveō* is used for the wielding of weapons and for the playing of musical instruments.

13–14: **tibi**: dative of possession (AG §373). **ambitiōse**: another example of the necessity for scansion; the *e* is short, not long, so *ambitiōse* is vocative, not an adverb.

15–16: **an**: a particle introducing a direct question, usually indicating some surprise or indignation (AG §335b). **quod ubīque, tuum est?**: i.e., *id, quod ubīque est, tuum est?* "Do you own everything everywhere?" **Helicōnia** < *Helicōnius, -a, -um*: "of Mount Helicon" (see note on *Aoniam*

---

1   See http://pleiades.stoa.org/places/540808. Historical maps for the location marked in blue are available at the Pleiades website.

above). **tempē** is an indeclinable neuter pl.; originally a proper name, for the Vale of Tempe in Thessaly, but used for any pleasant valley. **Phoebō**: dative of reference AG §376). **sua** refers to Phoebus, even though the subject of the sentence is *lyra*; *suus -a -um* can be used to place emphasis on the fact that a thing belongs to one person rather than another (AG §301c).

17–18: **surrexit** < *surgō -ere surrexī surrectum*, "to arise," used also of the beginning or expansion of literary works; there is probably also a sexual double entendre: "is aroused." We would expect the present tense of the indicative in a temporal *cum* clause, but the perfect emphasizes that the action is a completed one, in contrast to that described in the main clause (AG §473a). Translate, perhaps: "each time a new page has gotten going nicely with a first verse" (i.e. the first line of an elegiac couplet). **attenuat**: more double entendre; the poet gets going (the hexameter line), but then goes all weak (in the pentameter). **nervōs ... meōs**: *nervī* can be "strength," "the strings of a lyre," and "penises." **proximus ille**: refers either to the *inferior versus* of line 3, or less probably to Cupid.

19–20: **mihi**: dative of possession (AG §373). **numerīs**: as in line 1, *numerus* means "meter." **aut ... aut** = *nec ... nec*, because the *nec* on line 19 has made the whole sentence a negative one. **puer ... puella**: Ovid can assume that the elegiac meter and love poetry go together, thanks to his predecessors Catullus, Gallus, Propertius, and Tibullus. Of these, Catullus and Tibullus (as well as Horace, though not in elegiac couplets) wrote poems to both male and female lovers. **longās ... comās**: the so-called Greek accusative (also called accusative of part affected, accusative of specification, and accusative of respect), AG §397b. **compta** < *comptus, a, um* "adorned, done up" or *cōmō, cōmere, compsī, comptum* "adorn," (of hair) "arrange, 'do'" Note the chiasmus, here reflecting the meaning: the words for long hair surround those for the well-groomed girl.

21–22: **pharetrā ... lēgit** = *cum ille, pharetrā solūtā, legit*. **ille**: referring back to Cupid. **solūtā** < *solvō solvere solvī solūtum*, "open up"; Cupid's quiver had a top on it. **lēgit**: *lēgō* can mean "select, choose" (OLD 6a). **in exitium**: *in* + acc. can express purpose. **spīcula** < *spīculum, ī,* n. "point, tip"; "arrow"; Ovid will regularly use singulars for plurals and vice versa, often with no obvious significance for the meaning.

23–24: **genū**: ablative of means (AG §409). Cupid used his knee to help with bending the bow: when stringing a composite bow you push the bow away from you with your knee (or thigh) to break the initial stiffness. (I am grateful to a former student, David Stifler, for his advice on composite bows.) **sinuōsum**: Cupid's bow (a composite bow) looks wavy rather than crescent-shaped when unstrung. **quod ... canās**: relative clause of purpose (AG §531.2), or characteristic (AG §534). The line is written with intentional staccato to reflect Cupid's abrupt and violent response.

25–26: **mē miserum**: accusative of exclamation (AG §397d). **in vacuō pectore**: the author's heart had been empty, up to this point. **Amor** = *Cupīdō*.

27–28: **mihi**: dative of advantage (AG §376). **surgat ... resīdat**: hortatory subjunctives (AG §439; also called jussive subjunctives). **sex ... numerīs, in quīnque**: the reference, as in lines 1–3, is to the elegiac couplet, consisting of a line of dactylic hexameter followed by a line of dactylic pentameter. **ferrea ... bella**: vocative. **modīs**: as in line 2 *modus* means "meter."

29–30: **cingere** < *cingō cingere cinxī cinctum* "to encircle, to wreathe"; second person singular passive imperative. **lītoreā** < *lītoreus -a -um* "of the seashore." Notice the scansion, which reveals that *lītoreā* modifies *myrtō* (on which see below). The chiastic word order reflects the meaning, with the words for the myrtle surrounding those for the Muse's hair. **tempora** < *tempus -oris*, n. "the temple" (of the head), "forehead." Greek accusative/accusative of specification, as above in line 20 (AG §397b). **myrtō**: the myrtle was sacred to Venus, who was born out of sea foam (hence *lītoreā*). The names of trees in Latin are regularly second declension, but feminine (AG §32). **Mūsa**: vocative. **per**: for *per* + accusative to indicate instrument see OLD 15. **undēnōs**: an elegiac couplet has eleven feet in all, whereas two lines of hexameters would have twelve. **ēmodulanda**: the word is used only here in Classical Latin.

8. *Amores* 1.2: Conquered by Cupid

It is not clear whether we are to read each poem in *Amores* 1 as building directly on the poem that precedes it. There can be little doubt that Roman poets constructed their poetry books with care, and probably assumed that the poems would be read, often, one after the other. But it does not follow from this that the book as a whole was supposed to provide a consistent storyline, with the poet telling us more and more about his (no doubt fictional) private life.

Fig. 5 "Cupid and Pan," detail. Attributed to Federico Zuccaro (around 1600). http://commons.wikimedia.org/wiki/File:Cupid_and_Pan.JPG

Nonetheless it seems natural at least to try to read the poems as providing a more or less coherent story, and in the discussions that follow I will assume that we are supposed to read each poem in order, with each one adding something to our picture of the poet and his love life. *Amores* 1.2 certainly picks up and develops one aspect of the poem that precedes it—the idea of the lover as Cupid's victim. We may have ended *Amores* 1.1 with the introduction of the poet's new love interest as muse, but we learn no more about her now. Instead, the poet offers us a display of the self-absorption

© William Turpin, CC BY   http://dx.doi.org/10.11647/OBP.0067.07

that sometimes seems all too typical of young lovers, especially perhaps if they are also poets.

Once he realizes the truth, he has to decide whether or not to resist. He concludes, quickly enough, that resistance is generally a mistake (line 9–10), and supports this proposition with another rhetorician's list of *exempla* (compare *Amores* 1.1.5–16): fire, cattle, and horses, all have easier lives if they take what comes to them (lines 11–16). And the poet, too, has to submit to the domination of a master, in this case Cupid: it will be easier for him if he accepts his new position as a slave (*servitium*) to *Amor* (lines 17–18).

The first eight lines of the poem connect it more or less directly with *Amores* 1.1. The poet has been unable to sleep, and at first does not know why; it might be love, but, he says, surely he would have noticed (lines 5–6). This suggests to some readers that the poem is *not* connected directly to *Amores* 1.1, in which we were told of Cupid's arrow and its consequence; Ovid, we might think, shouldn't be so confused. But we need not be so literal, and indeed it makes little sense to take Cupid's arrow literally. People who can't sleep do not necessarily think all that clearly, and we can forgive our poet a little confusion about what his problem is. At any rate he figures it out, or perhaps remembers (*sic erit*, line 7): it's the arrow(s), it's Cupid/Amor, and it's the poet's captive heart (lines 7–8).

Slavery for the Romans was always associated with conquest, and the poet's slavery is quickly recast as military surrender to Cupid (lines 19–22). This sets up the astonishing image that occupies about half the poem: the triumphal procession of Cupid (lines 23–49), leading as his captives young men and women in love (line 27), not least the poet himself (29–30).

At the risk of stating the obvious, it is worth noting how wonderfully funny this is. The Romans took their triumphs very seriously; the triumph was the peak of any politician's career, and it enacted the ruthless militarism of Rome for all the city to see; the captives, after all, were led up the Capitoline to be executed. And this most serious of Roman institutions is invoked by the poet to express the potentially happy, and certainly private, thought that Cupid has won the day: the poet has fallen in love. The centerpiece of his image is both charming and silly: the *triumphator*, in this poem, is no battle-hardened Roman general, but a beautiful, and naked, boy-god of love (lines 38–42). But we should not forget the extraordinary juxtaposition of a potentially difficult love-affair, on the one hand, and, on the other, the abject physical subjugation at the heart of a Roman triumph.

Fig. 6 The triumph of Vespasian and Titus (71 CE). Relief from Arch of Titus, Rome, showing the spoils from the Temple in Jerusalem. Wikimedia, https://commons.wikimedia.org/wiki/File:Fra-titusbuen.jpg

The last four lines contain the poet's plea for mercy: although he could appropriately be part of Cupid's triumph, he's not really worth the effort (49–50); Cupid should emulate his relative Augustus (the Julii were supposedly descended from Venus), and should protect his victim, not punish him.

Is this a satisfying way to end? Augustus did pride himself on his clemency, and even if we ignore the fact that his enemies told stories about his ruthlessness it is surprising, and perhaps even jarring, for reality to intrude so suddenly after the long fantasy of Cupid's triumph.

But the reference to Augustus perhaps makes more sense if we see it as something we've been waiting for since the beginning of *Amores* 1.1. The poet had started out trying to write patriotic poetry—poetry reminiscent of Vergil's great epic—but was ambushed by Cupid and sidetracked to love and elegy. *Amores* 1.2 offers a kind of substitute for that patriotic poetry: we get an account of a triumph, but its outrageousness only raises more questions about the poet's patriotism, or loyalty to the regime. Those questions, in turn, prepare us for the final couplet: Augustus, it turns out, matters after all.

Fig. 7 Statue of Augustus from Prima Porta. Marble copy of a bronze original, c. 20 BCE. Note Cupid riding on a dolphin (dolpins were associated with Venus). Wikimedia, https://commons.wikimedia.org/wiki/File:Augustus_of_Prima_Porta_(2984423197).jpg

Suggested reading

Athanassaki, Lucia. "The Triumph of Love and Elegy in Ovid's *Amores* 1.2," *Materiali e discussioni per l'analisi dei testi classici* 28 (1992): 125–141. http://dx.doi.org/10.2307/40236002

Moles, J. "The Dramatic Coherence of Ovid, *Amores* 1.1 and 1.2," *Classical Quarterly* 41 (1991): 551–554. http://dx.doi.org/10.1017/s0009838800004766

Amores 1.2

Esse quid hoc dīcam, quod tam mihi dūra videntur
  strāta, neque in lectō pallia nostra sedent,
et vacuus somnō noctem, quam longa, perēgī,
  lassaque versātī corporis ossa dolent?
nam, puto, sentīrem, sī quō temptārer amōre— 5
  an subit et tectā callidus arte nocet?
sīc erit: haesērunt tenuēs in corde sagittae,
  et possessa ferus pectora versat Amor.
cēdimus, an subitum luctandō accendimus ignem?
  cēdāmus: leve fit, quod bene fertur, onus. 10
vīdī ego iactātās mōtā face crescere flammās
  et vīdī nullō concutiente morī.
verbera plūra ferunt, quam quōs iuvat ūsus arātrī,
  dētractant prensī dum iuga prīma bovēs.
asper equus dūrīs contunditur ōra lupātīs: 15
  frēna minus sentit, quisquis ad arma facit.
ācrius invītōs multōque ferōcius urget,
  quam quī servitium ferre fatentur, Amor.
ēn ego, confiteor, tua sum nova praeda, Cupīdō;
  porrigimus victās ad tua iūra manūs. 20
nīl opus est bellō: pācem veniamque rogāmus;
  nec tibi laus armīs victus inermis erō.
necte comam myrtō, māternās iunge columbās;
  quī deceat, currum vītricus ipse dabit;
inque datō currū, populō clāmante triumphum, 25
  stābis et adiunctās arte movēbis avēs.
dūcentur captī iuvenēs captaeque puellae:
  haec tibi magnificus pompa triumphus erit.

ipse ego, praeda recens, factum modo vulnus habēbō
   et nova captīvā vincula mente feram. 30
Mens Bona dūcētur manibus post terga retortīs,
   et Pudor, et castrīs quicquid Amōris obest.
omnia tē metuent, ad tē sua bracchia tendens
   vulgus "iō" magnā vōce "triumphe" canet.
Blanditiae comitēs tibi erunt Errorque Furorque, 35
   assiduē partēs turba secūta tuās.
hīs tū mīlitibus superās hominēsque deōsque;
   haec tibi sī dēmās commoda, nūdus eris.
laeta triumphantī dē summō māter Olympō
   plaudet et appositās sparget in ōra rosās. 40
tū pinnās gemmā, gemmā variante capillōs
   ībis in aurātīs aureus ipse rotīs.
tum quoque nōn paucōs, sī tē bene nōvimus, ūrēs;
   tum quoque praeteriens vulnera multa dabis.
nōn possunt, licet ipse velīs, cessāre sagittae; 45
   fervida vīcīnō flamma vapōre nocet.
tālis erat domitā Bacchus Gangētide terrā:
   tū gravis ālitibus, tigribus ille fuit.
ergō cum possim sacrī pars esse triumphī,
   parce tuās in mē perdere, victor, opēs! 50
aspice cognātī fēlīcia Caesaris arma:
   quā vīcit, victōs prōtegit ille manū.

 Listen to the *Amores* 1.2
http://dx.doi.org/10.11647/OBP.0067.24

Notes on *Amores* 1.2

1–2: **Esse quid hoc dīcam**: *dīcam* is deliberative subjunctive (AG §444), governing an indirect statement, the subject of which is *hoc*: "I should say that this is what?" i.e., "What should I say this is?" "What's going on?" **quod**: "that"; for *quid quod?*, "what of the fact that?" **nostra** = *mea*.

3–4: **vacuus somnō**: *vacuus* can govern an ablative of separation to mean "free from a thing" (AG §400). **quam longa**: perhaps = *tam longa quam fuit*, but more likely a parenthetical exclamation, with *nox* understood as its subject; = *et vacuus somnō noctem—quam longa!—perēgī*. **versātī** < *versō -āre* "to turn round, to spin," used of tossing and turning one's body.

5–6: **puto**: the *o* of first person singular endings is long by nature, but is often regarded as short by the poets. **sentīrem, sī quō temptārer amōre**: a present contrary to fact condition; *quō* = *aliquō* (AG §310a), with *amōre*. **an**: as in *Amores* 1.1.15, *an* introduces a rather surprised question (AG §335b). **subit** < *subeō, -īre, -iī, -itum* can mean "steal in on"; the subject is *amor/Amor*.

7–8: **erit**: sometimes called the future of surprised realization: "That'll be it!" **versat** < *versō -āre*, here "push something this way and that," i.e., "control."

9–10: **cēdimus, an ... accendimus**: both verbs are interrogative; *an* can introduce a second question asked as an alternative to the first one. Take *accendō* as "intensify, aggravate." **leve fit, quod bene fertur, onus**: a "sententia" or proverb. **bene**: "with fortitude."

11–12: **vīdī ego**: remember that *ego* is intensive: "I myself have seen." **nullō concutiente**: "when no one shakes them." **morī**: the subject is *flammās*. Ovid has seen the flames of love extinguished on their own.

13–14: **verbera** < *verber, verberis*, n. "whip" or "the blow of a whip" (rare in the singular); *ferre verbera* means "endure beatings." **quōs** = *eī bovēs quōs*. **ūsus arātrī**: *ūsus, usūs*, m. "employment, use." **dētractant prēnsī dum iuga prīma bovēs**: "while cattle when they have been rounded up (*prēnsī*) refuse to submit themselves to their first yokes." The point is that oxen who don't cause difficulties when they are first yoked up, and who actually enjoy the *ūsus arātrī*, suffer far less than oxen who resist.

15–16: **ōra**: the Greek accusative (accusative of specification), AG §397b. **quisquis**: i.e., *quisquis equus*. **ad arma facit**: "adapts itself to its harness"; *faciō* here means "be effective in dealing with"; *arma* here means "equipment."

17–18: **multōque**: ablative of degree of difference (AG §414); *multō* is to be taken with both *ācrius* and *ferōcius*. **quī** = *eōs quī*; antecedent pronouns are often omitted in poetry when they can be understood from the context. **fatentur**: "agree to."

19–20: **ēn**: "look!" **porrigimus**: *manūs porrigere* more typically means "stretch out the hands to take something," but here, with *ad tua iura*, the gesture is apparently one of submission.

21–22: **nīl opus est bellō**: "there is no need for war"; *opus est* is impersonal (+ ablative, AG §411). *nīl* is accusative with adverbial force (AG §390 n.2). **nec tibi ... erō** = *nec (tibi) erō laus armīs, victus inermis*. *tibi* is probably an ethical dative (AG §380); translate as something vague, such as "you see, you know" or as if Ovid had written *armīs tuīs*. **laus** < *laus, laudis,* f. "praise" but also "cause of praise, glory"; predicate nominative.

23–24: **māternās iunge columbās**: *iungō, iungere, iunxī, iunctum* "harness, yoke" (to a chariot, etc.); doves were sacred to Venus, Cupid's mother. **quī deceat**: subjunctive in a relative clause of purpose (AG §531) or characteristic (AG §534); the antecedent of *quī* is *currum*; understand *tē* as the direct object. **vītricus**: "step-father," probably Vulcan, who was married to Venus. Cupid's father was Jupiter. **dabit**: Vulcan, as the Gods' craftsman, will build a chariot for Cupid.

25–26: **triumphum**: object of *clamante*; the people shout that Cupid is a victorious general marching in his triumph. **arte**: construe with *movēbis* as an ablative of manner (*cum* understood), AG §412; best translated adverbially, "skillfully." **movēbis**: i.e., Cupid will drive the team of birds harnessed to the chariot; *moveō* is not a normal word for "drive," and seems intentionally awkward, i.e., "you'll get those birds moving."

27–28: **haec ... trumphus erit** = *haec pompa magnificus triumphus erit tibi*. **pompa**: *pompa, ae,* f. "procession."

29–30: **factum modo**: "only just made/inflicted"; reinforces *praeda recens*. **captīvā**: notice the scansion, which reveals that *captīvā* modifies *mente*, ablative of manner (AG §412).

31–32: Mens Bona: *Mens* was the personification of good counsel, and had a temple on the Capitoline Hill in the center of Rome. **post terga**: plural for singular. **Pudor**: unlike *Mens Bona*, Pudor is personified only by the poets; there was no actual cult of Pudor in Rome, though there was a cult of Pudicitia (more explicitly female chastity). **castrīs quidquid Amōris obest** = *quidquid obest castrīs Amōris*, i.e., "any enemy of Amor"; *castrīs* means not only "camp" but also, by metonymy, "army"; ablative of place where, with the preposition omitted, as often in poetry (AG §429.4). The theme of "Love's War" will be taken up more extensively in *Amores* 1.9.

33–34: omnia: the neuter makes this a more sweeping claim than *omnēs* would have done: *every thing* will be afraid of Cupid. **'iō ... triumphe'**: the ritual cry shouted at a triumphal procession.

35–36: Blanditiae: "flattery, charm" (the plural is regularly translated by the singular); here personified. **partēs ... tuās**: "your side"; *partēs* is the normal word for a political faction, or for one side in any dispute. **turba**: "crowd," especially in a procession; in apposition to *Blanditiae*, *Error* and *Furor* of the preceding line. The point is that without *Blanditiae*, *Error*, and *Furor* Cupid would be powerless (*nūdus*); the joke is that Cupid is usually *nūdus* anyway.

37–38: hīs ... mīlitibus: we would expect a preposition (ablative of agent), but here the soldiers are apparently treated as an instrument (AG §409). **tibi**: dative of separation (AG §381). **dēmās**: indefinite subjunctive, with a generalizing second person subject: "if you should remove," i.e., "should anyone remove." **commoda**: *commodum* in the plural often means "assets," including military ones; *Blanditiae*, *Error* and *Furor* are thus no longer personifications (attendants in Cupid's triumph), but abstractions (his weapons). **eris**: the apodosis of a future less vivid condition can be in the present or future indicative; the shift indicates that the speaker becomes more certain that the event will take place (AG §516b).

39–40: triumphantī: sc. tibi; dative with plaudet. **plaudet** < *plaudō, plaudere, plausī, plausum* "applaud for, show one's approval for," here with dative. **appositās sparget in ōra rosās**: Venus will shower Cupid's head with roses. The roses are "laid out" (*appositās*) because they have been laid out at a banquet of the gods (Barsby), or perhaps have been placed on Venus's altars by her worshippers. **in ōra**: plural for singular, and metonymy: *ōs* often means "face" or "head."

41–42: **pinnās … capillōs** = *gemmā variante pinnās, gemmā variante capillōs* (ablative absolutes). Note the asyndeton, the chiasmus, and the anaphora (repetition). **rotīs** < *rota, -ae*, f. "wheel"; in plural, by metonymy, "vehicle in motion," here "chariot."

43–44: **nōn paucōs**: litotes: "not a few" means "some."

45–46: **licet**: "although, even if." **vīcīnō** < *vīcīnus, a, um* "close at hand." **flamma**: Cupid has a torch as well as a bow and arrow.

47–48: **domitā … Gangētide terrā**: ablative absolute. **Gangētide**: "of the Ganges, Indian." Bacchus/Dionysus was famous for his triumphant arrival, complete with tigers, from India. **tū gravis ālitibus**: ambiguous, since *gravis* can mean either physically heavy or emotionally burdensome, and since *ālitibus* can be either dative or ablative; either "you are a heavy load for the birds (drawing your chariot)," taking *ālitibus* as a dative of disadvantage; or "you are a heavy burden (for other people) because of your birds," taking *ālitibus* as an ablative of cause; or "you oppress (i.e. *gravis*) with your birds …"(Barsby), taking *ālitibus* as an ablative of means. **tigribus**: note the chiasmus and the asyndeton. There is the same ambiguity about Bacchus as for Cupid: either "he was a heavy burden for the tigers (drawing his chariot)," or "he was a heavy burden because of his tigers," i.e. "he oppressed with his tigers."

Fig. 8 The Triumph of Bacchus, by Jan Thomas, c. 1660. Buenos Aires, National Museum of Fine Arts. Wikimedia, https://commons.wikimedia.org/wiki/File:Jan_Thomas_-_The_Triumph_of_Bacchus.jpg

49–50: **ergō**: note the logic: the poet has been giving arguments for the plea he makes now. **cum possim**: concessive *cum* clause. **parce**: *parcō* can be used with the infinitive to mean "refrain from." **in mē**: *in* + acc. can be used with a verb of spending (here, *perdere*, "waste") to mean "on" or "upon." **perdere ... opēs**: "waste your resources"; < *ops, opis*, f. "might, power" but often, in the plural, "resources."

51–52: **cognātī ... Caesaris**: the Caesar referred to is the emperor Augustus (C. Julius Caesar Augustus), who was the great-nephew and adopted son of Julius Caesar the dictator. The *gens Iūlia* traced its ancestry to Iulus, the son of Aeneas, and Aeneas was the son of Anchises and Venus. **quā**: agrees with *manū* (prolepsis, i.e. a dramatic anticipation of a word that comes later in the sentence). **victōs prōtegit**: *clementia* was one of the virtues for which Augustus was celebrated.

Fig. 9 Bust of Gaius Julius Caesar Augustus, first Roman Emperor, 27 BC–14 AD. Rome, Capitoline Museums. Wikimedia, http://commons.wikimedia.org/wiki/File:Bust_of_augustus.jpg

9. Amores 1.3: Just give me a chance

The first two poems have made it abundantly clear that the poet has fallen head over heels in love, and we also assume that things are not going well: lovers whose affections are reciprocated might speak of their passion (*uror*, 1.1.26), but they do not exclaim *me miserum!* and complain about Cupid's arrows (1.1.25), or talk about being wounded (*factum modo vulnus habebo*, 1.2.29).

Thus as *Amores* 1.3 opens we are not surprised to find the poet speaking of himself as the stereotypical unrequited lover, in ways that strongly remind us of Catullus and Propertius in their more abject modes. The poem begins with a cry of unrequited love: the poet prays first that the girl will love him or at least not reject him outright, but then even that second hope seems too presumptuous, and he is reduced to hoping that she will at least allow him to love her (lines 1–4).

This diffidence does not keep him from making his case: he's looking for a long-term relationship (line 5), and his love is the real thing (line 6). He may not be rich and he may not be an aristocrat (lines 7–10), but he has other qualities which should work in his favor: he's a poet (line 11), and, as he's already said, he's in it for the long haul (lines 12–18). He doesn't flit from girl to girl (line 15, *non sum desultor amoris*) and, looking far down the road, he wants her there when he dies (lines 17–18). Readers may find him sincere and persuasive, but they may also wonder whether he does not protest too much.

And there is a more immediate problem. The speaker's status as a poet is offered as the first argument in his favor (line 11), but then it seems to get dropped, as he turns instead to the long-term relationship argument. And although the two arguments are not obviously related, he writes as if they are, listing his "supporters" without any suggestion that they are

© William Turpin, CC BY   http://dx.doi.org/10.11647/OBP.0067.08

in different categories: Apollo, the Muses, and Dionysus (line 11); Amor, *fides*, *mores*, *simplicitas* and *pudor* (lines 12–14). It is poetry that in fact turns out be the crucial argument. After claims to fidelity, culminating with his dramatic "till death do us part" argument, the poet suddenly returns to poetry. The logic seems to be that the relationship, and especially the girl's part in it, will be the kind of thing that inspires poetry (lines 19–20).

Ovid, ever the rhetorician, drives this point home with three *exempla*, all heroines made famous by poets (lines 21–24). But the poet's choices are spectacularly inappropriate, given the case he is trying to make. A girl interested in declarations of fidelity and commitment will not want to be compared to three (no less!) of Jupiter's one-night stands. And the poet's language makes it hard to take this mythology seriously: Io is afraid of her new horns (line 21), Leda is deceived by her "riverine adulterer" (line 22), and Europa holds on with her "maiden hand" (line 24). The poet's persuasive skills, which at first seemed so powerful, seem now to have deserted him.

The final couplet offers us useful guidance on how to read this poem. After offering his poetry as an inducement to the girl, as it is *she* who will be immortalized, the poet ends up focused on himself: "we" (*nos*) not she, will be sung throughout the world, and it is *his* name, now, that will always be linked to hers (lines 25–26). A person, of course, can be passionately in love with someone else and completely self-involved at the same time. But if what other people see is the self-absorption they're not going to be very sympathetic.

Moreover, once we see that our poet is more interested in himself than in the girl he offers to write about, his claims to *sexual* fidelity look even more suspicious. The poet knows what to say to women: they love all that talk about sincerity and commitment, perhaps even more than they want poetic immortality. But, we learn, the arguments are just that: the rhetoric of persuasion rather than the language of love.

Suggested reading

Curran, Leo. "*Desultores Amoris*: Ovid *Amores* 1.3," *Classical Philology* 61 (1966): 41–49. http://dx.doi.org/10.1086/365081

Holleman, A. W. J. "Notes on Ovid *Amores* 1.3, Horace *Carm*. 1.14, and Propertius 2.26," *Classical Philology* 65 (1970): 177–180, at 177–179. http://dx.doi.org/10.1086/365624

Amores 1.3

Iusta precor: quae mē nūper praedāta puella est,
    aut amet aut faciat, cūr ego semper amem.
ā, nimium voluī: tantum patiātur amārī;
    audierit nostrās tot Cytherēa precēs.
accipe, per longōs tibi quī dēserviat annōs;   5
    accipe, quī pūrā nōrit amāre fidē.
sī mē nōn veterum commendant magna parentum
    nōmina, sī nostrī sanguinis auctor eques,
nec meus innumerīs renovātur campus arātrīs,
    temperat et sumptūs parcus uterque parens: 10
at Phoebus comitēsque novem vītisque repertor
    hāc faciunt, et mē quī tibi dōnat, Amor
et nullī cessūra fidēs, sine crīmine mōrēs,
    nūdaque simplicitās, purpureusque pudor.
nōn mihi mille placent, nōn sum dēsultor amōris: 15
    tū mihi, sī qua fidēs, cūra perennis eris;
tēcum, quōs dederint annōs mihi fīla sorōrum,
    vīvere contingat tēque dolente morī!
tē mihi māteriem fēlīcem in carmina praebē:
    prōvenient causā carmina digna suā.   20
carmine nōmen habent exterrita cornibus Īō
    et quam flūmineā lūsit adulter ave,
quaeque super pontum simulātō vecta iuvencō
    virgineā tenuit cornua vāra manū.

nōs quoque per tōtum pariter cantābimur orbem 25
iunctaque semper erunt nōmina nostra tuīs.

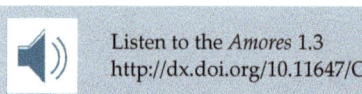

Listen to the *Amores* 1.3
http://dx.doi.org/10.11647/OBP.0067.25

Notes on *Amores* 1.3

1–2: quae ... puella est = *puella quae mē nūper praedāta est*. Notice the return to the martial terminology in *praedāta est*; see *Amores* 1.2, where Ovid refers to himself as the spoils (*praeda*, 19) of Cupid. **aut faciat cūr ego semper amem**: i.e., if she will not love him outright, let her at least give him reasons to keep on hoping. *Amet* and *faciat* are both jussive subjunctive (AG §439). *Amem* is subjunctive in an indirect question (AG §574).

3–4: ā: "oh me!"; an interjection indicating powerful feeling, including misery. **tantum**: "only, just." **patiātur**: jussive subjunctive; understand *puella* as the subject. **amārī**: understand *sē* as the subject of this infinitive. **audierit**: syncopated form of *audīverit*, probably future perfect (AG §181b); the clause functions almost as the apodosis of a condition: "if she would just allow herself to be loved, Venus will have heard my many prayers." **nostrās**: plural for singular. **Cytherēa** = Venus; the Greek island of **Cythera**[1] was sacred to Venus.

5–6: per longōs ... annōs: for *per* + accusative as "throughout" a period of time, see OLD 7. **quī dēserviat**: the antecedent is an implied *eum*, i.e., *accipe eum quī tibi dēserviat*. The verb *dēservīre*, "to devote oneself," can take a dative; it presumably retains some of its original meaning of "be enslaved to." The relative clauses of characteristic here and in the next line put the emphasis on Ovid's character. **nōrit** = *nōverit*, "knows how to."

7–8: veterum ... parentum: "of a long line of ancestors." **sī** = *etsī*. **eques**: "equestrian," a member of the *ordo equester*; take as a predicate nominative

---

1   http://pleiades.stoa.org/places/570186

with *est* understood. A family founded by a member of the equestrian order was highly respectable, but it had distinctly less prestige than a senatorial family.

9–10: **campus**: normally refers to an open field as a site of sport or warfare, but here it clearly refers to land under cultivation, an estate. **temperat et** = *et temperat*; poets often postpone conjunctions for metrical or stylistic reasons. **sumptūs**: accusative plural, object of *parcus uterque parens temperat*.

11–12: **at**: the poet since line 7 has been listing possible reasons for rejecting him as a lover; *at* introduces his response (see OLD 3). **comitēs ... novem**: the nine companions of Apollo are the Muses. **vītisque repertor**: the discoverer of the vine is Bacchus/Dionysus, god of wine and, here, a god of poetry. **hāc faciunt**: if this reading is right it means *faciunt hāc ex parte*, "act on this side," i.e., "are on my side." **mē quī tibi dōnat Amor** = *Amor quī mē tibi dōnat*, i.e., Amor is handing the poet over, as a slave; compare *dēserviat* (line 5).

13–14: **fidēs ... mōrēs ... simplicitās ... pudor**: these four Roman virtues parallel the divinities of poetry mentioned above (*Phoebus ... comitēs novem ... vītis repertor ... Amor*) and are also subjects of *hāc faciunt* (12). **cessūra**: "that will yield to," "second to," (+ dat.). **sine crīmine**: the basic meaning of *crīmen, crīminis*, n. is "charge, accusation." **purpureus pudor**: note the repetition of the *pu-* sound, perhaps suggestive of an embarrassed stammer; *pudor* is purple because it is modestly blushing.

15–16: **mille**: supply *puellae*. **dēsultor**: "circus rider" (in the Circus Maximus, who would jump from horse to horse at full gallop). This imagery suggests the opposite of fidelity, jumping from bed to bed. **sī qua fidēs**: understand *est*, i.e., "if there exists any loyalty at all"; *qua* = *aliqua*.

17–18: **quōs ... annōs** = *annōs, quōs fīla sorōrum dederint mihi*. *annōs* has been attracted into the relative clause, but functions with *vīvere* as an accusative of duration of time. **dederint**: possibly future perfect, but more likely perfect subjunctive in a conditional relative clause (AG §519). **sorōrum**: the three Parcae (the Fates), who spun and cut the threads of life (*fīla*). **vīvere contingat**: "may it befall me to live," "may I be allowed to live"; optative subjunctive (AG §441). **morī**: infinitive of *morior*, depending on *contingat*.

19–20: tē mihi māteriem: adversative asyndeton: the complete absence of connecting words indicates an abrupt change of topic. *māteriem fēlīcem* is a predicate accusative with *tē*: "Offer yourself as…" **in carmina**: "for songs"; *in* + acc. can mean "for the purpose of." **causā carmina digna suā**: "songs worthy of their inspiration"; *dignus* regularly takes an ablative (AG §418b).

21–22: carmine: "in poetry" or "because of poetry"; Ovid proceeds to give examples of women whose names live on through poems. **habent**: plural because there are three subjects: Io; the suppressed antecedent of *quam* in line 22 (Leda); and the suppressed antecedent of *quaeque* in line 23 (Europa). **Īō**: the daughter of Inachus, from Argos. Zeus fell in love with her, raped her, then changed her into a cow in an attempt to conceal his actions from Juno. Ovid elsewhere describes Io's shock at seeing her horns reflected in water (*Metamorphoses* 1.640–641). **quam** = *ea quam*; the reference is to Leda, raped by Zeus after he took the form of a swan (*flūmineā … ave*).

23–24: quaeque = *et ea quae* "and she who"; the reference is to Europa, whom Zeus, transformed into a bull, carried off to Crete.[2] **cornua vāra**: *vārus, a, um* means "bent outwards"; the detail makes the scene more vivid.

25–26: nōs: apparently = *ego et tu*, though we might suspect that poet mostly means *ego*. **pariter**: "equally," i.e., just as much as Zeus and his mistresses; the word may also suggest that Ovid and Corinna will be remembered *together*. **nostra**: here plural for singular.

---

2   http://pleiades.stoa.org/places/589748

10. *Amores* 1.4: Secret signs

If Ovid's book is telling us the story of a love affair, the fourth poem suggests at first that the poet has made a lot of progress. The previous poem gave us nothing but arguments, which did not in the end seem to be those likely to win a girl's heart; in *Amores* 1.4, it seems, she is the poet's willing lover. But of course there is a snag: she is not free to be with the poet, much as she might want to, as she has a man.

The identity, or rather the legal status, of this man is unclear. The Romans could use *vir* to mean "boyfriend" as well as "husband," just as "stand by your man" is ambiguous in English, at least in country-western music. We will discuss this problem after we have considered the poem as a whole.

The poem opens with the poet speaking, at least in theory, to the girl. He's heard that the *vir* is going to be at dinner with her, and he's jealous. In the best traditions of male jealousy he focuses on the physical facts: the *vir* will be able to touch the girl, and he (the poet) won't (lines 1–6). But it is harder to sympathize with our poet when he goes on to compare their situation to that of the Lapiths and Centaurs. This famous battle was provoked, supposedly, when the centaurs got drunk at the wedding feast in honor of Pirithous and Hippodamia, and tried to abduct the bride; the story (immortalized at Athens on the Parthenon metopes) exemplified primal conflict, between humans (the Lapiths) and the grotesquely semi-human centaurs. For the poet to compare himself to a centaur is a grotesque exaggeration: we can only laugh at the poet's attempt to compare a fairly pedestrian sexual jealousy with a clash between civilization and chaos. Our amusement is only heightened when he explains, with the heavy-handed clarity of the truly self-absorbed, that of course he is not *really* a centaur (line 9).

© William Turpin, CC BY   http://dx.doi.org/10.11647/OBP.0067.09

Fig. 10 Lapith fighting a centaur. South Metope 30, Parthenon, ca. 447–433 BC. London, British Museum. Wikimedia, http://commons.wikimedia.org/wiki/File:South_metope_30_Parthenon_BM.jpg

Most of the poem consists of the poet's "instructions" to the girl. The poet tells her to arrive as early as possible, not because they can have any real contact but because he just can't wait to see her; all he can hope for is some quick footsie when they take their places at the table (lines 13–16). The poet then gives the girl elaborate instructions for secret communications (lines 17–28). And it is here that we get our first clear sense that he is not being reasonable or realistic. The notion that lovers could get away with writing notes on the table with wine is absurd (line 20), and that detail calls into question the practicality of the whole discussion: surely a husband, and the other guests, would notice if the girl watched our poet with the intensity that he demands.

Once we start wondering about practicalities, we perhaps ask ourselves an even more fundamental question: whether the girl is actually listening. Is she even present at all? Could this simply be an internal monologue? The earlobe signal (lines 23–24) could be a real signal. But some of the poet's other suggestions seem oddly ambiguous: a girl could touch her cheek (lines 21–22), twist the ring on her finger (lines 25–26) or touch the table (lines 27–28) without thinking of these instructions at all. If a modern dinner guest were to decide that a woman who asked for the sugar was making a coded statement about him we might suspect he was fooling himself. Lovers, especially unrequited lovers, are notorious daydreamers.

The poet moves gradually from his fantasies about communication to simple jealousy (lines 33–34), and he becomes increasing preoccupied with the physical contact between the girl and her *vir* (lines 35–44). He knows about this physical stuff, he says, because he's done it himself (lines 45–48), with his mistress (*dominaeque meae*). This sudden use of the third person presents a problem, since up to this point, supposedly, he has been talking to the girl herself (note the striking return to the second person in line 49: *hoc tu non facies*). The solution offered by McKeown is to see these four lines as an aside: the poet, like a character in comedy, comments on his own speech in words not to be heard by the addressee. If this is right it has an important consequence: we learn for the first time that the poet and the girl really have been having an affair.

The alternative is to see this *domina* as a different girl, with whom the poet had had exactly the kinds of dalliances he's worried about here. This, as McKeown observes, would hardly be tactful: we would not expect an ardent lover to remind his new girl of her predecessors. But, in my view, this is precisely the point. The poet has lots to say, including things that in real life would be tactless: he can say what he wants in his own head.

The "instructions" continue: get the *vir* as drunk as possible, because that will give them a chance to be together (lines 51–54), and perhaps they can do some touching (whatever body parts happen to be available) when everyone gets up from the table (lines 55–58). Then comes, apparently, a dose of reality: the poet realizes that whatever fun he can have during dinner will be trivial compared to what happens when the girl has to go home with her *vir* (lines 59–62). The *vir* is going to be kissing her, and much more. All the poet can do is urge the girl not to show herself willing: the *vir* should not enjoy himself, much less the girl herself (lines 63–68).

Finally, in the last couplet, the poet asks her to lie to him: whatever happened at home with her *vir*, she should say categorically that nothing happened. The poet, in other words, *wants* to be deceived, at least on this crucial point. This works well enough if we really are to see this as a real, if one-sided, conversation: there is a certain charm in a lover *asking* to be lied to, at least in these particular circumstances. But it works even better if we read the poem as fantasy. The poet's imagination deals with the ultimate affront in two complementary ways: he first imagined the girl giving in to her *vir* only because she had to, and now he imagines her as so sensitive to his feelings that she will lie about it. She's the perfect lover, at least in the poet's own mind.

Appendix: the *vir*

Given the prominence of adultery in the western literary tradition, it is difficult for us to read *Amores* 1.4 without thinking of the *vir* as the girl's husband. This might seem to be confirmed by the clear suggestion that the girl *has* to go home with her *vir* (lines 61–62), who will then exercise his legal rights (lines 63–64).

But in his authoritative commentary James McKeown accepts the suggestion (made by Ian Du Quesnay) that the girl is a freedwoman, and the *vir* is her patron (i.e. her former owner), who has retained legal rights over her. McKeown observes that in *Amores* 2.5 Ovid uses similar legal language about his *own* girl, who is certainly not his wife. More important, McKeown finds it hard to believe that anyone would imagine a *married* couple furtively having sex at a dinner party (lines 47–50); as he says, on the authority of Ovid himself (*Ars Amatoria* 3.585f), "husbands do not have to seize fleeting opportunities" (McKeown 2, 77). It is worth remembering, too, that adultery was more than just one of the sexual vices that so offended the puritanical Augustus: in a remarkable intrusion into Roman legal tradition, Augustus made adultery a state crime, prosecuted in the same manner as treason, forgery, and poisoning. An extended fantasy about adultery is about as anti-Augustan as a poet could get.

I would suggest, nonetheless, that "husband" remains the most likely translation of Ovid's *vir*. As McKeown observes, the Roman dinner party had become a stereotypical venue for adultery (see esp. Horace, *Carm.* 3.6.25ff). And his argument about husbands and "fleeting opportunities" is not necessarily convincing. In the first place, outrageous sexual activity is not always, or even often, prompted merely by *opportunity*; it is easy enough to imagine a dissolute married couple flaunting their sexuality purely for the fun of it, especially in Rome.

More important, McKeown's argument depends on a relatively "literal" reading of the poem as a whole. If it is a "real" set of instructions given to a "real" girl actually expected to pay attention, then the dinnertime behavior is, at least, very surprising. But if the whole speech is purely in the poet's head, then the *vir*'s behavior makes perfect sense: with his beloved and his rival sharing a couch at dinner, our poet's imagination simply gets the better of him.

Fig. 11 Fresco from Herculaneum with banquet scene. Mid-first century CE. Naples, National Archaeological Museum. Wikimedia, https://commons.wikimedia.org/wiki/File:Scène_de_banquet,_fresque,_Herculanum.jpg

Suggested reading

Ford, G. B., Jr. "An Analysis of *Amores* 1.4," *Helikon* 6 (1955): 645–652.

Tracy, V. A. "Dramatic Elements in Ovid's *Amores*," *Latomus* 36 (1977): 496–500.

Davis, J. T. "*Amores* 1.4.45–48 and the Ovidian Aside," *Hermes* 107 (1979): 189–199.

Yardley, J. C. "Four Notes on Ovid, *Amores* 1," *L'Antiquité classique* 49 (1980): 265–268 http://dx.doi.org/10.3406/antiq.1980.1980

Stapleton, M. L. *Harmful Eloquence*: *Ovid's* Amores *from Antiquity to Shakespeare*. Ann Arbor: University of Michigan Press, 1996, 11–15.

Miller, P. A. *Subjecting Verses: Latin Love Elegy and the Emergence of the Real*. Princeton: Princeton University Press, 2004, 169–183.

Amores 1.4

Vir tuus est epulās nōbīs aditūrus eāsdem:
  ultima cēna tuō sit, precor, illa virō.
ergō ego dīlectam tantum convīva puellam
  aspiciam? tangī quem iuvet, alter erit,
alteriusque sinūs aptē subiecta fovēbis? 5
  iniciet collō, cum volet, ille manum?
dēsine mīrārī, positō quod candida vīnō
  Ātracis ambiguōs traxit in arma virōs;
nec mihi silva domus, nec equō mea membra cohaerent:
  vix ā tē videor posse tenēre manūs. 10
quae tibi sint facienda tamen cognosce, nec Eurīs
  dā mea nec tepidīs verba ferenda Notīs.
ante venī quam vir; nec quid, sī vēneris ante,
  possit agī videō, sed tamen ante venī.
cum premet ille torum—vultū comes ipsa modestō 15
  ībis ut accumbās—clam mihi tange pedem;
mē spectā nūtūsque meōs vultumque loquācem:
  excipe fūrtīvās et refer ipsa notās.
verba superciliīs sine vōce loquentia dīcam;
  verba legēs digitīs, verba notāta merō. 20
cum tibi succurret Veneris lascīvia nostrae,
  purpureās tenerō pollice tange genās;
sī quid erit, dē mē tacitā quod mente querāris,
  pendeat extrēmā mollis ab aure manus;

cum tibi, quae faciam, mea lux, dīcamve, placēbunt,   25
　　versētur digitīs ānulus usque tuīs;
tange manū mensam, tangunt quō mōre precantēs,
　　optābis meritō cum mala multa virō.
quod tibi miscuerit, sapiās, bibat ipse iubētō;
　　tū puerum leviter posce, quod ipsa volēs: 30
quae tū reddiderīs, ego prīmus pōcula sūmam,
　　et, quā tū biberīs, hāc ego parte bibam.
sī tibi forte dabit, quod praegustāverit ipse,
　　rēice lībātōs illius ōre cibōs.
nec premat impositīs sinitō tua colla lacertīs,   35
　　mīte nec in rigidō pectore pōne caput;
nec sinus admittat digitōs habilēsve papillae;
　　oscula praecipuē nūlla dedisse velīs.
oscula sī dederis, fīam manifestus amātor
　　et dīcam "mea sunt" iniciamque manum.   40
haec tamen aspiciam, sed quae bene pallia cēlant,
　　illa mihī caecī causa timōris erunt.
nec femorī committe femur nec crūre cohaerē
　　nec tenerum dūrō cum pede iunge pedem.
multa miser timeō, quia fēcī multa protervē,   45
　　exemplīque metū torqueor ipse meī:
saepe mihī dominaeque meae properāta voluptās
　　veste sub iniectā dulce perēgit opus.
hoc tū nōn faciēs; sed nē fēcisse putēris,
　　conscia dē tergō pallia dēme tuō.   50

vir bibat usque rogā (precibus tamen oscula dēsint),

    dumque bibit, fūrtim, sī potes, adde merum.

sī bene compositus somnō vīnōque iacēbit,

    consilium nōbīs rēsque locusque dabunt.

cum surgēs abitūra domum, surgēmus et omnēs,   55

    in medium turbae fac memor agmen eās:

agmine mē inveniēs aut inveniēris in illō;

    quidquid ibī poteris tangere, tange, meī.

mē miserum! monuī, paucās quod prōsit in hōrās;

    sēparor ā dominā nocte iubente meā.   60

nocte vir inclūdet; lacrimīs ego maestus obortīs,

    quā licet, ad saevās prōsequar usque forēs.

oscula iam sūmet, iam nōn tantum oscula sūmet:

    quod mihi dās furtim, iūre coacta dabis.

vērum invīta datō (potes hoc) similisque coactae: 65

    blanditiae taceant sitque maligna Venus.

sī mea vōta valent, illum quoque nē iuvet optō;

    sī minus, at certē tē iuvet inde nihil.

sed quaecumque tamen noctem fortūna sequētur,

    crās mihi constantī vōce dedisse negā.

 Listen to the *Amores* 1.4
http://dx.doi.org/10.11647/OBP.0067.26

Notes on *Amores* 1.4

1–2: Vir: can mean either "husband" or "boyfriend/lover"; the ambiguity is perhaps intentional (see the introductory essay). The oblivious *vir* as a woman's "significant other" is a standard figure in Roman love elegy. **nōbīs**: dative of reference with *eāsdem* (AG §376; OLD **īdem** 2c); he will be attending the same banquet as you and I will be. **sit precor** = *precor ut sit*, "I pray that (that dinner) will be." Verbs of praying, ordering, etc., usually introduce indirect commands with *ut* + subj., but occasionally *ut* is omitted (AG §565). Ovid's prayer is rather harsh, considering that the *vir* is the wronged individual.

3–4: tantum: can be construed either with *convīva* ("only a dinner guest") or with *aspiciam* ("Shall I only look upon?"). **convīva**: in apposition to *ego*: "Shall I, a mere table companion, look upon?" **tangī quem iuvet** = *is quem iuvet ā tē tangī*, "he who enjoys being touched by you."

5–6: sinūs ... fovebis: "will you warm the chest." *sinus* refers to the fold produced by the draping of clothes; the folds of clothing most commonly referred to (for men and women alike) are those at the breast, hence "bosom, breast," and therefore "embrace," in plural as well as singular. **subiecta**: "snuggling closely against." A dining-couch could accommodate two or three people. **iniciet ... manum**: a double entendre: *manum inicere* + dative can mean "to put one's hand on" or, in a legal sense, "to seize," as a way of making a formal claim on a person or thing. **collō**: dative with the compound verb *iniciō* (AG §370).

7–8: positō quod ... vīnō: construe *quod* first, "that"; verbs of perceiving, such as *sciō*, *crēdō*, *videō* and even *mīror* often introduce a *quod* clause acting as the direct object of that verb. **positō ... vīnō**: "after wine was served," ablative absolute (AG §420). Drunkenness was a factor in the centaurs' attack. **Ātracis** < *Ātracis, -idis*, f. "the woman from Atrax"[1] (a town in Thessaly). The reference is to Hippodamia, whose wedding to Pirithous, king of the Lapiths, turned violent when the centaurs, who were guests, were so aroused by her beauty that they tried to carry her off. **ambiguōs ... virōs**: the centaurs, half-man/half-horse creatures; hence, humorously, "ambiguous men."

---

1 http://pleiades.stoa.org/places/540682

9–10: nec mihi silva domus: understand *est*; dative of possession. The poet explains that he is not an uncivilized beast prone to uncontrolled acts (as the centaurs are). **equō**: dative with the compound verb *cohaerent* (AG §370); again, a reference to the centaurs. **ā tē**: "from you," with *tenēre manūs*. **tenēre**: "to keep (away), to restrain, to hold back."

11–12: quae tibi sint facienda: "(the things) which must be done by you," i.e., what you must do. The gerundive injects a matter-of-fact tone. **sint** is subjunctive in an indirect question (AG §574). **nec Eurīs ... nec tepidīs ... Notīs**: "neither to the east winds nor to the warm south winds." **ferenda**: the gerundive with a verb meaning "give" expresses purpose (AG §500.4).

13–14: ante ... quam = *antequam* "before, early, in advance"; the splitting of a compound word is called tmesis. **venī**: present imperative; note the scansion (*āntĕ vĕnī*). **nec quid ... video** = *nec videō quid possit agī, sī vēneris ante*. *quid possit* is impersonal "what can be done"; subjunctive in an indirect question. The repetitions of *ante* convey a sense of urgency.

15–16: torum: "couch"; at formal dinners the Romans ate lying down. **vultū ... accumbās**: this clause is a second *cum* clause, with the *cum* supplied by *cum premet ille torum*; the asyndeton suggests that the speaker is in a highly emotional state. **comes**: note that *comes, comitis* "companion" can be feminine as well as masculine. **accumbās**: "take your place (reclining) at the table." **mihi**: dative of advantage (AG §376).

17–18: furtīvās ... notās: with both *excipe* and *refer*. *referō* can mean "return" (see OLD 12); for *nota, -ae*, f. as "signal," see OLD 7.

19–20: superciliīs ... digitīs: ablative of means with *notāta* (AG §409). < *supercilium, i(ī)* "eyebrow." **merō**: "with wine," ablative of means; *merum* strictly speaking is "wine not mixed with water" but is often used to mean wine in general.

21–22: cum: here and at 25 and 28 *cum* means "whenever." **Veneris** = *amōris* (metonymy); here *amor* clearly means sex. **purpureās**: as in 1.3.14 "purple" implies "blushing."

23–24: quid = *aliquid* (AG §310a); antecedent of *quod*. **dē mē tacitā quod mente querāris** = *quod dē mē, tacitā mente, querāris*; poets sometimes postpone conjunctions for metrical or stylistic reasons. **tacitā ... mente** = *tacitē* (an anticipation of the Romance languages' use of the *–mente* ending to create adverbs, e.g. Italian *facilmente*. *querāris* is potential subjunctive (AG §447.2). **extrēmā ... aure**: scansion shows that these words are to be taken together; *extrēmus* can mean "the lowest part," so she is presumably supposed to touch her earlobe.

25–26: **quae** = *ea quae*; the antecedent of the relative pronoun is often omitted, AG §307c. **mea lux**: a term of endearment; vocative case. **usque**: "continuously" (OLD 5).

27–28: **tangunt**: understand *mensam*, normally "table" but also "altar"; touching an altar was a normal gesture of prayer. **quō mōre**: "in the manner in which." **optābis ... cum**: "when(ever) you hope for"; *cum* is postponed. *cum* takes the indicative when it means "on every occasion which." **meritō**: "deservedly, as he deserves."

29–30: **quod** = *id quod*. **miscuerit**: future perfect; the subject is the *vir*. Romans normally drank their wine mixed with water; the implication here is that the *vir* will add relatively little water, but our poet wants the *puella* to drink a weaker mixture. **sapiās**: hortatory subjunctive, used to express a proviso: "may you be wise" means "if you are wise" (AG §528a). But the expression seems to be a colloquial way of saying "be wise," "be sensible." **bibat ipse iubētō** = *iubētō ut bibat ipse*. *iubētō* is second person singular future imperative (AG §449); the future imperative suggests the language of formal legislation. *iubeō* normally takes accusative + infinitive, but can also take *ut* + subjunctive. For the omission of *ut* with verbs of commanding see AG §565a (cf. line 2 above). **puerum**: i.e. the cupbearer; a male slave, of whatever age, could be called *puer*. **leviter**: "quietly" (adverb). **posce**: "call for, demand," with double accusative (ask *x* for *y*, AG §396); the word is often used of asking for wine in particular. **quod** = *id quod*, as in line 29: "that (only) which."

31–32: **quae**: the antecedent is *pōcula*. **reddiderīs ... biberīs**: future perfect, but translate as imperative, "return." The final syllable of the second person singular in the future perfect is often lengthened in poetry immediately before the caesura. **quā**: "on whatever part (of the cup)"; construe with *parte* (line 32); ablative of place where.

33–34: lībātōs < *lībō* (1) here "nibble, taste." **illius**: in poetry the second i is sometimes long, sometimes short, as here (see OLD).

35–36: nec premat ... sinitō = *nec sinitō (ut) premat*, "do not allow him to press"; *sinitō* (future imperative) is mock formal in tone, like *iubētō* in line 29. **colla**: plural for singular. Note the chiastic word order, with words for arms surrounding the words for neck. **mīte ... caput** = *nec pōne mīte caput in rigidō pectore*. **nec pōne** = *nē pōne*; for this archaic and poetic form of a negative command see AG §450a; here it has a religious or legal tone. **mīte** < *mītis, mite* "soft, gentle."

37–38: sinus: "the fold of your dress." Refer to the note on *sinus* in line 5. **digitōs** = *digitōs eius*. **papillae**: understand *admittant*, from the preceding *sinus admittat*. **nulla dedisse velīs**: "may you wish to have given no (kisses)," i.e., don't give any. The tone is mock formal, as with the future imperatives above.

39–40: sī dederis: future perfect indicative, in a future more vivid condition (AG §516c). **manifestus amātor**: a play on legal language; *fūr manifestus* is the technical term for a thief caught red-handed. **iniciamque ... manum**: for *manum inicere* see above on line 6.

41–42: pallia < *pallium, iī* n. "cloak." **illa**: refers to *quae bene pallia cēlant*.

45–46: protervē: "boldly" or "shamelessly."

47–48: mihī dominaeque meae: datives of advantage (AG §376). **voluptās**: used explicitly of the pleasure connected with sex, see OLD 5; here possibly personified (OLD 3). **veste sub iniectā** = *sub iniectā veste*. **perēgit opus**: an explicit sexual reference, with *dulce opus* as a euphemism for sexual intercourse

49–50: nē fēcisse putēris: a negative purpose clause (AG §531); *putēris* is present passive subjunctive. **pallia**: here probably plural for singular. **dēme** < *dēmō, dēmere, dempsī, demptum* "remove."

51–52: vir bibat usque rogā = *rogā (ut) vir bibat usque*; for the omission of *ut* with verbs of commanding, see AG §565a. **merum**: here perhaps undiluted wine (contrast line 20); the point then would be that she is secretly making his drink stronger than he expects. But it is possible that she is simply supposed to keep adding ordinary wine, secretly, so that he will drink more.

53–54: **compositus**: "settled in a position of rest." **somnō vīnōque** = *somnō vīnī*, by hendiadys (the use of two substantives connected by a conjunction, instead of a substantive with an adjective or genitive). **cōnsilium**: accusative; here "plan of action" (OLD 4b).

55–56: **surgēmus et omnēs** = *et (cum) omnēs surgēmus*. **in medium turbae ... agmen**: "into the middle part of the crowd's line of march"; *agmen, agminis* n. can refer to any group of people or things moving in the same direction together, but is often used of a column of soldiers on the march. **fac memor ... eās** = *fac ut memor sīs ut eās*; *eās* is present subjunctive of *eō*. For the omission of *ut* with certain verbs of commanding see AG §565a.

57–58: **inveniēris**: future passive indicative; the future perfect active would be *invenieris*. **in illō** = *in agmine*. Notice that the words for the poet and the *puella* are placed within the words for the *agmen*. **meī**: partitive genitive, with *quidquid* (AG §346a3).

59–60: **mē miserum**: accusative of exclamation (AG §397d). Ovid speaks to himself in an aside. **paucās quod prōsit in hōrās**: "I have given the sort of advice which is useful (only) for a few hours." *prosit* is subjunctive in a relative clause of characteristic (AG §535). **nocte iubente**: ablative absolute (AG §420).

61–62: **inclūdet**: understand *tē* as direct object; the address to the *puella* resumes. **quā**: "where, to what extent"; adverb. **prōsequar**: "I will accompany (you)." **saevās ... forēs**: the "savage doors" are the front doors of his girlfriend's house; front doors provide the typical setting in Roman poetry for expressions of unrequited love by an excluded lover (*exclūsus amātor*). See further on *Amores* 1.6.

63–64: **iūre**: this may indicate that the woman is bound "by law" to kiss her *vir*, who would then have to be a husband; but it is also possible that Ovid is speaking more metaphorically of the "rights" of a rival lover.

65–66: **vērum**: "but." **invīta**: feminine nominative singular, agreeing with the subject of *dato*. **datō**: another future imperative (AG §449) like *iubētō* in line 29; understand *ōscula* (line 63) as the direct object. **potes hoc**: *possum* can be construed with a simple accusative, meaning "be able to do." **similisque coactae**: "like a woman who has been compelled"; participles, like all adjectives, can be used as nouns (AG §494a).

67–68: **illum quoque nē iuvet optō** = *optō nē iuvet illum quoque*. *iuvet* is impersonal: *mē iuvat*, for example, means "it helps me," i.e. "it's good for me to" or "I enjoy it." So the poet hopes that the *vir* (*illum*) "won't enjoy it." The point of *quoque* becomes clearer after the next line: the poet claims that his mistress won't enjoy her encounter with her *vir*, and here he hopes that this will be true for the *vir* as well (*quoque*). **sī minus** = *sī mea vōta minus valent*; *minus* here = *nōn*. **at certē**: "then at least," an emphatic and colloquial way of introducing the apodosis of a condition. **inde**: "from there, thence," but used sometimes to express causation; adverb. **nihil**: internal accusative with the impersonal *iuvet* (*me nihil iuvat* means "I enjoy it *not at all* when").

69–70: **quaecumque ... noctem fortūna sequētur**: "whatever fortune attends the night," i.e., whatever happens tonight. The verb is future in Latin—regular, and more logical than English, which uses the present tense in this type of clause. **constantī**: agrees most naturally with *voce*; it could also agree with *mihi*, which would add a distinct note of irony to the poem. **dedisse**: picks up *das*, *dabis*, and *datō* in lines 64–65; but *dō* can also be used absolutely to mean "grant sexual favors."

11. *Amores* 1.5: The siesta

This short poem is important as the one in which we "meet" the main object of all the poet's attention; *Amores* 1.1 raised questions about the girl who prompted his shift to elegiac poetry, and now we learn her name. We also get a detailed description, indeed almost an inventory, though it is a description of her body rather than of her appearance as a whole, much less of her as a person. The poem is unique in Roman poetry in being erotic in the modern sense of the word: it is about the physicality of love rather than love itself.

Readers will perhaps differ on the appeal of this poem, depending not least on their reaction to an eroticism that is so unapologetically male. But even if we set aside as purely modern our concerns about the treatment of Corinna, the poem presents a problem, precisely because it does seem so straightforward. It is not easy to see the poem as a satisfactory artistic whole.

The poem begins with an elaborate description of the setting (lines 1–8). It is midday, the poet is having his siesta, and the room is dark and tranquil (Roman shutters were very effective). The light is beautiful for its own sake, even magical, but it is also particularly suitable for girls who are "modest" (lines 7–8). Girls and their modesty suggest that there is more to the siesta than meets the eye; it may be that for the Romans the siesta was the ideal time for adultery.

Then Corinna suddenly appears (line 9). The language of procession (*Ecce, Corinna venit*, line 9) associates her with divinity, as does her name: the Greek poet Corinna, like the more famous Sappho, was associated with the Muses. *Amores* 1.1 invited us to expect a girlfriend who inspired the poet to write, and here she is: the poet's new muse, all ready for bed.

© William Turpin, CC BY   http://dx.doi.org/10.11647/OBP.0067.10

She is wearing only a tunic, and an unbelted one at that, and her hair is down (a more dramatic signal of intimacy in days of elaborate hairdos than it is today). The poet, rhetorical training at the ready, cannot resist two literary allusions (lines 11–12): Corinna is like queen Semiramis, an allusion with at least latent sexual allusion, and Lais, with whom the connection with sex is obvious. Lais was a famous name for a courtesan.

So we are prepared, to some extent, for the abrupt transition to sex, though perhaps not for the violence (*deripui tunicam*, line 13). The poet describes Corinna as resisting, but the resistance was not serious (lines 13–16). The trope is disturbing to modern readers, for whom no means no, but we should remember that, at least in Roman poetry, there was a place (rightly or wrongly) for *pretend* sexual violence. And Corinna did, after all, come into the room without many clothes to join the poet in bed.

The poet goes on to describe Corinna's naked body in minute detail, starting with shoulders and moving down to the thighs (lines 17–22). Here too modern readers will probably be offended by the egregious objectification. But since *Lady Chatterley's Lover* we have grown used to descriptions with far more explicit sexual detail. And it is important to remember that the "catalog of body parts," as in Marvell's beloved "To His Coy Mistress," mocks the observer more than the observed.

The poet's obsessive focus makes the most sense, I think, if this is their first time in bed together. Of course this reading works only if we accept that *Amores* 1.4 is fantasy rather than "reality," with the poet only imagining that the girl cares about him at all. But this reading gives some point to what follows. The poem ends abruptly; unlike D. H. Lawrence and his successors, Ovid can leave the crucial facts to our imaginations (*cetera quis nescit*, line 25). The happy couple rest, and perhaps even doze off, and the poet says he hopes there will be many more such siestas (line 26).

So what is the point here? One possibility is that we are to focus on the fact that at long last the poet is willing to talk of Corinna, however briefly, as if she mattered too (*lassi requievimus ambo*, line 25). Another possibility (not excluded by the first) is that our focus is on the hope for the future (line 26); he's finally gotten her into bed, they had a great time (or at least he did), and he wants the affair to continue. But is it possible that we are to be struck by the pure physicality? All our poet wants from the affair, at least so far, is uncomplicated sex in the afternoon. It is not easy, as we have seen, to defend the sexual violence, and the objectification of Corinna. Is it possible that we are not supposed to? We see the poet's "love" for Corinna for exactly what it is: masculine, physical, and shallow.

Suggested reading

Nicoll, W. S. M. "Ovid, *Amores* I.5," *Mnemosyne* 30 (1977): 40–48. http://dx.doi.org/10.1163/156852577x00248

Papanghelis, T. D. "About the Hour of Noon: Ovid, *Amores* 1.5," *Mnemosyne* 42 (1989): 54–61. http://dx.doi.org/10.1163/156852589x00056

Amores 1.5

Aestus erat, mediamque diēs exēgerat hōram;
    apposuī mediō membra levanda torō.
pars adaperta fuit, pars altera clausa fenestrae,
    quāle ferē silvae lūmen habēre solent,
quālia sublūcent fugiente crepuscula Phoebō   5
    aut ubi nox abiit nec tamen orta diēs.
illa verēcundīs lux est praebenda puellīs,
    quā timidus latebrās spēret habēre pudor.
ecce, Corinna venit tunicā vēlāta recinctā,
    candida dīviduā colla tegente comā,   10
quāliter in thalamōs fōrmōsa Semīramis īsse
    dīcitur et multīs Lāis amāta virīs.
dēripuī tunicam; nec multum rāra nocēbat,
    pugnābat tunicā sed tamen illa tegī;
cumque ita pugnāret tamquam quae vincere nollet,   15
    victa est nōn aegrē prōditiōne suā.
ut stetit ante oculōs positō vēlāmine nostrōs,
    in tōtō nusquam corpore menda fuit:
quōs umerōs, quālēs vīdī tetigīque lacertōs!
    fōrma papillārum quam fuit apta premī!   20
quam castīgātō plānus sub pectore venter!
    quantum et quāle latus! quam iuvenāle femur!
singula quid referam? nīl nōn laudābile vīdī,
    et nūdam pressī corpus ad usque meum.

cētera quis nescit? lassī requiēvimus ambō.   25

prōveniant mediī sīc mihi saepe diēs.

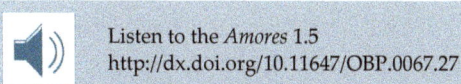
Listen to the *Amores* 1.5
http://dx.doi.org/10.11647/OBP.0067.27

Notes on *Amores* 1.5

1–2: aestus < *aestus, -ūs*, m. "tide; heat"; here "a hot spell, hot season." This could simply be describing the weather, or it could have sexual connotations. **exēgerat** < *exigō, -ere, -ēgī, -actum*, "to drive out"; here (of a period of time) "to bring to an end." **levanda** < *levō -āre*, "to lighten, relieve"; *membra levāre* means "to rest"; the gerundive is used as a simple participle to express purpose (AG §500.4), "I had laid my limbs to rest." *membra*, especially in the singular, can also have a sexual connotation. **torō**: dative of direction with a verb of motion (AG §428h).

3–4: pars adaperta ... pars ... clausa: *adaperta* means "open." The window was a double one, with one side open and the other closed; the structure of the line reflects the double nature of the window. **quāle ... lūmen**: "like the light which"; this is in apposition to all of line 3.

5–6: quālia ... crepuscula: "like the twilight which"; subject of *sublucent*, also in apposition to line 3. Note the languid *l*, *u*, and *a* sounds. **fugiente ... Phoebō**: "as Apollo is fleeing," i.e., "as the sun is setting," ablative absolute. Apollo was the god of the sun, which his steeds and chariot pulled across the sky from east to west. **nec ... orta**: understand *est*, "has not risen."

7–8: quā ... spēret: relative clause of characteristic (AG §535); *quā* (its antecedent is *lux*) is an ablative of means (AG §409); "the kind of light in which."

9–10: Corinna: here the poet's lover is finally introduced by name. Corinna was the name of a real-life Greek poet, just as the name Lesbia, which

Catullus gave to his lover, was an allusion to the poet Sappho. "Corinna" may be based on the Greek word κόρη ("maiden"), the Greek equivalent of *puella*. **vēlāta** < *vēlō -āre*, "to cover, clothe"; the juxtaposition of *vēlāta* and *tunicā recinctā* produces an ironic oxymoron: "clothed in an unfastened tunic." **dīviduā** < *dīviduus, a, um* "divided"; we thus infer that Corinna had long hair, and that her hairdo was undone, with her hair hanging over each shoulder. **colla**: plural for singular (as in 1.4.35).

11–12: **quāliter**: "in which way, so" (adverb). **Semīramis** < *Semīramis, -idis*, f. the legendary queen of Assyria; she was famous for her regal nature, her beauty, and lust. **Lāis** < *Lāis, -idis* or *-idos*, f. the name of two famous Greek courtesans. **virīs**: dative of agent, as often with perfect participles (AG §375).

13–14: **multum**: "much" (adverbial), modifying *nocēbat*. **rāra**: modifies an understood *tunica*; here "thin" or possibly "scanty." **nocēbat** < *noceō, nocēre, nocuī, nocitum* "harm" but here "detract," i.e., the tunic didn't present much of an obstacle. **pugnābat tunicā sed tamen illa tegī** = *sed tamen illa pugnābat tunicā tegī*; the postponed conjunction (*sed*) highlights the words placed in front of it (*pugnābat, tunicā*). *tegī* is an infinitive of purpose with *pugnābat* (AG §460).

15–16: **cumque ita pugnāret tamquam quae vincere nollet** = *cum ita pugnāret tamquam (aliquis pugnāret) quae vincere nollet*. The *cum* clause is perhaps causal, or concessive (AG §549). For relative clauses of characteristic, see AG §535. **nōn aegrē**: both "with no difficulty" (on the part of the speaker) and "with no reluctance" (on the part of Corinna).

17–18: **nostrōs** = *meōs*. **menda**: "fault, blemish." Ovid is the only poet to use this word to mean a physical blemish; in other authors it refers to literary faults.

19–22: **quōs … quāles … quam … quantum**: anaphora. Ovid here describes Corinna's charms, starting with her shoulders and working his way down.

19–20: **quōs umerōs**: exclamatory *quis*, "what!" **quam**: exclamatory *quam*, "how!", modifying an adjective (*apta*). **apta**: "suitable, proper," here construed with *premī* (passive infinitive).

21–22: **castīgātō** < *castīgātus -a -um* "tightly drawn, controlled." Notice that this line is entirely spondaic except for the fifth foot, presumably suggestive of the poet's careful admiration. **quantum et quāle latus** < *latus, lateris* n., "side"; accusative of exclamation (AG §397d). In referring to the human body *latus* most often refers to the upper trunk (OLD 1a), but since the poet seems to be working his way down Corinna's body it perhaps here means "hip"; this would explain why he admired its size, since the Romans seem to have preferred big hips on women.

23–24: **quid** = *cūr*. **referam**: deliberative subjunctive (AG §444a). **nūdam pressī**: "I clasped her, naked as she was" (Barsby). **corpus ad usque meum** = *usque ad meum corpus*; hyperbaton (a violent disruption of the natural word order for dramatic effect).

25–26: **proveniant**: optative subjunctive, "I hope that middays may turn out." Ryan and Perkins suggest a double entendre, since *prōveniō*, when referring to plants, can mean "spring up, arise."

12. *Amores* 1.6: On the doorstep

The poet has been at dinner party, and has been drinking. In the approved mode of a Greek or Roman lover, he has gone on to the house of his mistress, where he is confronted with closed doors and a doorkeeper (*ianitor*) who won't open up. The poem presents us with a long speech, mostly to the doorkeeper, and as with *Amores* 1.4 there is some doubt as to whether we are to see this as a real speech, or an interior monologue. Perhaps in this case, though, our decision does not matter much: one crucial aspect of the poem is the fact there are no signs that anyone is listening.

To understand the general situation it is helpful to have a mental picture of the huge defensive doors characteristic of a Roman town house, closer to the gates of a castle or a Cambridge college than to anything we know from our own domestic architecture, and accurately recreated in the HBO series "Rome." The important thing for this poem is that a poet could declaim all night on such a doorstep without necessarily being heard by occupants other than the doorkeeper.

Discussion of the poem requires particular attention to the question of genre. Just as Roman readers of *Amores* 1.1 would have recognized it as a form of *recusatio*, *Amores* 1.6 would have been read within its generic context, for which classicists have yet more technical language. A lover kept outside the doors of his mistress is known as an *exclusus amator*, and a poem on such a theme is known by the ponderous but unavoidable Greek word *paraclausithyron* ("next to a closed-door"). In the typical *paraclausithyron* the *exclusus amator* sings to the door itself; Ovid offers a striking variation, singing to the *ianitor* instead. (The classic study of this theme is the short monograph by Copley.)

The persistence of this genre in Greek and Latin literature, especially in Roman comedy and Latin elegy, raises an important question, on which scholars seem flatly to disagree. For some, the generic elements are purely literary: there are garlands, torches, drunken lovers, and closed doors in Greek literature, and they persist in Latin, but Roman lovers in real life, however heartbroken, normally went home to bed. Others (especially Jasper Griffin) imagine that at least some Roman lovers in real life (perhaps not the poets themselves) would have done exactly what the poets show them doing: not singing poems to doors or doorkeepers, necessarily, but definitely spending part of the night in a kind of amatory vigil. The problem is similar, perhaps, to that of the serenade: presumably in real life men have in fact gone with their guitars to sing to their girlfriends, but few of us have seen it done.

Fig. 12 François-Adolphe Grison (1845–1914), "The Serenade." Image from Sothebys. Wikimedia, https://commons.wikimedia.org/wiki/File:Fran%C3%A7ois-Adolphe_Grison_The_Serenade.jpg

An unusual feature of this poem is its refrain: *tempora noctis eunt; excute poste seram* occurs at lines 24, 32, 40, 48, and 56, i.e. every 8th line for roughly the middle third of the poem. This has been seen as a reflection of the *komos*, the kind of song sung by drunken lovers (whether in reality or in literature) outside the doors of girls. But Lindsay Watson has argued that the refrain also reflects the language of hymns, and that part of the joke is that instead of a god the "hymn" is addressed to a humble, but for the poet all-powerful, *ianitor*.

There is no need to explain the poet's various arguments, though it may be helpful to state the obvious: they are not supposed to be serious ones. He argues, for example, that the door only needs to be opened a very little, because the poet, like all unrequited lovers, has lost weight (lines 3–6). And he argues that he deserves a break, because love has made him brave; the only thing he's defeated by is the *ianitor* himself (lines 7–18). He also claims that in the past he persuaded the mistress of the house not to give the *ianitor* a whipping (lines 19–22), though this sounds like a desperate lie; nothing in the first five poems, at least, suggests that he has that kind of relationship with the *puella*.

Perhaps surprisingly, the refrains do not provide much of an organizing principle; one might have expected five "verses" of seven lines, each marked off by the refrain, but instead the speaker seems to have a short attention span, moving from argument to argument as one thought suggests another. Thus after the first use of the refrain (line 24), the poet moves from pleading to a kind of argument: the *ianitor* is defending his door as though there were was a war on (lines 25–31). After the second refrain (line 32) the poet develops that thought: a lover's siege is like warfare in some ways (a theme that will be explored in *Amores* 1.9), except that the lover is harmless (lines 33–39). After third refrain (line 40) the poet suggests two reasons why the *ianitor* might not be listening: he might be asleep, or he might have a girl himself (lines 41–47). The fourth refrain (line 48) is followed by a moment of wild optimism (the poet hears something: maybe the door is moving), but he's wrong (it's only the wind), which is followed by other thoughts about other winds (lines 49–55).

After the final refrain (line 56) the poet moves from persuasion to threats of violence (lines 57–60), but that doesn't work either. Nothing, neither pleading nor threatening, has had any effect (lines 61–64). In defeat the poet, as dawn breaks, shifts his focus, and addresses his garland (lines 65–70), but he then returns briefly to the *ianitor*, and bids him farewell.

The last couplet is a puzzle. The poet changes addressee one more time, and says goodbye to the doors themselves, in all their physicality: doorposts, threshold, and bars. But the doors have also been given an epithet far more appropriate for the *ianitor*: the doors are now "fellow slaves" (*conservae ... fores*, line 75). What is going on? The "fellow slave" joke has been hovering in the background throughout the poem: the *ianitor* is a real slave, and the poet is a slave of love (as we saw in *Amores* 1.2, esp.

line 18, and lines 17–30). But what does it mean to say that *doors* are fellow slaves?

Part of the solution, perhaps, resides in the reader's awareness of genre, and the expectations that come with it. For more than 70 lines Ovid has been amusing us by exploring his own unique version of the *paraclausithyron*: instead of addressing the doors, his *exclusus amator* has been talking to the *ianitor*. Part of the point in this last couplet, therefore, is that we have a sense of relief: we're finally back to what we are more comfortable with.

But what is the point, then, of putting the "fellow slave" joke here, of all places? I can only suggest that it makes us think harder about what has been going on in the poem. The poet has been talking, endlessly, to the *ianitor*. But has anyone, even a *ianitor*, been paying any attention? Has the poet not, in fact, been doing what *other* poets do in this situation (other *exclusi amatores*), namely talking only to big wooden doors—to doorposts, threshold, and bars. Calling those doors *conservae*, reminding us of the *ianitor*, reminds us that they are absolutely not listening.

Suggested reading

Copley, F. O. *Exclusus Amator: A Study in Latin Love Poetry*. Madison: American Philological Association, 1956.

Griffin, Jasper. "Genre and Real Life in Latin Poetry," *Journal of Roman Studies* 71 (1981): 39–49, reprinted in his *Latin Poets and Roman Life*. Chapel Hill: University of North Carolina Press, 1986. http://dx.doi.org/10.2307/299495

Watson, Lindsay C. "Ovid *Amores* 1.6: A Parody of a Hymn?" *Mnemosyne* 35 (1982): 92–102. http://dx.doi.org/10.1163/156852582x00639

Amores 1.6

Iānitor (indignum) dūrā religāte catēnā,
  difficilem mōtō cardine pande forem.
quod precor exiguum est: aditū fac iānua parvō
  oblīquum capiat sēmiadaperta latus.
longus amor tālēs corpus tenuāvit in ūsūs   5
  aptaque subductō pondere membra dedit;
ille per excubiās custōdum lēniter īre
  monstrat, inoffensōs dērigit ille pedēs.
at quondam noctem simulācraque vāna timēbam;
  mīrābar, tenebrīs quisquis itūrus erat: 10
rīsit, ut audīrem, tenerā cum mātre Cupīdō
  et leviter "fīēs tū quoque fortis" ait.
nec mora, vēnit amor: nōn umbrās nocte volantēs,
  nōn timeō strictās in mea fāta manūs;
tē nimium lentum timeō, tibi blandior ūnī: 15
  tū, mē quō possīs perdere, fulmen habēs.
aspice (utī videās, immītia claustra relaxā)
  ūda sit ut lacrimīs iānua facta meīs.
certē ego, cum positā stārēs ad verbera veste,
  ad dominam prō tē verba tremente tulī.   20
ergō, quae valuit prō tē quoque grātia quondam,
  heu facinus! prō mē nunc valet illa parum?
redde vicem meritīs: grātō licet esse, quod optās.
  tempora noctis eunt; excute poste seram.

excute: sīc umquam longā relevēre catēnā, 25
    nec tibi perpetuō serva bibātur aqua.
ferreus ōrantem nēquīquam, iānitor, audīs:
    rōboribus dūrīs iānua fulta riget.
urbibus obsessīs clausae mūnīmina portae
    prōsunt: in mediā pāce quid arma timēs? 30
quid faciēs hostī, quī sīc exclūdis amantem?
    tempora noctis eunt; excute poste seram.
nōn ego mīlitibus veniō comitātus et armīs:
    sōlus eram, sī nōn saevus adesset Amor;
hunc ego, sī cupiam, nusquam dīmittere possum: 35
    ante vel ā membrīs dīvidar ipse meīs.
ergō Amor et modicum circā mea tempora vīnum
    mēcum est et madidīs lapsa corōna comīs.
arma quis haec timeat? quis nōn eat obvius illīs?
    tempora noctis eunt; excute poste seram. 40
lentus es, an somnus, quī tē male perdat, amantis
    verba dat in ventōs aure repulsa tuā?
at, meminī, prīmō, cum tē cēlāre volēbam,
    pervigil in mediae sīdera noctis erās.
forsitan et tēcum tua nunc requiescit amīca: 45
    heu, melior quantō sors tua sorte meā!
dummodo sīc, in mē dūrae transīte catēnae.
    tempora noctis eunt; excute poste seram.
fallimur, an versō sonuērunt cardine postēs
    raucaque concussae signa dedēre forēs? 50

1.6: On the doorstep

fallimur: impulsa est animōsō iānua ventō.
    ei mihi, quam longē spem tulit aura meam!
sī satis es raptae, Boreā, memor Ōrīthyiae,
    hūc ades et surdās flāmine tunde forēs.
urbe silent tōtā, vitreōque madentia rōre   55
    tempora noctis eunt; excute poste seram,
aut ego iam ferrōque ignīque parātior ipse,
    quem face sustineō, tēcta superba petam.
nox et Amor vīnumque nihil moderābile suādent:
    illa pudōre vacat, Līber Amorque metū.   60
omnia consumpsī, nec tē precibusque minīsque
    mōvimus, ō foribus dūrior ipse tuīs.
nōn tē formōsae decuit servāre puellae
    līmina: sollicitō carcere dignus erās.
iamque pruīnōsōs mōlītur Lūcifer axēs,   65
    inque suum miserōs excitat āles opus.
at tū, nōn laetīs dētracta corōna capillīs,
    dūra super tōtā līmina nocte iacē;
tū dominae, cum tē prōiectam māne vidēbit,
    temporis absumptī tam male testis eris.   70
quāliscumque valē, sentīque abeuntis honōrem:
    lente nec admissō turpis amante, valē.
vōs quoque, crūdēlēs rigidō cum līmine postēs
    dūraque conservae ligna, valēte, forēs.

Listen to the *Amores* 1.6
http://dx.doi.org/10.11647/OBP.0067.28

Notes on *Amores* 1.6

1–2: Iānitor ... religāte: vocative. The doorkeeper is a slave, chained (*religāte*) to his door, a custom that was apparently common but not universal (Suetonius would later call the practice "old fashioned," *On Rhetors* 3). Ovid, as the excluded lover (*exclūsus amātor*), begins a *paraclausithyron*, a song sung in front of the locked door of a mistress, a genre with a long tradition among both Greek and Roman writers. The author will plead his case to the stern doorkeeper to win admittance to his mistress's home. **(indignum)**: a parenthetical accusative of exclamation (AG §397d), "for shame!" **difficilem**: the door is almost personified. **forem**: one half of a double door; the word is more often found in the plural.

3–4: exiguum: "a tiny thing" (predicate nominative). **aditū fac iānua parvō...capiat** = *fac ut iānua parvō aditū ... capiat*; *ut* is omitted from the indirect command, as we have seen before (AG §565a). The word order is intentionally difficult (hyperbaton, see on 1.5.24), to emphasize the difficulty of the act in question. *iānua*, in contrast to *foris* or *forēs*, refers to the doorway as a whole. **capiat**: "receive." **sēmiadaperta** < *sēmiadapertus, -a,-um* "half-open" (rare); the *i* is treated here as a consonant (i.e. *sēmjadaperta*). **latus** = *latus meum*.

5–6: tālēs ... in ūsūs: "for such purposes"; *in* + acc. can mean "for the purpose of," as in 1.3.19 **aptaque ... membra dedit**: sc. *tālēs in ūsūs*. **subductō pondere**: "since weight has been lost," i.e., "since I have lost weight," ablative absolute (AG §420). **dedit**: "has made"; *dō* with a noun and an adjective in the accusative can mean "make X (noun) Y (adj.)."

7–8: ille = *amor* (or *Amor*), now more obviously personified. **custōdum**: genitive plural. **īre**: the infinitive depends on *monstrat*. **monstrat**: sc. *mihi*; *monstrō* can mean "show the way" (see OLD 6). **inoffensōs**: "unhindered."

9–10: simulācraque vāna: i.e., ghost-like forms that (he now knows) were figments of his imagination. **mīrābar**: supply *eum* or *illum*. **tenebrīs**: "through the darkness"; the ablative of place where (without a preposition) is used freely in poetry (AG §429.4); another possibility is that the ablative here indicates time when, i.e., when the night is casting shadows. See AG

§423. **itūrus erat**: "was about to go" or "intended to go"; the future active periphrastic, constructed from the future active participle and forms of *sum*, AG §194.

11–12: **ut audīrem**: purpose clause.

13–14: **nec mora**: "nor (was there) a delay," i.e., without delay, a common idiom. **nōn umbrās**: understand *timeō* from the following line. **nōn timeō**: note the asyndeton (the lack of conjunction) and anaphora (repetition of *nōn*), which emphasize the speaker's new-found bravery. **strictās ... manūs** < *stringō, stringere, strinxī, strictum* often means "to unsheathe" (a sword, etc.); here that meaning is transferred to very different weapons, the hands. **in mea fāta**: *in* + acc. here means "in order to cause, produce, obtain" (OLD 21a); *fātum, -ī,* n. here means "death," here plural for singular. With his newly acquired bravery the narrator is not afraid of being assaulted and possibly killed at night.

15–16: **tē ... tibi ... tū**: emphatic repetition (anaphora). "*You're* the one I fear": gross and comic flattery of the slave. **lentum**: "immovable"; modifies *tē*, which is emphatic. **quō possīs perdere**: potential subjunctive (AG §447.3). **fulmen**: "thunderbolt"; McKeown suggests a pun, since *fulmen* might be thought of as the equivalent of *fulmentum*, "prop, support" and thus "the bar of a door."

17–18: **utī** = *ut*; introduces a purpose clause. **relaxā**: imperative. **ūda sit ut lacrimīs iānua facta meīs** = *ut iānua facta sit ūda lacrimīs meīs*. *ut* here means "how" and introduces an indirect question. **lacrimīs ... meīs**: ablative of means or cause.

19–20: **positā** = *depositā*. **stārēs ad verbera** < *verber, -eris,* n. "whip" or "blows"; *stāre ad verbera* = "stand at the whipping post." **dominam**: another pun, since the *ianitor's* "mistress" is also the speaker's mistress in the sexual sense. **prō tē**: "on your behalf."

21–22: **quae valuit ... grātia**: the antecedent (*grātia*), "favor, influence," lies within the relative clause itself (AG §307b); in such cases the antecedent is usually reinforced by a demonstrative pronoun, in this case *illa* in the next line. **prō tē quoque**: i.e., the poet had formerly (*quondam*) had plenty of *grātia* with his mistress: enough (it is implied) for himself, and for the *iānitor* as well (*quoque*). **heu facinus!**: "what a crime!" parenthetical. The speaker affects to find the doorkeeper's lack of reciprocity shocking. **illa**: *grātia*, the favor that the poet thinks he has with the doorkeeper. **parum**: "too little, not enough" (adverb).

23–24: **redde vicem meritīs**: "give me back a return for my services," i.e. return the favor. **grātō ... optās**: either "you have the chance you want to show your gratitude" (Barsby); or "it is possible for you, (if you are) grateful, to get what you want," namely freedom (McKeown). The premise here is that the doorkeeper is *ungrateful*, so the second option seems preferable; and the carrot of freedom is dangled at 25–26. Either way, *tibi* is assumed with *grātō*. **quod**: the relative pronoun, = *id quod*. **tempora noctis eunt; excute poste seram**: this line is repeated four more times, at eight-line intervals; the use of a refrain suggests the singing of the *kōmos* (κῶμος), the song of the party-going lover. **seram**: the *sera* was a removable bar that could be fitted into the doorposts from the inside.

25–26: **sīc**: "thus," but also "on these terms, in this way" (adverb). The word is often used in making requests. A speaker expresses a willingness to *pray* or *hope* for something, on condition that his own request is granted, e.g., "If you get me out of this mess, then (*sīc*) may your praises be sung for ever more." In this case the poet hopes that the *iānitor* will be free some day, on condition (*sīc*) that he responds to the word *excute*: "Open the door (please)! If you do (*sīc*) then may..." **umquam**: "at some time in the future," a very rare sense. Normally this word means "ever." **longā ... catēnā**: "long-suffered chain" (Barsby), or simply "long chain"; ablative of separation (AG §400). **relevēre**: present subjunctive = *relevēris* (AG §184), in an optative sense (AG §441), "may you be released." **tibi**: dative of agent (AG §375a). **perpetuō**: "permanently." **serva**: "of slavery, servile."

27–28: **ferreus ōrantem**: understand *tū* and *mē*. *ferreus* used figuratively, "hard-hearted, unfeeling" (OLD 4a), but also reminds us that the doorkeeper is in chains. **nēquīquam**: "to no avail"; construe with *ōrantem*. **rōboribus durīs**: "hardwood bars" < *rōbur*, *-oris* n. "oak"; thus anything made out of oak or other hardwood; here = the *sera* and *postēs* of line 24. **fulta**: "bolstered, reinforced by."

29–30: mūnīmina ... prōsunt: "are useful as fortifications," i.e., for defense; **mūnīmina** is in apposition to *clausae ... portae*, subject of *prōsunt*. **portae:** *portae* are city gates rather than doorways. **quid:** "why" (OLD *quis* 16).

31–32: quid faciēs hostī, quī: "what will you do to an enemy, if...." For *quid faciēs* (and the like) + dat. in exasperated questions, see OLD 22b. The antecedent of *quī* is the doorkeeper, subject of *faciēs*.

33–34: mīlitibus ... et armīs = *mīlitibus armātīs* (hendiadys, for which see on 1.4.53). **eram, sī nōn ... adesset:** a mixed contrary to fact condition (AG §517b): use of the imperfect indicative instead of the imperfect subjunctive in the apodosis indicates that the action was intended to happen, likely to happen, or already begun.

35–36: hunc: referring to *Amor*. **sī cupiam, nusquam ... possum:** a mixed condition: *cupiam* is probably present subjunctive (as opposed to future indicative), and thus the protasis of a future less vivid condition, with the change to present indicative in the apodosis indicating a shift in the point of view (AG §516b). *sī* = *etsī* with a concessive force; *nusquam* here means "never." **ante:** adverb, not preposition, "first," i.e., "sooner." **vel:** "even," used to introduce what might be thought an extreme or unlikely possibility. **dīvidar:** potential subjunctive (AG §447.3).

37–38: Ovid lists the lover's "equipment" and companions—not weapons and fellow hooligans, as would be the case if he were a robber, but Cupid, some wine, and a garland of flowers askew on his hair, which has been anointed with perfume—indications that he has come from a party. **circa mea tempora:** *tempora* are the temples of the head, i.e. the wine has "gone to his head." **madidīs ... comīs:** ablative of place (or cause).

39–40: timeat ... eat: potential subjunctives (AG §447.3). **obvius:** *obvius īre* (+ dat.) = "go out to meet (in battle)."

41–42: lentus: "unyielding" (see 1.6.15). **an:** introduces an alternative question. **quī tē male perdat:** parenthetical; *perdat* is optative subjunctive (AG §441): "who I hope will..." **amantis** goes with *verba* in the next line. **verba dat in ventōs:** "to give" a thing "to the winds" is to render them useless or meaningless. **aure ... tuā:** ablative of separation (AG §400).

43–44: tē cēlāre: "to keep (a secret) from you (acc.)," "to elude you." Ovid knows from experience that the doorkeeper does not sleep on the job. **in mediae sīdera noctis**: *in* + acc. here means "up to (a point in time)" (OLD 13b).

45–46: quantō: ablative of degree of difference (AG §414). **sorte mea**: ablative of comparison (AG §406).

47–48: dummodo sīc = *dummodo sīc (rēs sē habeat)* means "on this condition," "provided that this is the case," referring to the situation of line 45, i.e. *tēcum tua nunc requiēscit amīca*. **transīte catēnae**: i.e., on this condition (only) Ovid is willing to trade places with the *iānitor*; note the apostrophe (direct address) to the *catēnae* (vocative).

49–50: fallimur: 1st plural for 1st singular. 'Am I deceived?' 'Is it just my imagination, or?' In line 51 the narrator answers his own question with *fallimur*. **dedēre** = *dedērunt*.

51–52: ei: one syllable, an exclamation of misery, esp. common with *mihi*: "Woe is me." **quam**: with *longē*, "how far!" **tulit**: *ferō* can mean "to take away, carry off"; note the tense.

53–54: Boreā < *Boreās, -ae*, m. the god of the North Wind; here in the vocative (for the forms of Greek nouns in the third declension, see AG §81). **Ōrīthyiae** < *Ōrīthyia, -ae* f. Orithyia was a daughter of Erechtheus, king of Athens, abducted by Boreas (Ovid tells the story at *Metamorphoses* 6.675 ff.). The word has four long syllables, with *yi* as a dipthong (= Greek υι); the hexameter line with a spondaic fifth foot is unusual in the *Amores*. **satis ... memor**: "sufficiently mindful of." The poet hopes that Boreas, a former lover himself, will swoop in and help a fellow sufferer. **ades**: second person singular imperative of *adsum, adesse*.

55–56: silent: the subject is *tempora noctis*. The connection to the previous line is not stated. The absence of a connective (asyndeton) can indicate "but" or "however" (adversative asyndeton); Boreas *might* have come to blow down the doors, (but) all is quiet.

Fig. 13 The Abduction of Orithyia by Boreas, after a 1701 painting by Francesco Solimena (1657–1747). Baltimore, Walters Art Museum. Wikimedia, https://commons.wikimedia.org/wiki/File:Francesco_Solimena_-_The_Abduction_of_Orithyia_-_Walters_371695.jpg

57–58: "Or else I myself, now quite ready, will attack the arrogant house with sword and fire, which I carry in my torch." Humorously empty bluster, given that he has earlier admitted to being unarmed. "Sword and fire" are the traditional weapons of a rampaging army. **aut** picks up on the refrain, i.e. *"excute poste seram* or else…." **parātior ipse**: either we have to understand *quam Boreās*, or the comparative means simply "quite prepared" (for the use of the comparative as a kind of positive without an object of comparison, see AG §291). **quem**: the antecedent is *ignīque*. **petam**: *petō* often means "to attack."

59–60: **nihil moderābile suādent**: "suggest/urge no restraint" < *moderābilis* "controllable" (rare); *suādeō* can take a direct object, i.e., "suggest" a particular course of action. **illa**: refers back to *nox*; remember that *ille, illa, illud* are often used to mean "the former," while *hic, haec, hoc* can mean "the latter" (AG §297a-b). **vacat**: "is devoid of," "lacks" + abl. of separation. **Līber** is the Roman Bacchus; = *vīnum* by metonymy. The god's alternate name hints at the "freeing" effect wine has.

61–62: omnia consumpsī: "I have tried everything," i.e., "those are all the arguments I have" (uttered in exasperation); *consūmō* can mean "to use up" resources, money etc., or even "waste, squander." **foribus ... tuīs**: ablative of comparison (AG §406). **ipse**: understand *tū*.

63–64: nōn tē ... decuit servāre: "it was not fitting that you protect," i.e., you do not deserve to protect. The past tenses of *decuit* and *erās* in the next line are equivalent to presents, but emphasize that Ovid can do nothing about the situation. **sollicitō carcere dignus**: *dignus* can be construed with the ablative ("deserving of a thing," AG §418b); *sollicitus* here means "associated with trouble," i.e. "troubling."

65–66: mōlītur: "is setting in motion." **Lūcifer** < *Lūcifer, -erī*, m. Lucifer is the morning star; in myth he was the son of Aurora (Dawn) and Cephalus. **axēs**: literally "axles," (plural for singular) but by metonymy "chariot." **inque suum ... opus**: *in* + acc. expressing purpose,"for their work"; the reflexive refers not to the subject (*āles*), but to an implied *quemque*, in apposition to *miserōs*. **miserōs**: adjective, used as a noun. **āles**: a rooster.

67–68: at tū: apostrophe; Ovid addresses his garland (*corōna*) in the vocative case. **nōn laetīs** = *miserīs* (litotes). **capillīs**: dative with *dētracta*. **super**: governs *dūra līmina*. **tōtā ... nocte** = *per tōtam noctem*; the ablative of time (time within which) can be used to express duration of time (AG §424b).

69–70: dominae: dative of reference/advantage (AG §376) removed from its logical complement (*testis eris*) and foregrounded for emphasis. **māne**: (indeclinable neuter) "morning; in the morning."

71–72: quāliscumque valē: "goodbye (doorkeeper), such as you are," (vocative); i.e., "no matter what your attitude towards me is." **sentīque abeuntis honōrem**: "and listen to the compliment of a departing man." The disappointed lover grudgingly admits that the doorkeeper has done his job well. *Honōrem* = "courtesy, compliment" is very rare. **lente**: "unyielding" (vocative). **nec admissō turpis amante**: "and not disgraced through granting a lover admission"; *turpis* is vocative. **conservae ... forēs**: in apposition to *dūra ... ligna*, but also to *crūdēlēs rigidō cum līmine postēs* in the previous line. See for example Frank Olin Copley, "*Servitium amoris* in the Roman Elegists," *TAPhA* 78 (1947): 285–300.

13. *Amores* 1.7: Violence and love

This poem, like *Amores* 1.5, plays with a topic about which it is hard for modern readers to be playful: physical abuse. The poet has used violence on his girlfriend, and now expresses his deep remorse. But scholars are divided on the extent to which that remorse is supposed to be sincere. No one doubts that there is *some* element of playfulness here, and for many readers that playfulness remains problematic. But some scholars have read the poem as expressing an underlying anxiety: the poet has committed assault, and tries to cover up his shame and embarrassment with a pathetic attempt at humor.

The question of what we do with our modern sensibilities about subjects like sexual violence is complicated, and one that readers will have to answer for themselves. Here I will focus on a more preliminary question: what exactly has the poet done? What, in other words, is he apologizing so abjectly *for*? It is one thing if he has caused real physical harm, and then apologizes and tries to minimize the offense. It is quite another if the pain was trivial and accidental. The poem itself is unclear, and it may be that Ovid is inviting us to make up our own minds about it. At the risk of reading the poem too literally, I believe we should focus on the fact that the poet apologizes not for a serious physical assault on his girlfriend, but for messing up her hair (lines 11 and 49), even if he also scratched her face in the process (lines 40 and 50).

The first eleven lines provide an obvious exploration of Latin sarcasm: the poet describes his offense in dramatic terms: he was insane (lines 2–4), and he committed an offense on a par with assaulting his parents or the gods (lines 5–6). This put him on a par with Ajax in his murderous insanity, and with Orestes pursued by the Furies (lines 7–10). And what did he do that was so terrible? He tore, or tore at, or messed up, her hair: *ergō ego dīgestōs potuī laniāre capillōs?* (11). If we take *laniāre* ("tear") literally, then he has been violent (and oddly unmanly). But his own focus is on the fact that he messed up her elegant hairdo (*dīgestōs ... capillōs*). So either he is downplaying a savage assault by calling it a trivial one, it else he is humorously exaggerating something that, if it was an assault at all, was of a very different kind. In Roman poetry, as we have already seen, the language of sex includes the language of violence.

The messy hair, says the poet, was attractive (line 12). He then elaborates, this time with three learned *exempla*: Atalanta and Ariadne (neither of whom is actually named), and Cassandra, who were all famous for their disordered hair (lines 13–18). The reasons were different: Atalanta lived in the wild, Ariadne had messy hair at the moment that Theseus abandoned her, and Cassandra was possessed. But all three women were also sex objects: Milanion won Atalanta in the famous footrace, Ariadne was in disarray because she had been asleep with Theseus on Naxos, and Cassandra ended up as the concubine of Agamemnon. We saw in *Amores* 1.5 (line 10) that Corinna came to bed with her hair down, and it seems clear that the poet is thinking of that kind of intimacy here. This could be a mere passing thought. But it seems more likely that it was a desire for intimacy that prompted him to touch her hair in the first place, and that they weren't fighting at all. The poet had made a move, not an attack.

If so, the exaggerated remorse makes much more sense: there is an obvious parallelism between seduction and assault, but a seducer, if successful, sees the parallel as rhetorical rather than real. The poet continues with even deeper expressions of remorse: other people would call him names, and she reproached him with silent tears (lines 19–22). The poet cannot forgive himself for his offense: he'd rather lose his arms, what he did was worse than assaulting a Roman citizen, and worse even than sacrilege (lines 23–34). Indeed the assault was a kind of sacrilege, since the girl herself is a goddess (line 32). The remorse is described in terms that suggest serious violence, and it is easy to forget that this all started because of a hairdo.

The sarcasm goes up yet another notch as the poet sarcastically imagines himself as a *triumphator*, proudly celebrating this "assault" (lines 35–40). The girl was his prisoner, complete with the dishevelled hair of a captive (line 39), and, we now learn, with marks of some kind on her face (*laesae genae*, line 40). If this is anything approaching the bruising of a battered woman, the poet's sarcasm here is simply grotesque. But we soon learn that what caused the marks (or mark) was only a fingernail (*ingenuas ungue notare genas*, line 50; see line 64). And the marks (or mark) was a byproduct of the messing up of the hair, not, apparently, an end in itself. Is the joke, then, that the girl is making a fuss about, literally, a mere scratch? This is not an easy conclusion, perhaps; even a scratch inflicted by an ardent lover is not a ready subject for humor.

What follows is perhaps the most difficult and disturbing section of a difficult and disturbing poem, as the poet goes on to describe forms of assault that would have been "better" (lines 41–50). The first alternative he thinks of is love-bites, confirming that it is sex rather than fighting that is uppermost in his mind (lines 41–42). But talk of lovemaking then turns, apparently, into talk about fighting: if he was going to be angry, there were better alternatives; for example, he could simply have yelled at her and threatened her (lines 43–46). But his second possibility reveals that they were not really *fighting* at all: he could also, he says, have taken off her top (lines 47–48). What he wanted, it turns out, was sex, and he could have threatened her, or he could have stripped her to the waist. What he did was mess with her hair, which was his big mistake.

The poet follows with even more abject apology: he paints a touching picture of a dazed and weeping victim and invites her to take her revenge (lines 51–66). She should scratch him back and go for his eyes as well as his hair (lines 65–66). Is this a final attempt to get what he had wanted all along?

It is striking that in the last couplet the poet begs his victim to fix her hair: doing so will remove all traces of his crime (lines 67–68). Again, we are faced with a choice: either he is spectacularly heartless, ignoring entirely that scratched face, or his offense was indeed a trivial one. We might also wonder when the hair was to be fixed: immediately, or after that final encounter?

Suggested reading

Greene, Ellen. "Travesties of Love: Violence and Voyeurism in Ovid *Amores* 1.7," *Classical World* 92 (1999): 409–418. http://dx.doi.org/10.2307/4352311

Korenjak, Martin and Florian Schaffenrath. "Snowmelt in the Alps: Corinna's Tears at Ovid, *Amores* 1.7.59," *Classical Quarterly* 62 (2012): 874–877. http://dx.doi.org/10.1017/s0009838812000420

Amores 1.7

Adde manūs in vincla meās (meruēre catēnās),
    dum furor omnis abit, sī quis amīcus ades:
nam furor in dominam temerāria bracchia mōvit;
    flet mea vēsānā laesa puella manū.
tunc ego vel cārōs potuī violāre parentēs   5
    saeva vel in sanctōs verbera ferre deōs.
quid? nōn et clipeī dominus septemplicis Aiax
    strāvit dēprensōs lāta per arva gregēs,
et vindex in mātre patris, malus ultor, Orestēs
    ausus in arcānās poscere tēla deās?   10
ergō ego dīgestōs potuī laniāre capillōs?
    nec dominam mōtae dēdecuēre comae:
sīc fōrmōsa fuit; tālem Schoenēida dīcam
    Maenaliās arcū sollicitasse ferās;
tālis periūrī prōmissaque vēlaque Thēseī   15
    flēvit praecipitēs Crēssa tulisse Notōs;
sīc, nisi vittātīs quod erat, Cassandra, capillīs,
    prōcubuit templō, casta Minerva, tuō.
quis mihi nōn "dēmens," quis nōn mihi "barbare" dīxit?
    ipsa nihil: pavidō est lingua retenta metū.   20
sed tacitī fēcēre tamen convīcia vultūs;
    ēgit mē lacrimīs ōre silente reum.
ante meōs umerīs vellem cecidisse lacertōs;
    ūtiliter potuī parte carēre meī:
in mea vēsānās habuī dispendia vīrēs   25
    et valuī poenam fortis in ipse meam.

quid mihi vōbīscum, caedis scelerumque ministrae?
    dēbita sacrilegae vincla subīte manūs.
an, sī pulsassem minimum dē plēbe Quirītem,
    plecterer: in dominam iūs mihi maius erit? 30
pessima Tȳdīdēs scelerum monimenta relīquit:
    ille deam prīmus perculit; alter ego.
et minus ille nocens: mihi quam profitēbar amāre
    laesa est; Tȳdīdēs saevus in hoste fuit.
ī nunc, magnificōs victor mōlīre triumphōs, 35
    cinge comam laurō vōtaque redde Iovī,
quaeque tuōs currūs comitantum turba sequētur,
    clāmet "iō, fortī victa puella virō est!"
ante eat effūsō tristis captīva capillō,
    sī sinerent laesae, candida tōta, genae. 40
aptius impressīs fuerat līvēre labellīs
    et collum blandī dentis habēre notam.
dēnique sī tumidī rītū torrentis agēbar
    caecaque mē praedam fēcerat īra suam,
nonne satis fuerat timidae inclāmasse puellae, 45
    nec nimium rigidās intonuisse minās,
aut tunicam ā summā dīdūcere turpiter ōrā
    ad mediam? (mediae zōna tulisset opem)?
at nunc sustinuī raptīs ā fronte capillīs
    ferreus ingenuās ungue notāre genās. 50
astitit illa āmens albō et sine sanguine vultū,
    caeduntur Pariīs quālia saxa iugīs;

exanimēs artūs et membra trementia vīdī,
  ut cum pōpuleās ventilat aura comās,
ut lēnī Zephyrō gracilis vibrātur harundō   55
  summave cum tepidō stringitur unda Notō;
suspensaeque diū lacrimae fluxēre per ōra,
  quāliter abiectā dē nive mānat aqua.
tunc ego mē prīmum coepī sentīre nocentem;
  sanguis erat lacrimae, quās dabat illa, meus.   60
ter tamen ante pedēs voluī prōcumbere supplex;
  ter formīdātās reppulit illa manūs.
at tū nē dubitā (minuet vindicta dolōrem)
  prōtinus in vultūs unguibus īre meōs;
nec nostrīs oculīs nec nostrīs parce capillīs: 65
  quamlibet infirmās adiuvat īra manūs.
nēve meī sceleris tam tristia signa supersint,
  pōne recompositās in statiōne comās.

 Listen to the *Amores* 1.7
http://dx.doi.org/10.11647/OBP.0067.29

Notes on *Amores* 1.7

1–2: adde manūs: *addō* can mean "insert"; binding the hands was the traditional treatment for the insane. The poem begins with a request that some friend put the speaker in chains. **meruēre** = *meruērunt*. **catēnās**: whereas *vincla* are chains or restraints in general, *catēnae* are long and heavy chains. **dum:** *dum* + indicative can mean "until." **sī quis amīcus ades:** the second person singular verb makes this hard to put into English: perhaps, "if any of you, my friends, are present." For the use of indefinite *quis, quid* with *sī, nisi, nē* and *num* see AG §310a.

3–4: **in dominam**: *in* can mean "against" (OLD 9).

5–6: **tunc**: *tunc* can be used to refer to a hypothetical situation: "if I could do X, *then*." **saeva vel … deos** = *vel ferre saeva verbera in sanctōs deōs*. **verbera ferre**: a variation of the idiom *arma ferre*, which means "make war on."

7–8: **clipeī dominus septemplicis**: "lord of the seven-layered shield," a reference to Ajax's famous "tower" shield of seven ox hides (Homer, *Iliad* 7.219–223). **Aiax**: the *i* is a vowel, and part of the dipthong *Ai*. Ajax went insane with anger because he had not been awarded the prize in the funeral games held in honor of Achilles; he destroyed a flock of sheep because he mistook them for the Greeks who had done him the (as he saw it) injustice.

Fig. 14 Fresco from Akrotiri, on the island of Thera (modern Santorini), with warriors with "tower shields" (before 1500 BC). Athens, National Archaeological Museum. Wikimedia, https://commons.wikimedia.org/wiki/File:Akrotiri_assembly.jpg

9–10: **in mātre**: "in the matter of his mother"; *in* + abl. used in a judicial context (e.g., *in re*). **patris**: objective genitive with *vindex* (AG §348). **malus ultor, Orestēs**: Orestes, driven temporarily mad by the Furies, avenged the murder of his father Agamemnon by killing his mother Clytemnestra; the morality of this vengeance was of course highly problematic, hence *malus ultor*. **ausus**: understand *est*. **arcānās … deās**: the Furies, who were associated with the underworld (i.e. "secret," "mystical," or "hidden" from mortal view). **poscere tēla**: Orestes asked for a bow with which to defend himself from the Furies (Euripides, *Orestes* 268).

11–12: **ergō**: introduces an indignant rhetorical question. Despite the mythological precedents just mentioned, the speaker is shocked at his own actions. **dīgestōs**: "carefully arranged." **nec … dēdecuēre**: "were not unbecoming to" + acc. (litotes). **motae … comae**: "her locks having been moved," i.e., her disheveled hair.

13–14: sīc fōrmōsa fuit: *sīc* points to an action or a situation: "she was lovely thus" (= "in the way that I have just described her, with her hair messed up"). The narrator now proceeds to describe several women from mythology (Atalanta, Ariadne, and Cassandra) who were beautiful despite their messy hair; the tone shifts from self-reproach to a clueless romanticism. **Schoenēida**: Atalanta, literally "the daughter of Schoeneus," a king of Boeotia. For the Greek form of the accusative case, see AG §81. **dīcam**: potential subjunctive (AG §447.1). **Maenaliās** < *Maenalius, -a, -um* "of Mount Maenalus"[1] (a range of mountains in Arcadia), "Arcadian." **sollicitasse**: syncopated form of *sollicitāvisse*, perfect active infinitive in an indirect statement: "I would say that she were such a one as the daughter of Schoeneus (i.e., Atalanta), who harassed...."

15–16: tālis ... Notōs = *tālis Cressa flēvit praecipitēs Notōs prōmissaque vēlaque periūrī Thēseī tulisse (eam)*. **tālis ... Cressa**: *tālis* is an adjective, but in English we need to supply extra words, e.g. "such a one (was) the Cretan (maiden, when she) lamented." **flēvit** ("wailed, lamented") introduces an indirect statement. The Cretan princess Ariadne fell in love with Theseus when he came to face her brother the Minotaur, and helped him kill the Minotaur and escape from the Labyrinth; Theseus then abandoned her on the island of Naxos. See especially the description of Ariadne in Catullus 64.63–70, where much is made of the disordered state of her hair and clothes as she watches Theseus sailing away. **prōmissaque vēlaque**: zeugma: these two nouns are subjects of *tulisse*, which applies to each in a different sense. An English example would be, "she gave him her heart and her purse." **Thēseī**: two syllables, by synizesis (the running together of two vowels in different syllables without full contraction) (AG §603c).

17–18: sīc: i.e. with hair similarly messy. **nisi ... quod**: "except for the fact that." **vittātīs ... capillīs** < *vittātus -a -um*, "bound up by a fillet"; the *vitta* was a headband worn by priestesses; ablative of description (AG §415). **Cassandra**: Cassandra, a daughter of Priam, was a priestess of Athena (Minerva), from whose temple she was taken at the fall of Troy; she was an inspired prophetess (cursed with being always accurate and always ignored) and was therefore often depicted as having messy hair. **templō ... tuō**: ablative of place where (AG §421). **casta Minerva**: vocative.

---

1   http://pleiades.stoa.org/places/570449

Fig. 15 Emma, Lady Hamilton, as Cassandra, by George Romney (1734–1802). Wikimedia, https://commons.wikimedia.org/wiki/File:Lady_Emma_Hamilton,_as_Cassandra,_by_George_Romney.jpg

19–20: **dixit**: note the tense. **ipsa nihil**: understand *dīxit*.

21–22: **vultūs**: nominative plural; *vultūs* here has its original meaning of "facial expression, look." **ēgit mē ... reum**: *reum agere* means "to accuse, prosecute, put on trial"; the subject is inferred from *ipsa* (line 20). **ōre silente**: a concessive ablative absolute, "even though her mouth was silent" (AG §420).

23–24: **ante**: "beforehand" (adverbial). **umerīs**: ablative of separation (AG §400). **vellem**: potential subjunctive, AG §447.1 (first person singular expressions of cautiously saying, thinking or wishing), = *utinam lacertī cecidissent*. **carēre**: "to be without, lack," regularly construed with the ablative of separation (here *parte*). **meī**: partitive genitive (AG §346a1).

25–26: **in mea ... dispendia** < *dispendium, -(i)ī*, n. "loss"; with *in* + acc. it means "so as to produce my own loss," i.e., at a cost to myself. **et ... meam** = *et ipse, fortis, valuī in poenam meam*: "and I was (physically) powerful, strong (enough) for my own punishment myself," i.e., strong enough to punish myself. The contorted word order foregrounds *ipse*, which accentuates the paradox. For *fortis in* + acc. = "strong (enough) for" a task, see Ovid, *Metamorphoses* 4.149–50 and OLD *in* 20.

27–28: **quid mihi vōbīscum**: apostrophe (the poet addresses his hands); *quid mihi (est) cum...?* means "what have I to do with...?" *mihi* is dative of reference (AG §376). **caedis scelerumque**: objective genitives (AG §348). **ministrae**: vocative. **sacrilegae ... manūs**: vocative. **subīte**: imperative, "endure, submit to."

29–30: an: *an* is a particle used to introduce questions, often with a sense of surprise or indignation (AG §335b). **pulsassem** = *pulsāvissem*, syncopated form of the pluperfect subjunctive. **minimum**: *minimus* can be used of social status to mean "least important, lowest, humblest." **Quirītem** < *Quirīs, Quirītis*, m. the formal term for a Roman citizen, used particularly in legal situations to emphasize civic rights. **plecterer** < *plectō, plectere*, "to beat, punish" (occurs only in the passive); a mixed contrary to fact condition (AG §517a). He would have been beaten as punishment for striking a Roman citizen. **in dominam**: "over my mistress"; *in* + acc. is used with words indicating power or control over someone. Note the asyndeton. Note also the paradox produced by the double meaning of *domina*: the poet may have power over his girlfriend, but he should not have rights over a *domina* (in the original meaning of the word). **maius**: the a is long by position; see AG §11d: "a syllable whose vowel is a, e, or or u, followed by the consonant i, is long whether the vowel itself is long or short."

31–32: Tydīdēs: *Tȳdīdēs, -ae*, m. "the son of Tydeus," i.e. Diomedes, who wounded Aphrodite/Venus when she took part in the battle before Troy (Homer, *Iliad* 5.334–351). **monimenta**: "reminders, examples," perhaps also with overtones of "warning" (the word is derived from *moneō*). In the *Aeneid* (11.275–280) and the *Metamorphoses* (14.477–495) Diomedes tells of the punishment he suffered for his violence to Venus. **ille ... ego**: antithesis and chiasmus. **alter ego**: understand *deam perculī. alter* means "the second of two."

Fig. 16 Venus (Aphrodite), supported by Iris, complaining to Mars, and showing the wound she has received from Diomed in her attempt to rescue Aeneas, by George Hayter (1792–1871). Chatsworth House, Derbyshire. Wikimedia, https://commons.wikimedia.org/wiki/File:Venus_supported_by_Iris,_complaining_to_Mars_1820.jpg

33–34: nocens: "guilty." **mihi ... / laesa est** = *laesa est mihi (ea) quam profitēbar amāre*. **mihi**: dative of agent, with *laesa est* (AG §375). **profitēbar** < *profiteor, profitērī, professus* (+ inf.), here "to claim." **in hoste**: "when dealing with an enemy" as at line 9 above.

35–36: ī nunc, magnificōs victor molīre triumphōs: the poet sarcastically addresses himself as if he were a victorious general celebrating a triumph. **victor**: here used as an adjective or in apposition to the subject. **molīre**: imperative singular. **vōtaque redde**: *vōtum reddere* means "to discharge a vow"; in a triumph the victorious general would offer prayers and sacrifices in the temple of Jupiter Optimus Maximus on the Capitoline.

37–38: quaeque ... sequētur = *quaeque turba comitantum tuōs currūs sequētur*. **quaeque** = *et quae*, the antecedent of *quae* being *turba*. **tuōs currūs**: plural for singular. **comitantum** = *comitantium* (see McKeown); substantivized participle of *comitor* (1) "accompany." **clamet**: hortatory subjunctive. **io ... est!**: a parody of the kinds of ritual cries made by the crowds at triumphal processions. **fortī ... virō** is dative of agent (AG §375).

39–40: ante eat: "let her go before you" (in the triumphal procession). *eat* is hortatory subjunctive (AG §439). **effūsō** < *effūsus, -a, -um* "flowing." **capillō**: *capillus*, though more commonly plural, can be a collective noun, "the hair." **candida tōta**: in apposition to *trīstis captīva*. The protasis of the condition is replaced by a hortatory subjunctive (AG §521b): *ante eat ... candida tōta, sī sinerent laesae ... genae*, i.e., "Let her go before you... all white, if her wounded cheeks permitted it."

41–42: aptius: neuter singular comparative of *aptus, -a, -um*, "appropriate." **fuerat** = *fuisset*; the indicative is used in certain expressions where we might expect a potential subjunctive, e.g. *satius erat*, "it would have been better" (AG §437a). **līvēre** < *līveō, līvēre* "to be livid, to be black and blue with bruises"; the subject is *collum* in the next line. **labellīs**: the Roman poets speak often of love bites. **collum**: subject of *līvēre* in the preceding line and of *habēre*. **blandī dentis**: oxymoron.

43–44: dēnique: "at least" (adverb). **rītū**: *rītus, -ūs*, m. in the ablative singular can mean "in the manner of, like" (+ genitive).

45–46: fuerat = *fuisset*; see on line 41. **inclāmasse**: "to shout abuse" + dat. For the form of the perfect infinitive (*inclāmasse* = *inclāmāvisse*), see AG §184.

nec nimium rigidās ... minās = *et minās nōn nimium rigidās; rigidus* here means "stern, strict."

47–48: **turpiter**: "in a way that brings discredit"; the primary reference is apparently to the discredit that such an act would bring on the woman, but there may also be an implication that it would bring discredit to the perpetrator as well. **ōrā** < *ōra, ōrae*, f. here in its original sense of "edge, border" (including the border of a piece of clothing). **mediae zōna tulisset opem**: "her belt would have come to the rescue at the middle"; *mediae* is dative of end of motion (Ryan and Perkins), or perhaps locative (AG §43c).

49–50: **at nunc**: "but as it is," *nunc* can have an adversative sense introducing a fact contrary to previous possibilities. **sustinuī** < *sustineō, sustinēre, sustinuī*, "to allow oneself to, be cruel enough to" + infin. **ingenuās** < *ingenuus -a -um*, "tender, delicate." Notice the play on words with *genās*.

51–52: **albō ... vultū**: "her face white and bloodless"; abl. of description (AG §415). **Pariīs** < *Parius, -a, -um* "of Paros"; the island of Paros[2] was famous for its marble; the *puella* was as white (*albō ... vultū*, 51) as a statue made of Parian marble.

53–54: **exanimēs** < *exanimis -e* "scared stiff, frightened out of one's wits." **ut cum**: "as when," introducing a simile.

55-56: **stringitur** < *stringō, stringere, strinxī, strictum* "draw tight"; here "graze, scratch" (OLD 5).

57–58: **suspensaeque diū**: "long pent up." **abiectā** < *abiciō, abicere, abiēcī, abiectum*, "to throw down"; the text has been suspected, but if correct *abiecta dē nive* means "from snow that has been thrown down into a pile," i.e., "piled up." Martin Korenjak and Florian Schaffenrath have recently suggested reading *Alpina de nive manat aqua. Classical Quarterly* 62 (2012), 874–877.

59–60: **sanguis erat lacrimae ... meus**: we would say "the tears were my blood," but Ovid reverses the predicate nominative for emphasis, "it was my blood that those tears were."

---

2 http://pleiades.stoa.org/places/599868

61–62: **tamen**: the reading has been suspected, since there is no obvious contrast with what precedes; an obvious alternative is *tandem*. If *tamen* is right the point seems to be "it took me a long time to feel any pity (*tunc ego mē prīmum coepī sentīre nocentem*), at which point her tears were my blood, but nevertheless (I eventually did)."

63–64: **at tū**: the poet now addresses his girlfriend directly for the first time. **nē dubitā**: "do not hesitate" = *nōlī dubitāre*; the use of *nē* + present imperative in prohibitions is poetic (AG §450a), but also legal. **vindicta**: "vengeance, punishment." **prōtinus**: "at once, immediately" (adverb). **in vultūs ... meōs**: plural for singular.

65–66: **parce** < *parcō, parcere, pepercī* + dative, "to act forbearingly towards, show consideration for." **quamlibet**: modifies *infirmās*, i.e., "weak though they are."

67–68: **in statiōne** < *statiō, statiōnis*, f. "position"; the word is often used in military contexts for guard duty, garrisons, etc.

14. *Amores* 1.8: The bad influence

This is the longest of all the *Amores*, and occupies the central position in Book 1. It is, therefore, an important poem, and it is intriguingly different. The central speech, by far the longest speech Ovid gives to any female character in the *Amores*, is delivered by an anti-heroine. Dipsas is an old woman and a *lena*, a stock character of the comic stage variously translated as "bawd," "procuress," "brothel-keeper," or "madam." A better translation might be "panderess" (if the word were used these days) or perhaps "enabler," since Dipsas is not actually an employer of prostitutes; she is an aged dependent and confidante of the poet's girlfriend, presumably a slave or freedwoman, and perhaps originally the girlfriend's nurse. She is now trying to control the girl's sex life, for entirely mercenary reasons.

Fig. 17 Drunken old woman. Roman marble copy of third- or second-century B.C. original. Munich, Glyptothek. Kikimedia, http://en.wikipedia.org/wiki/File:Old_drunkard_Glyptothek_Munich_437_n1.jpg

© William Turpin, CC BY   http://dx.doi.org/10.11647/OBP.0067.13

One of the less attractive features of Roman literature, and indeed of Roman society, was its selection of elderly women as the objects of scorn and hostility (Richlin, 1984 provides a good introduction). Poets could be unsparing in their references to wrinkles, bad hair, and worse, and they associated the physical degeneration of such women with sexual dissolution and drinking (the Romans regarded the two vices as closely associated with each other); particularly vivid is the Roman copy of a famous Hellenistic sculpture of a drunken old lady, now in the Munich sculpture museum. Ovid's character draws from this traditional stereotype: the name Dipsas itself suggests drunkenness, and the first thing we learn about her is that the name is completely appropriate. But Dipsas is also dangerous: the name evokes a snake as well as thirst, and the next thing we learn about her is that she is a witch. Some witches in classical literature are young and beautiful, but others, like Dipsas, are old and ugly.

This is not an easy poem to like. Even if we get past the unpleasant demonization of an elderly female retainer, there remains the problem of subtlety. The poet begins by telling us who Dipsas is: a drunk (lines 3–4), a witch (lines 5–18), and an eloquent corruptor of chaste girls (lines 19–20), and he tells us about overhearing her speech (lines 21–22). Most of the poem is devoted to Dipsas' speech—we have to imagine that the girl herself never says anything at all—on the subject of rich and generous lovers (lines 23–108). The speech comes to a sudden end when, we are told, Dipsas senses that she has been overheard (line 109). The poem then comes to an end almost as abrupt, with the poet wishing he had beaten Dipsas up (lines 110–112), praying instead that she should be a homeless, cold and drunken pauper in what remains of her old age. As conclusions go, this is certainly clear and definitive, but it is not, at first sight, very interesting, or attractive.

It is the speech of Dipsas that provides the most obvious moments of interest, and even wit. As should be clear by now, Ovid in the *Amores* is nothing if not rhetorical, and the most surprising thing about Dipsas is that she is too: *nec tamen eloquio lingua nocente caret* (line 20). The formal rhetorical qualities of her speech have been well discussed by Nicolas Gross (1995–96), who even provides a formal outline (here given with some modifications):

23–26 *exordium*. Dipsas begins by telling the girl that she has attracted a rich suitor because she is so beautiful (*captatio benevolentiae*).

27–28 *propositio*. The basic argument of the speech is that Dipsas would be less poor if her mistress were rich.

29–34 *egressio*. Dipsas digresses, on reasons why the girl can and should accept a wealthy lover; the right stars are in alignment and the rich suitor is also handsome. (I suggest that this is part of the *propositio*.)

35–104 *argumentatio*. How to get the lover you want, and how to control him.

- 35–38. While pretending to look down modestly, evaluate the present he's bringing.
- 39–40. The Sabine women might have been chaste, but they were primitive.
- 41–48. Chastity now is obsolete (*casta est quam nemo rogavit*, line 43), and Roman women only pretend to be chaste. Even Penelope wasn't really chaste: the contest with Odysseus' bow was really about male sexual endowments.
- 49–56. Life is short, and girls in particular have only a limited time to profit (literally) from their good looks. In fact they should maximize profits by taking multiple lovers.
- 57–68. (Gross regards this section as part of the preceding one). This brings us (*ecce*, line 57) to your lover the poet: poetry is no good, and aristocratic birth is no good, if the lover is poor (*pauper amator*, line 66). Even being attractive is no good: nobody gets a night with you for free.
- 69–86. How to get what you want from your lover: start with small requests, then ask for more once you've got him hooked. Play hard to get, but not so much that he loses interest; play lovers off against each other; go on the offensive when you quarrel, and don't let arguments go on too long. Fake tears can be helpful, and lies are acceptable in love affairs.
- 87–94. (Gross regards this section as part of the preceding one). Your servants and your relatives are all part of the process: they can advise your lover on what presents to give, and if they are subtle about it they can acquire presents for themselves.

- 95–102. Also, you can invent reasons for your lover to give you presents: you can pretend it's your birthday, and you can make him jealous; above all, show him the presents you get from his rival, and if there aren't any go buy them yourself. And, finally, if he's given you a lot already, you can switch to asking for loans, and simply never pay him back.
- 103–104. Finally, you should learn the appropriate rhetorical skills.

105–108 *conclusio*. The girl should listen to Dipsas, and if she does she will be extremely grateful.

Part of the joke here is that of course we do not expect an aged and dissolute retainer to be an expert in rhetoric. It is the same joke, very roughly, as when Cockney ladies in Monty Python argue about the relative merits of French and German philosophers. But Dipsas' rhetoric also brings her intriguingly close to the poet himself; it is the poet, after all, who relies on his rhetorical skills. Moreover, the arguments with which Dipsas begins (before she gets too preoccupied with presents) are the typical ones of the poet-lover, the famous *carpe diem* theme: chastity is overrated in general (lines 39–48), and a girl's beauty does not last long (lines 49–50). Thus Dipsas sounds more and more like a projection of the poet rather than a "real" old woman.

This perhaps suggests that we should read the poem not as a story, but as fantasy, rather like the address to an unresponsive doorkeeper in *Amores* 1.6. Consider the plight of a poet-lover whose girlfriend is unavailable or uninterested. A young man in this situation might, in theory, assess the situation objectively: he might accept that he is not handsome, or interesting, or even much of a poet. But our bumptious and self-confident poet has an explanation that is much more flattering to his own ego. There is Dipsas talking to the girl, corrupting her with all that talk about money and presents. He might be handsome, and interesting, and a great poet, but he is not rich. The mystery of his failure is solved.

Thus the poem can be read as a study in delusion. Such a reading, I believe, gives more point to the long speech of Dipsas: we are appalled not by Dipsas herself (too easy a target), but by a lover who simply can't face reality. He should be angry at himself, or perhaps simply at life itself, but he transfers that anger (he is all too human) to his invented nemesis (lines 110–115). And such a reading perhaps gives more point to the elaborate description of Dipsas' magical powers (lines 5–18). The poet *ought* to be able to get the girl, because he's wonderful. If he can't, it's not just that Dipsas is persuasive. She's also a witch.

Suggested reading

Gross, N. "Ovid *Amores* 1.8: Whose Amatory Rhetoric?" *Classical World* 89 (1995–96): 197–206. http://dx.doi.org/10.2307/4351784

Meyers, K. S. "The Poet and the Procuress: The Lena in Latin Love Elegy," *Journal of Roman Studies* 86 (1996): 1–21. http://dx.doi.org/10.1017/s0075435800057403

Richlin, A. "Invective Against Women in Roman Satire," *Arethusa* 17 (1984): 67–80.

Amores 1.8

Est quaedam (quīcumque volet cognoscere lēnam,
    audiat), est quaedam nōmine Dipsas anus.
ex rē nōmen habet: nigrī nōn illa parentem
    Memnonis in roseīs sōbria vīdit equīs.
illa magās artēs Aeaeaque carmina nōvit,   5
    inque caput liquidās arte recurvat aquās;
scit bene quid grāmen, quid tortō concita rhombō
    līcia, quid valeat vīrus amantis equae.
cum voluit, tōtō glomerantur nūbila caelō;
    cum voluit, pūrō fulget in orbe diēs.   10
sanguine, sī qua fidēs, stillantia sīdera vīdī;
    purpureus Lūnae sanguine vultus erat.
hanc ego nocturnās versam volitāre per umbrās
    suspicor et plūmā corpus anīle tegī.
suspicor, et fāma est; oculīs quoque pūpula duplex   15
    fulminat et geminō lūmen ab orbe venit.
ēvocat antīquīs proavōs atavōsque sepulcrīs
    et solidam longō carmine findit humum.
haec sibi prōposuit thalamōs temerāre pudīcōs;
    nec tamen ēloquiō lingua nocente caret.   20
fors mē sermōnī testem dedit; illa monēbat
    tālia (mē duplicēs occuluēre forēs):
"scīs here tē, mea lux, iuvenī placuisse beātō?
    haesit et in vultū cōnstitit usque tuō.

1.8: The bad influence

et cūr nōn placeās? nullī tua fōrma secunda est. 25
    mē miseram! dignus corpore cultus abest.
tam fēlix essēs quam fōrmōsissima vellem:
    nōn ego tē factā dīvite pauper erō.
stella tibi oppositī nocuit contrāria Martis;
    Mars abiit; signō nunc Venus apta suō. 30
prōsit ut adveniens, ēn aspice: dīves amātor
    tē cupiit; cūrae, quid tibi dēsit, habet.
est etiam faciēs, quā sē tibi comparet, illī:
    sī tē nōn emptam vellet, emendus erat.
ērubuit! decet alba quidem pudor ōra, sed iste, 35
    sī simulēs, prōdest; vērus obesse solet.
cum bene dēiectīs gremium spectābis ocellīs,
    quantum quisque ferat, respiciendus erit.
forsitan immundae Tatiō regnante Sabīnae
    nōluerint habilēs plūribus esse virīs; 40
nunc Mars externīs animōs exercet in armīs,
    at Venus Aenēae regnat in urbe suī.
lūdunt fōrmōsae: casta est quam nēmō rogāvit;
    aut, sī rusticitās nōn vetat, ipsa rogat.
hās quoque, quae frontis rūgās in vertice portant, 45
    excute, dē rūgīs crīmina multa cadent.
Pēnelopē iuvenum vīrēs temptābat in arcū;
    quī latus argueret corneus arcus erat.
lābitur occultē fallitque volātilis aetās,
    ut celer admissīs lābitur amnis aquīs. 50

aera nitent ūsū, vestis bona quaerit habērī,
  cānescunt turpī tecta relicta sitū:
fōrma, nisi admittās, nullō exercente senēscit;
  nec satis effectūs ūnus et alter habent.
certior ē multīs nec tam invidiōsa rapīna est;   55
  plēna venit cānīs dē grege praeda lupīs.
ecce, quid iste tuus praeter nova carmina vātēs
  dōnat? amātōris mīlia multa legēs.
ipse deus vātum, pallā spectābilis aureā,
  tractat inaurātae consona fīla lyrae.   60
quī dabit, ille tībi magnō sit māior Homērō;
  crēde mihī, rēs est ingeniōsa dare.
nec tū, sī quis erit capitis mercēde redemptus,
  despice: gypsātī crīmen ināne pedis.
nec tē dēcipiant veterēs circum ātria cērae: 65
  tolle tuōs tēcum, pauper amātor, avōs.
quī, quia pulcher erit, poscet sine mūnere noctem,
  quod det, amātōrem flāgitet ante suum.
parcius exigitō pretium, dum rētia tendis,
  nē fugiant; captōs lēgibus ūre tuīs.   70
nec nocuit simulātus amor: sine crēdat amārī
  et cave, nē grātīs hic tibi constet amor.
saepe negā noctēs: capitis modo finge dolōrem;
  et modo, quae causās praebeat, Īsis erit.
mox recipe, ut nullum patiendī colligat ūsum   75
  nēve relentescat saepe repulsus amor.
surda sit ōrantī tua iānua, laxa ferentī;
  audiat exclūsī verba receptus amans;

et, quasi laesa, prior nonnumquam īrascere laesō:
    vānescit culpā culpa repensa tuā.   80
sed numquam dederis spatiōsum tempus in īram:
    saepe simultātēs īra morāta facit.
quīn etiam discant oculī lacrimāre coactī,
    et faciant ūdās illa vel illa genās;
nec, sī quem fallēs, tū periūrāre timētō: 85
    commodat in lūsūs nūmina surda Venus.
servus et ad partēs sollers ancilla parentur,
    quī doceant, aptē quid tibi possit emī,
et sibi pauca rogent: multōs sī pauca rogābunt,
    postmodo dē stipulā grandis acervus erit.   90
et soror et māter, nūtrix quoque carpat amantem:
    fit cito per multās praeda petīta manūs.
cum tē dēficient poscendī mūnera causae,
    nātālem lībō testificāre tuum.
nē sēcūrus amet nullō rīvāle cavētō: 95
    nōn bene, sī tollās proelia, dūrat amor.
ille virī videat tōtō vestīgia lectō
    factaque lascīvīs līvida colla notīs;
mūnera praecipuē videat, quae mīserit alter:
    sī dederit nēmō, Sacra roganda Via est.   100
cum multa abstulerīs, ut nōn tamen omnia dōnet,
    quod numquam reddās, commodet, ipsa rogā.
lingua iuvet mentemque tegat: blandīre nocēque;
    impia sub dulcī melle venēna latent.
haec sī praestiterīs ūsū mihi cognita longō   105
    nec tulerint vōcēs ventus et aura meās,

saepe mihi dīcēs vīvae bene, saepe rogābis

    ut mea dēfunctae molliter ossa cubent—"

vox erat in cursū, cum mē mea prōdidit umbra;

    at nostrae vix sē continuēre manūs   110

quīn albam rāramque comam lacrimōsaque vīnō

    lūmina rūgōsās distraherentque genās.

dī tibi dent nullōsque Larēs inopemque senectam,

    et longās hiemēs perpetuamque sitim!

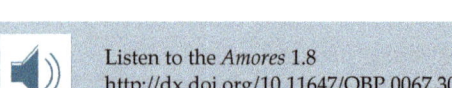 Listen to the *Amores* 1.8
http://dx.doi.org/10.11647/OBP.0067.30

Notes on *Amores* 1.8

1–2: lēnam < *lēna -ae*, f., "brothel-keeper, madam, procuress, go-between." The *lēna*, who profited financially from arranging sexual liaisons between men and young women, was a stock character in comedy and mime, and also appeared frequently in love elegy. In this poem, a *lēna* gives advice to a young woman on how to get more gifts out of her lover/clients, as the poet listens from behind a door. **Dipsas**: "Dipsas by name." *nōmine* is ablative of specification (AG §418). Dipsas is derived from the Greek διψάς meaning a small snake, the bite of which supposedly makes its victim extremely thirsty. It indicates the "poisonous" nature of the *lēna* who makes the *puella* "thirsty" for monetary rewards, and it points a drinking problem. **anus**: *anus, anūs*, f. "old woman."

3–4: ex rē: "based on fact," "for good reason." **nigrī ... parentem / Memnonis**: Dipsas is always drunk at dawn: the mother (*parentem*) of Memnon, King of Ethiopia (*nigrī ... / Memnonis*), is Aurora, goddess of the dawn, who arrives every morning in a horse-drawn chariot (*in roseīs ... equīs*). **sōbria**: postponed for emphasis: Dipsas has never seen the dawn *sober*.

5–18: the narrator describes the magical powers of the *lēna*, which recall those of similar characters in Tibullus and Propertius.

5–6: **magās** < *magus, -a, -um*, "magic" (rare; the usual word is *magicus*). **Aeaeaque** < *Aeaeus -a -um*, "of Aeaea." Aeaea was the island of the witch Circe, who used her magical powers to turn Odysseus' men into animals. **carmina** < *carmen, carminis* n. "chant, spell, incantation." **caput**: "the source" (of a river). **recurvat**: the ability to reverse the course of rivers was one of the proverbial powers of witches.

7–8: **grāmen** < *grāmen, grāminis* n., "herbs" (a collective singular), especially magical ones. *grāmen*, *līcia* and *vīrus* are all subjects of *valeat* (line 8). **tortō** < *torqueō, torquēre, torsī, tortum*, "to cause to rotate, spin." **rhombō** < *rhombus, -ī* m., a wooden object which, when attached to a string and twirled in the air, produced a loud hissing sound, the volume of which depended on the force of the motion. It was used in the mysteries of Dionysus, Cybele, and Demeter, and as a tool of magic (see Theocritus, *Idyll* 2.30). Cupid is depicted as employing one in the fresco below, from Pompeii, found in the *Casa di Amore Punito*. See A. S. F. Gow, "ΙΥΓΞ, ΡΟΜΒΟΣ, Rhombus, Turbo," *Journal of Hellenic Studies* 54 (1934), pp. 1–13. **quid valeat**: "what power... has." **vīrus** < *vīrus, -ī* n., "bodily fluid, secretion," especially a magical potion or love charm. **amantis equae**: "of a mare in heat." Fluid from a mare in heat could be used as a love charm.

Fig. 18 Venus and Mars. Fresco from the Casa dell'Amore Punito, Pompeii. Naples, National Archaeological Museum. Cupid (Amor) is holding a rhombus on a string stretched between his hands. Wikimedia, https://commons.wikimedia.org/wiki/File:Seduzione_tra_marte_e_venere,_alla_presenza_di_un_amorino_e_ancella,_da_casa_dell'amore_punito_a_pompei,_9249,_02.JPG

9–10: cum voluit: *cum* (also *ubi, ut* and *quandō,* with or without *-cumque*) can be used as an indefinite relative ("whenever") and introduce a conditional relative clause, which functions as the protasis of a condition (AG §542). The condition here is present general, with a perfect indicative in the protasis and present indicative in the apodosis (AG §514d1). **tōtō ... caelō**: ablative of place where; the preposition is regularly omitted with *tōtus* (AG §429.2). **pūrō ... in orbe**: *orbis* can mean "the vault of heaven."

11–12: sī qua fidēs: "if there is any trustworthiness (in me)," supply *est*; see 1.3.16. **stillantia** < *stillō -āre,* "to drip with" (+ ablative). **purpureus**: predicate adjective; *purpureus* can be used of things stained with blood.

13–14: versam < *vertō, vertere, vertī, versum,* "to transform" (by magic). **volitāre** < *volitō, -āre,* "to fly around." For the formation of intensive or iterative verbs by adding *-tō* or *-itō,* see AG §263.2.

15–16: oculīs: locative, or ablative of place where, often without a preposition poetry (AG §429.4). **pūpula duplex** < *pūpula, -ae,* f. "the pupil" (of the eye); certain remote barbarians were thought to have amazing eyesight because of having double pupils. **orbe**: "eyeball," contrasted with *orbe* (10), "vault of heaven." **geminō lūmen ab orbe venit**: the Romans spoke of light coming *from* the eyes, not to them.

17–18: antīquīs ... sepulcrīs: ablative of place from which (AG §428g). **longō carmine**: *carmen* can mean "magical spell" (cf. line 5); *longō* indicates that the spell is a long and elaborate one. **findit** < *findō, findere, fidī, fissum* "to split apart"; this is presumably another way to bring back the spirits of the dead. **humum** < *humus, -ī,* f. "earth," modified by the feminine adjective form *solidam*.

19–20: haec ... pudīcōs: "this woman has set herself to defile a pure marriage," ironic because, as emerges from her speech, the "pure marriage" in question is actually a temporary liaison between the narrator, an impecunious poet, and a quasi-prostitute. **tamen**: take with *nocente*: "nor did her tongue lack eloquence, harmful though it was."

21–22: mē ... dedit: "gave me the opportunity (to be)." **occuluēre** < *occulō, occulere, occuluī, occultum* "conceal"; perfect 3rd person plural.

23–24: **herī**: "yesterday," a colloquial form of *herī*; adverb. **mea lux**: vocative; a term of endearment the *lēna* uses when addressing the *puella*, similar to our "light of my life." **iuvenī ... beātō**: "a rich young man," dative object of *placuisse*. The rival for the *puella*'s attentions is a common figure in love elegy, and the fact that this rival is well off financially gives the narrator a real cause for concern. **haesit ... tuō**: "he stood stock-still and fixed his gaze unwaveringly on your face" (Barsby).

25–26: **placeās**: deliberative subjunctive, here expressing indignation (AG §444). **nullī** = *nullī formae* or *formae nullīus*. **mē miseram**: accusative of exclamation (AG §397d). **corpore**: either ablative with *dignus* ("worthy of"), or ablative of separation with *abest* ("is lacking from"), or both. **cultus**: *cultus, cultūs*, f. here "style of dress, get-up" (OLD 5b).

27–28: **tam fēlix essēs** = *vellem (ut) tam fēlix essēs quam fōrmōsissima (es)*. *fēlix* here means "wealthy"; for the omission of *ut* from a substantive clause of purpose with *volō*, see AG §565a. The personal fortunes of the *lēna* are tied to those of the *puella*, i.e., she proposes to be her madam and enrich herself as the *puella* is enriched.

29–30: **stella ... contrāria**: *stella* often means "planet"; in astrology Mars was often the bringer of bad luck. **tibi**: with *nocuit* (*noceō* takes a dative), but also with *oppositī*. **oppositī**: "hostile, opposed" in the astrological sense. **signō nunc Venus apta suō**: supply *est*, "favorable Venus is now established in her own corner of the sky" (Barsby). For the ablative without the preposition see on line 15 above. Venus has now entered one of the signs of the Zodiac (*signō*) favorable to her—clearly a good sign for the *puella*.

31–32: **prōsit ut adveniēns, ēn aspice** = *ēn aspice, ut prōsit adveniēns*, "see now, how she helps you by her coming." For *ut* as an exclamatory adverb ("how!") see OLD 2b. **prōsit** < *prōsum, prōdesse, prōfuī* "to be beneficial"; subjunctive in an indirect question. **cūrae, quid tibi dēsit, habet** = *habet cūrae quid tibi dēsit*; *cūrae* is dative of purpose ("as a care," see AG §382), used instead of a predicate accusative; the object is *quid tibi dēsit*.

33–34: **est ... illī**: *illī* is a dative of possession (AG §373). **faciēs**: *faciēs* can mean "good looks." **comparet**: potential subjunctive (AG §447.3). **sī tē nōn emptam vellet**: "if he did not wish to buy your favors." *volō* in the sense of "want something to be done" can take a perfect passive participle as well as the more usual accusative and infinitive. *vellet* is imperfect subjunctive in the protasis of a present contrary to fact condition. **emendus erat**: "he would have to be bought"; i.e., if he wasn't willing to pay for you, you would be willing to pay for him. We would expect *emendus esset*, but if the verb in the apodosis of a contrary to fact condition implies a future it can be in the indicative (AG §517 n.1).

35–36: **ērubuit!**: "she blushed!" spoken as an aside. **pudor**: the modesty manifested by blushing, which looks good (*decet*) on a pale complexion. **iste** = *pudor*. **vērus**: i.e., *vērus pudor*. **obesse** < *obsum, obesse, obfuī*, "to be a disadvantage" (here used absolutely), i.e., it is a detriment to the trade.

37–38: **bene**: here "decorously, becomingly." **gremium**: supply *tuum*. Downcast eyes are a sign of modesty. **quantum quisque ferat**: either "you will have to look to see how much each one is bringing," or "however much each one might bring, to that extent (understanding a *tantum*, implied by *quantum*) he will have to be esteemed." The first option better preserves the antithesis between *deiectīs ocellīs* (37) and *respiciendus* (38). **respiciendus erit**: supply *tibi* (AG §196).

39–40: **immundae ... Sabīnae**: the Sabine[1] women, from Rome's remote past, were famous for their old-world chastity; they are also famous for being raped by the followers of Romulus, but that is not the point here. For Dipsas chastity was merely a lack of sophistication, just as Tacitus suggests that Romans in his day called adultery "modern" (*saeculum*, Tac. Germ. 19). **Tatiō regnante**: "in the reign of Tatius" (ablative absolute). Titus Tatius was a king of the Sabines, who became king along with Romulus following the rape of the Sabine women; the story is told in Livy, *History of Rome* 1.10–11. **nōluerint habilēs ... esse**: "did not wish to offer themselves," literally, "be easy to handle." **nōluerint**: potential subjunctive, as regularly with *forsitan* (AG §447.3a). **habilēs**: there are no obvious parallels for this use of the word, which has physical and sexual overtones at *Amores* 1.4.37 (*habilēs ... papillae*).

41–42: **externīs ... in armīs**: "for wars abroad"; Dipsas regards the wars of the time of Romulus and Titus Tatius as *internal* ones, since the Sabines had

---

1 http://pleiades.stoa.org/places/423028

for so long been incorporated into the Roman state. **animōs exercet**: either "is occupying his energies" (Barsby), or perhaps "is giving brave men some practice" or "is keeping their minds busy." In other words, the husbands are so busy preparing themselves for war that they are paying no attention to their wives' extramarital activities. *exerceō* traditionally has associations with military training. **Aenēae ... suī**: Aeneas was Venus' son; according to Dipsas that apparently makes sexual freedom all the more appropriate for the Rome of her day; Augustus, who traced his lineage back to Venus and Aeneas, would have been shocked by this deduction.

43–44: **lūdunt**: *lūdō* can have an explicitly sexual meaning, "to sport amorously," "to be promiscuous." **nēmo**: the o is normally long, but Ovid sometimes shortens it; see McKeown *ad loc.* **rogāvit**: here with an explicitly sexual meaning, "to proposition." **rusticitās**: "lack of sophistication," with an allusion to the simple country living of the Sabine women. **ipsa**: i.e. *(illa) quam nēmo rogāvit*.

45–46: **hās**: understand *fēminās*, object of *excute*. **frontis ... in vertice portant**: "on the tops of their their foreheads" (singular for plural). **rūgās**: "wrinkles"; prudish ladies (not necessarily old ones) would make wrinkly judgemental faces. **excute**: "shake out" the prudish ladies, like someone shaking out a garment—a bold metaphor. For the use of an imperative as the equivalent of a protasis in a condition, see AG §521b. **crīmina**: "many a guilty thought" (Barsby) or "many (sexual) misdeeds." Given the outrageous rewriting of the story of Penelope in the next couplet, the second option is probably meant.

47–48: **Pēnelopē**: The wife of Odysseus is normally considered a paragon of wifely chastity, but Dipsas gives a much racier and more cynical version of her relationship with her suitors. **vīrēs**: the plural of *vīs*, f., which can refer to sexual prowess. **temptābat** < *temptō, -āre*, "to test, try out." Since in the *Odyssey* there was only a single archery contest, this may be an inceptive imperfect, indicating that the action has begun but not been completed (AG §471c); but the imperfect also makes sense in the racier alternative version, given the sexual sense of *vīrēs*, since Penelope could be seen as working through the long list of suitors. **in arcū**: "with the bow," though *arcus* can also mean "penis," cf . McKeown *ad loc.*; *in* + ablative can mean "bearing" a weapon. **qui latus ... arcus erat** = *arcus qui latus arguerat erat corneus*. **latus** < *latus, lateris*, n. "side, flank," but here "physical strength, vigor," sometimes in the sexual sense of "prowess." **arguerat** < *arguō, arguere, arguī, argūtum*, "demonstrate, prove." **corneus**: "made of horn"; in Homer, the bow of Odysseus was made of horn (a composite bow), but *corneus* also has an explicitly sexual connotation (McKeown *ad loc.*)

49–50: lābitur ... aetās: Dipsas changes her subject here (adversative asyndeton, cf. on 1.3.19). Poets, in Latin elegy and throughout western literature, have used the transitory nature of youth as an argument in seduction; the tradition is encapsulated in Horace's *carpe diem* poem (*Odes* 1.11), and Marvell's "To his Coy Mistress." **occultē**: "without being noticed" (adverb). **fallitque** < *fallō, fallere, fefellī, falsum* "to trick, deceive" but also "elude, be unnoticed." **admissīs ... aquīs**: *admittō* can mean "to release, let loose." Some manuscripts and some editors read *admissīs ... equīs*.

51–52: aera: "(pieces of) bronze," i.e. money. **ūsū**: "from use," i.e., bronze becomes dull if it is not handled. **habērī**: "to be worn." **cānescunt**: "to become white" with dust etc., but here the allusion to the human body, which grows white-haired with age, is even more obvious than in the previous line. **turpī ... sitū** < *situs, ūs*, m. "neglect."

53–54: admittās: *admittō* can have the specific meaning of "receive a lover." The form can be explained as a generalizing second person singular in an indefinite subjunctive (Barsby), or as the protasis of a future less vivid condition, the apodosis of which is in the present indicative (AG §516b); in the latter case, Dipsas is addressing her mistress directly. **nullō exercente**: ablative absolute (AG §420); *exerceō* here means "to employ, put to use." Just as bronze loses its sheen when it isn't handled and used (51), so beauty (according to Dipsas) loses its youthful appeal if no one puts it to use sexually. **satis effectūs** < *effectus, effectūs*, m., "result, outcome"; *satis* is an indeclinable substantive, here accusative, with a partitive genitive (AG §346). **ūnus et alter**: "(just) one or two." Supply *amātor* with both adjectives. **rapīna** < *rapīna, ae*, f. "plunder" (of property but also "abduction" (especially of a woman); here the primary meaning is "plunder," as an exaggerated way of talking about profit. Having only two lovers is not enough; one should have many (*multīs*, 55) to keep one's sexual prowess keen and to make a more reliable profit.

55–56: Dipsas now turns to her interest in the financial profitability of having lovers. **cānīs ... lupīs**: both "to gray wolves" and "to white-haired prostitutes." *cānus, -a, -um* means "white, gray"; *lupīs* is either from *lupus* ("wolf") or *lupa* ("she-wolf" or "prostitute"). **dē grege**: "from a (whole) flock"; this is the point.

57–58: **iste tuus ... vātēs**: "that poet of yours." It is finally revealed that the narrator and the *puella* are lovers, and it is clear that the narrator has been more than simply a casual eavesdropper. The pejorative sense of *iste* underscores the *lēnā's* scornful contempt for a poet (presumably a man of few financial resources). **amātōris mīlia multa legēs**: *legō* here means either "collect" (Barsby) or "read" (McKeown). If "collect" is right, the point is both repetitive and unclear: her mistress will get lots of money (*mīlia nummōrum*) from a lover, who is different from the poet under discussion. If "read" is right, it comes as a surprise: we expect that a sentence beginning with "many thousands of a lover's things" (possibly *mīlia nummōrum*) will conclude with "you'll receive as presents," but "the lover's things" turn out to be something that, according to Dipsas, her mistress will *reading*: all the poet has to offer is lots of poetry.

59–60: **ipse deus vātum**: Apollo. The point of this couplet seems to be that a really good poet, like Apollo, would display obvious signs of worldly success, comparable to Apollo's golden cloak and lyre, and would thus be worthy of attention. **pallā**: "cloak"; ablative of cause (AG §404) or specification (respect) (AG §418). **aureā**: here two syllables by synizesis (AG §603c). **tractat ... fīla**: "plucks the strings." The chiasmus reflects an actual lyre: the *consona fīla* are tucked inside *inaurātae ... lyrae*.

61–62: **quī dabit**: "he who will give" gifts; the *amātor dīves* who will give gifts and money to his lover. **tibi**: dative of reference, expressing point of view: "as far as you are concerned" (AG §378); the second i of *tibi* is usually short, but it can be lengthened to accomodate the meter. **mihi**: as with *tibi*, the second i can be long. **rēs est ingeniōsa dare** = *dare est rēs ingeniōsa*; *dare* is a subjective infinitive with *est* (AG §461b). Dipsas has no use for the talents of a poets, only for the "talent" of gift-giving.

63–64: **nec tū .../ despice** = *nōlī despicere*. "Don't despise the man who has bought his freedom at the price of his head," refers to a former slave who grew rich enough to purchase his freedom. In Ovid's circles, this would be a somewhat disreputable class. **capitis**: *caput* can mean "the status of a free citizen." **mercēde** < *mercēs, mercēdis* f., "price"; ablative of price (AG §416).

redemptus < *redimō, redimere, redēmī, redemptum* "buy back," especially "buy out of slavery." **gypsātī crīmen ināne pedis**: supply *est*; "the accusation of (having had) a foot whitened with gypsum is pointless," i.e., "the taint of slavery is pointless." When foreign slaves were put up for sale for the first time their feet were whitened with gypsum. The genitive is perhaps best described as appositional (AG §343d), or genitive with words suggesting accusation (AG §352).

65–66: **ātria**: "atrium" (the main reception room in a Roman house); the plural is regularly used for the singular in poetry. **cērae**: "wax portrait busts," but here a reference to the *imāginēs*, wax masks of distinguished ancestors placed in the atrium of an aristocratic Roman house; to say that a Roman had *imāginēs* was to say that he was a member of the senatorial aristocracy. **tolle ... tēcum**: "pick up and take with you (as you leave)." Note the harsh alliteration of the "t" sounds, emphasizing the *lēna*'s contempt for potential suitors who offer a lover nothing more than an illustrious ancestry. **avōs**: a reference to the ancestors (65, *veterēs circum ātria cērae*) in whom an aristocrat would put so much stock.

67–68: **quī** = *(ille) quī*. **quia pulcher erit**: Dipsas now turns to the suitor who is so good-looking that he thinks he doesn't need to offer presents (or payment) for a night with the girl. **quod det, amātōrem flāgitet ante suum**: "let him first demand something from his own lover to give (to you)." *flāgitet* < *flāgitō -āre*, "to ask for repeatedly"; it can take a double accusative, "ask someone for something" (AG §396); hortatory subjunctive. The *lēna* makes the assumption that, if the potential lover is *pulcher*, he must have a (male) lover of his own (*amātōrem ... suum*), from whom he can wheedle the money he needs to pay his mistress; she should never give away her favors for free.

69–70: **parcius**: "rather sparingly"; comparative of parcē. **exigitō**: "demand payment"; future imperative (from the language of Roman law and religion). **dum rētia tendis**: a hunting metaphor; hunters regularly stretched out nets to catch anything from birds to boar and deer. **lēgibus ūre tuīs**: "torment them on your own terms." *lēgibus* is probably ablative of specification (respect), which can include expressions indicating that in accordance with which a thing is done (AG §418). Smitten Roman lovers were often said to be subject to the *lēgēs* of their mistresses. *ūrō* is used especially of passion.

71–72: nocuit: gnomic perfect, used sometimes to indicate that what has been true in the past is always true; translate as a present or present perfect (AG §475). **sine crēdat amārī** = *sine (ut) crēdat (sē) amārī*: "permit him to believe he is loved." **cave**: imperative of *caveō*, here as often with a short *e* (iambic shortening, a feature of colloquial speech). Prohibition can regularly be expressed by *cave* + present subjunctive, but *cave nē* sometimes occurs (AG §450 n.2). **nē grātīs hic tibi constet amor**: "lest this love be worth nothing to you," "lest you charge nothing for this love." **grātīs** is the ablative plural of *grātia*, usually occurring in this syncopated form (instead of *gratiīs*), and means "without payment, for nothing." For the ablative of price, see AG §416.

73–74: capitis ... dolōrem: "a headache." **modo ... / modo**: "now X, now Y." **causās**: "excuses" (for not having sex). **praebeat**: subjunctive in a relative clause of purpose (AG §531.2) "to provide excuses." **Īsis**: the cult of the Egyptian goddess was popular in Rome, and was particularly associated with women; devotees were required to abstain from sex for a period of time each year.

75–76: recipe: supply *eum*. Here the word means, specifically, "receive as a lover." **ut nullum patiendī colligat ūsum**: "so that he does not get in the habit of enduring (getting rejected)." **colligat**: *colligō* here means "acquire" (by natural processes). **ūsum** < *ūsus, ūsūs*, m. "frequent practice **nēve** = *nē* + *-ve*. **relentescat** < *relentescō, -ere*, "slacken, become less ardent" (rare). **saepe**: take with *repulsus*.

77–78: ōrantī ... ferentī: understand *amātōrī* with both participles; dative of reference or, more specifically, dative of disadvantage (*ōrantī*) and dative of advantage (*ferentī*) (AG §376). **ferentī**: understand a direct object, such as *dōna*. **exclūsī** = *amantis exclūsī*, i.e. the failed rival of the successful lover, described as an *exclūsus amātor* (on which see *Amores* 1.6.1–2). **amans** < *amans, amantis*, m. "lover" (not the participle).

79–80: et quasi ... laesō: "sometimes, when he is has been wronged, be angry with him, as if you have been wronged." **īrascere**: imperative. **laesō** < *laedō, laedere, laesī, laesum* "harm, hurt" but here "wrong in love" (see OLD 3b), i.e. "betray, cheat on"; here = *amantī laesō*, dative, with *īrascere*. **culpā culpa**: *polyptoton*, or repetition of a word in a different form. Translators treat *culpa* as though it meant "accusation," which produces clearer English, but the point is really that the *sense of guilt* (which the woman would otherwise feel) disappears when balanced by the man's sense of guilt that she should create (hence *tuā*). **repensa** < *rependō, rependere, rependī, repensum*, "to make up for, balance."

81–82: **numquam dederis**: prohibition can be expressed by *nē* + the perfect subjunctive, and other negatives can be used instead (AG §450 n.4). **in īram**: *in* with a verb of spending can mean "upon." **saepe ... facit**: "prolonged anger often creates bitterness" (Barsby). **simultātēs** < *simultās –tātis*, f. "state of animosity, a feud"; Dipsas does not want the quarrel to get out of hand. **morāta** < *moror, morārī* = "dwell on in thought or utterance" (OLD 11c).

83–84: **quīn etiam**: "and in fact"; when used to introduce a statement confirming what has just been said, *quīn* is often strengthened by *etiam*. **coactī**: "on demand," literally, "when compelled," from *cogō*. **illa vel illa**: supply (*alia*) *puella* for both adjectives. She is supposed to act as though the man's other girlfriends were making her cry.

85–86: **commodat ... nūmina surda Venus**: either "Venus turns a deaf ear" when lovers swear falsely (literally, "a deaf Venus lends her divinity"); or "Venus lends her deaf divinity"—a play on "lends an ear," (*aurem commodāre*); or "Venus arranges that the gods be deaf to" lovers' perjuries (taking *commodāre* in the sense of "provide" a witness at a trial, etc. **in lūsūs**: "for the games of love."

87–88: **ad partēs ... parentur**: *ad partēs parāre* means "to prepare one's part/role" (in a play). **sollers**: "clever, skilled"; construed with *servus* as well as with *ancilla*. **quī doceant**: the subjects are the *servus* and the *ancilla*; as object understand *illum* (i.e. her boyfriend); relative clause of purpose. **tibi**: dative of advantage (AG §376).

89–90: **rogent ... rogābunt**: the subjects are *servus* and *ancilla*. **multōs**: *rogō* can take an accusative of the person asked for a thing, as well as an accusative of the thing asked for. **stipulā** < *stipula, -ae*, f. "stubble," i.e., what is left over after the grain harvest. **acervus**: "heap, pile," esp. a pile of money. Dipsas is looking at the situation from the slaves' point of view: if the *servus* and the *ancilla* get a little bit from a lot of boyfriends (*multōs*), it mounts up.

91–92: carpat < *carpō, carpere, carpsī, carptum* normally "to pluck, harvest," but here "despoil, fleece." **fit cito per multās praeda petīta manūs** = *praeda petīta per multās manūs cito fit*; *fit cito* here means "quickly accumulates" or "is quickly produced." The whole process of plundering the boyfriend by servants and relatives alike will be successful when there are a lot of people involved.

93–94: nātālem: supply *diem*; "birthday." **lībō** < *lībum, ī,* n. "cake," usually offered as a sacrifice, especially on birthdays; hence, not quite our "birthday cake." **testificāre** < *testificor -ārī,* here "give proof of." Singular imperative: "indicate by a cake that it is your birthday."

95–96: nē ... cavētō = *cavētō nē nullō rīvāle sēcūrus amet*. The subject of *amet* is *ille*, i.e. the boyfriend. **rīvāle** < *rīvālis, -is,* m. and f. "rival" (in love). **nullō rīvāle**: ablative absolute (AG §420). *cavētō nē* is a variant of *cavē nē*, for which see on line 72 above. **nōn bene, sī tollās proelia, dūrat amor**: this has the ring of a proverbial truism. **proelia**: "battles." For military imagery in love poetry see especially the next poem.

97–98: tōtō ... lectō: suggesting that their sexual activities had been particularly energetic. **factaque ... notīs** = *(et videat) colla (tua) facta (esse) līvida lascīvīs notīs*: he should see that her neck has been bruised by "sexually unrestrained marks," i.e. by love bites.

99–100: mīserit: future perfect. **Sacra roganda Via est** = *Sacra Via roganda est*; the *Via Sacra* was the principal street of the Roman Forum, but it was also notable for jewelry shops.

101–102: ut nōn tamen = *ita tamen ut nōn* "but without its happening that," "yet not with the result that"; for the use of a result clause in a restrictive sense, see AG §537b. Dipsas now has advice on what to do if the man won't give everything he has. **quod numquam reddās, commodet, ipsa rogā** = *ipsa rogā ut commodet id quod numquam reddās*. For the omission of *ut* with verbs of commanding, etc., see AG §565a. Here *commodō* has its original sense of "lend": ask him to lend you things that you have no intention of returning.

103–104: lingua ... tegat: "let your tongue assist and conceal your intentions." **blandīre nocēque**: imperatives. **impia sub dulcī melle venēna latent**: another terse sentiment with the authority of a proverb.

105–106: praestiterīs: "bring to bear, apply"; for the long final syllable see on 1.4.31. **nec tulerint:** supply *sī*; a continuation of the protasis of the preceding line.

107–108: mihi dīcēs vīvae bene: "you will speak well of me (or kindly to me) while I am alive." *benedīcō* is a verb taking the dative, and Ovid here splits it into its parts, perhaps to emphasize the key word *vīvae*; for the scansion of *mihi* see 61–62 above. **dēfunctae:** "when I have died," parallel to *vīvae* in the previous line. **molliter ... cubent:** where we say "rest in peace" the Romans said "rest comfortably"; the formula *sit tibi terra levis* was common on tombstones, often abbreviated *s.t.t.l.*

109–110: in cursū: "in full flow" (Barsby). Probably the metaphor is of a river, but the word was often used of speech (OLD 3d). **prōdidit** < *prōdō, prōdere, prōdidī, prōditum*, here "betray" (OLD 8); the narrator's lurking presence has been discovered. **vix sē continuēre manūs:** the narrator reacts angrily but with restraint to the advice Dipsas has been giving to his girlfriend. **continuēre** = *continuērunt*; followed by the *quin* clause below.

111–112: quīn ... / ... distraherentque: "from ripping apart"; *quīn* here is a conjunction introducing a clause of hindrance (AG §558). **rāram comam:** "thin/sparse hair." **vīnō:** ablative of cause with *lacrimōsa* (AG §404).

113–114: dī tibi dent: the narrator puts a curse on Dipsas; *dent* is hortatory subjunctive. **nullōsque Larēs** < *Lār, Laris*, m. "Lar, household god"; in the plural it often (as here) means "home"; the use of *-que ... -que* (instead of *et ... que*) is poetic; i.e., "may the gods render you homeless." **sitim** < *sitis, sitis* f. "thirst"; probably the worst part of this curse, since she is an alcoholic.

15. *Amores* 1.9: Love and war

This is an easy poem to like. Part of the appeal is that, for once, we can place it within a specific literary tradition without the aid of commentaries. We all know that "all is fair in love and war," and poets have understood that young men in war and young men in love have much in common (see above all Henry Reed's *Lessons of the War*). Part of the appeal, too, is that the poem is so self-consciously rhetorical. But the poem also presents problems of coherence. I will argue that this, too, is part of the appeal: we have a ponderous rhetorical discussion of something that turns out to be very physical and basic.

Greek and Latin poets often compared lovers and soldiers. Often, too, the two professions are regarded as polar opposites: on the comic stage the hapless young lover is regularly confronted with the *miles gloriosus*, and a life of love is stereotypically one of laziness, contrasted with the exertions of a military career. The paradoxical claim that lovers are *like* soldiers is usually made rather delicately, as in Horace's famous *Ode* 3.26 (*vixi puellis nuper idoneus, et militavi non sine gloria*). But Ovid is taking the paradox and running it into the ground: we are, I think, *supposed* to be irritated by his obsession with this one point.

Ovid's poetry, as we have observed more than once already, often reflects the rhetorical techniques that were the foundation of a Roman literary education. In this poem he seems to be going out of his way to put his rhetorical skills on display, almost as though that were the real point. The poet speaks directly, in the vocative, to an unknown "Atticus" (line 2), serving notice that he now needs to be *persuasive*. The address to Atticus also invites us to wonder, at least in the backs of our minds, what it is the two men have been talking about.

© William Turpin, CC BY   http://dx.doi.org/10.11647/OBP.0067.14

The first thirty lines present almost a caricature of a formal speech in defense of a particular proposition: *militat omnis amans*. The phrase is repeated word for word, to underscore that it is a proposition (lines 1–2). There follows a long list of comparisons, which are clever but unconvincing; it is not actually true, after all, that every lover is a soldier, or even very similar (see Murgatroyd 1999). Lovers and soldiers are alike, supposedly, in eight different ways: they're young men (lines 3–6), they keep watch at night (lines 7–8), they travel (lines 9–14), they go on scouting expeditions (lines 15–18), they conduct sieges (lines 19–20), they conduct night maneuvers (lines 21–26), they evade guards (lines 27–28), and they have both successes and failures (lines 29–30). The poet uses a variety of verbal formulations to maintain our interest, but also to show us just how clever he can be. The high point of his rhetorical creativity is with the sudden direct address (apostrophe) to, of all things, the horses of Rhesus captured in the *Iliad* (line 24). It is soon followed by what we might regard as a conspicuous rhetorical failure, when the poet, offering the last of his eight arguments, stumbles into a sexual *double entendre* (lines 29–30).

The list of comparisons is followed by a tentative conclusion (*ergo*, line 31): people should not say that love is lazy, because it's not. This is a dramatically different claim from the one we thought we were dealing with, and it forces us to re-evaluate what has been going on. Our poet has been comparing soldiers and lovers, it turns out, only to support a more general proposition about lovers being lazy. He will return to this issue at the end of the poem.

A more difficult problem is what comes next, a sudden shift to Homer: Achilles, Hector, Agamemnon, and Mars all had love interests (lines 33–40). The logic is simply not obvious, and part of the explanation may be that, as we have seen, our poet is conspicuously *bad* at rhetoric. But even if this is right, we would like to understand better than we do what is going on in our poet's head.

One problem is that it is not clear what the Homeric examples are supposed to illustrate. McKeown takes the discussion of Homer as following directly from the claim that lovers are not lazy. But, as he says (in his commentary, *ad loc.*), "To point out that great warriors have been lovers is of only limited relevance to the thesis that lovers are active." It seems preferable, therefore, to take the discussion of Homer as an amplification of the central proposition about lovers and soldiers. There is still a problem: the fact that Homeric warriors were also lovers does not prove that lovers are also warriors (Murgatroyd 1999). But our speaker has spent most of his poem desperately trying to make the case that lovers are soldiers; that he should resort with climactic desperation to a logical fallacy seems to me to make a certain psychological and comic sense. Groucho Marx, examining a patient in *A Day at the Races*, famously says "Either this man is dead or my watch has stopped."

Part of the solution, too, may reside in a feature of Roman rhetorical structure, the *refutatio* (also called *confutatio*). Orators, after laying out their main arguments, sometimes mention an objection: "But you will say, I suppose, that my client has a long criminal record, and to that I say…." But the objection is often unstated: the audience is primed to *expect* an objection, usually about four-fifths of the way through the speech, and is thus prepared for an abrupt change in direction: "My client's criminal record is irrelevant, because …." It is easiest to spot a *refutatio* in an actual speech, but similar shifts of direction occur quite often in other prose works, and in some poetry. Thus in *Amores* 1.9 our poet has for 30 lines been insisting to "Atticus" that lovers are like soldiers. Once we see that the discussion of Homeric warriors is a *refutatio*, we can guess at Atticus' objection: "Don't be silly; soldiers and lovers are totally different," or, perhaps "So, give me some examples."

The last six lines change everything. The argument that has been unfolding since line 1 is "Lovers are soldiers, Atticus; so they're not lazy." But this, we now learn, has been a response to a personal attack: "I *used* to be lazy, but now I'm not, because I fell in love. Love is an excellent remedy for laziness." The poem is not really about lovers and soldiers at all; it's about the poet himself (ever self-absorbed), and about being in love.

Even more fundamentally, the poem is about *energy*; lovers need it, others don't. And it is this, perhaps, that provides the point at the end of the poem. The "lover as soldier" theme returns one last time. His girl's beauty made him enlist in her service (line 44). In particular, he is now an energetic participant in the "wars" that happen at night (*nocturnaque bella gerentem*, line 45). Sex emerged as a preoccupation at the end of his long list of comparisons (lines 29–30), and here too what really interests our poet are his night moves.

Suggested reading

Murgatroyd, P. "The Argumentation in Ovid *Amores* 1.9," *Mnemosyne* 52.5 (1999): 569–572. http://dx.doi.org/10.1163/156852599323224680

Amores 1.9

Mīlitat omnis amans, et habet sua castra Cupīdō;
  Attice, crēde mihī, mīlitat omnis amans.
quae bellō est habilis, Venerī quoque convenit aetās:
  turpe senex mīles, turpe senīlis amor.
quōs petiēre ducēs animōs in mīlite fortī, 5
  hōs petit in sociō bella puella virō:
pervigilant ambō, terrā requiescit uterque;
  ille forēs dominae servat, at ille ducis.
mīlitis officium longa est via: mitte puellam,
  strēnuus exemptō fīne sequētur amans; 10
ībit in adversōs montēs duplicātaque nimbō
  flūmina, congestās exteret ille nivēs,
nec freta pressūrus tumidōs causābitur Eurōs
  aptave verrendīs sīdera quaeret aquīs.
quis nisi vel mīles vel amans et frīgora noctis 15
  et densō mixtās perferet imbre nivēs?
mittitur infestōs alter speculātor in hostēs,
  in rīvāle oculōs alter, ut hoste, tenet.
ille gravēs urbēs, hic dūrae līmen amīcae
  obsidet; hic portās frangit, at ille forēs. 20
saepe sopōrātōs invādere prōfuit hostēs
  caedere et armātā vulgus inerme manū.
sīc fera Thrēiciī cecidērunt agmina Rhēsī,
  et dominum captī dēseruistis equī.

1.9: Love and war

nempe marītōrum somnīs ūtuntur amantēs 25
    et sua sōpītīs hostibus arma movent:
custōdum transīre manūs vigilumque catervās
    mīlitis et miserī semper amantis opus.
Mars dubius, nec certa Venus: victīque resurgunt,
    quōsque negēs umquam posse iacēre, cadunt. 30
ergō dēsidiam quīcumque vocābat amōrem,
    dēsinat: ingeniī est experientis Amor.
ardet in abductā Brīsēide magnus Achillēs
    (dum licet, Argēās frangite, Trōes, opēs);
Hector ab Andromachēs complexibus ībat ad arma, 35
    et galeam capitī quae daret, uxor erat;
summa ducum, Ātrīdēs vīsā Priamēide fertur
    Maenadis effūsīs obstipuisse comīs.
Mars quoque dēprensus fabrīlia vincula sensit:
    nōtior in caelō fābula nulla fuit. 40
ipse ego segnis eram discinctaque in ōtia nātus;
    mollierant animōs lectus et umbra meōs;
impulit ignāvum fōrmōsae cūra puellae,
    iussit et in castrīs aera merēre suīs.
inde vidēs agilem nocturnaque bella gerentem: 45
    quī nōlet fierī dēsidiōsus, amet.

 Listen to the *Amores* 1.9
http://dx.doi.org/10.11647/OBP.0067.31

Notes on *Amores* 1.9

1–2: amans = *amātor*. **castra**: "warfare," by metonymy. **Attice**: Ovid addresses a friend (not otherwise known) by name; note the chiastic structure of the first couplet (ABBA).

3–4: quae: the antecedent is *aetās*; "the (same) age which." **bellō est habilis, Venerī … convenit**: the adjective *habilis* ("suited") is linked to a dative of reference (*bellō*), and the verb *convenit* ("befits") takes a dative object (*Venerī*). **turpe**: neuter predicate nominative, supply *est*; "is a shameful thing." **senīlis amor** = *senex amans*.

5–6: petiēre = *petiērunt*; gnomic perfect (AG §475); see note on 8.71. **quos … animōs**: "the (same) courage which"; the antecedent (*animōs*) has been drawn into the relative clause. **sociō**: note that *socius* can have military overtones: "ally." **bella** < *bellus, -a, -um* "pretty."

7–8: forēs: Roman lovers supposedly conducted long vigils outside their mistresses' doors, as in *Amores* 1.6. **servat**: "guards." **ducis**: "of his general"; understand *forēs servat* from the previous clause.

9–10: via = *iter*; soldiers often had to travel long distances to reach the field of battle. **mitte puellam**: imperative as the equivalent of a protasis in a condition (AG §521b). **exemptō fīne**: "with end removed," i.e. "endlessly"; ablative absolute (AG §420).

11–12: ībit: the subject is the lover; *Amores* 3.6 is addressed to a stream swollen with rain that kept the poet from getting to his mistress. **nimbō** < *nimbus, -ī*, m. "rain-cloud" hence "cloud-burst, downpour"; ablative of cause/means. **ille**: the soldier.

13–14: freta < *fretum, -ī*, n. "strait" but also, in both plural and singular, "the sea"; *freta pressūrus* = "about to set sail." **tumidōs**: "swollen," i.e. "causing the sea to swell," or perhaps in the developed sense of "raging, angry." **causābitur** < *causor* (1) "plead as an excuse"; the subject is primarily (I think) the lover. **Eurōs**: "winds"; Eurus is technically the east or southeast wind, but the word is used of winds generally. **verrendīs … aquīs**: "for skimming the water," i.e., for sailing. The dative of the gerundive is used with certain adjectives (like *apta*), especially those expressing fitness or adaptability (AG §505a). **sīdera**: someone considering a sea voyage might claim to be waiting for weather in which he could see stars to steer by. **quaeret**: understand *nec* from line 13.

17–18: alter ... alter: "the one ... the other," "the soldier ... the lover." **speculātor**: "as a spy," in apposition to *alter*.

19–20: ille ... hic: "the soldier ... the lover." **gravēs**: "hard to capture." **hic ... ille**: "the soldier ... the lover."

21–22: sopōrātōs = *dormientēs*. **prōfuit**: gnomic perfect (AG §475). **caedere et** = *et caedere*. **armātā ... manū**: presumably an armed hand, rather than an armed band of men.

23–24: fera Thrēiciī cecidērunt agmina Rhēsī: in Book 10 of the *Iliad* Odysseus and Diomedes kill Rhesus, a Thracian[1] ally of the Trojans, steal his horses, and escape. < *cadō, cadere, cecidī, cāsum* "fall" (not *caedō, caedere, cecīdī, caesum* "strike; kill"). **captī dēseruistis equī**: in an apostrophe with mock tragic effect, the author now addresses the horses of Rhesus in the vocative.

25–26: nempe: "certainly," introducing a statement confirming what has just been said, with the expectation that it will not be contradicted. **somnīs**: ablative with *ūtuntur*, "take advantage of the sleep." **sua ... arma movent**: "wield their weapons," in this context a sexual double entendre. **sōpītīs hostibus**: ablative absolute (AG §420).

27–28: transīre: the subject of *opus* [*est*] in line 28. **manūs**: here "band, troop." **miserī**: agrees with *militis* and with *amantis*. **opus**: supply *est*, "it is the task of."

29–30: Mars ... Venus: supply *est* for both clauses. By metonymy, *Mars* = *bellum*, *Venus* = *amor*. The outcome of both war and love is uncertain. **quōsque negēs**: "and those whom you would deny," followed by indirect statement. **negēs**: potential subjunctive (AG §447.2). **iacēre**: "lie prostrate, be brought low."

---

1   http://pleiades.stoa.org/places/981552

31–32: dēsidiam: "idleness, inactivity"; part of a double accusative with *vocābat*, "whoever used to call love 'idleness.'" **ingeniī ... experientis**: "of an enterprising nature"; genitive of quality/description (AG §345).

33–34: ardet: historical present for vividness (AG §469). It represents both the anger of Achilles at Agamemnon (for taking away Briseis) and his passion for Briseis, the first of several famous examples of love mixing with war. **in abductā Brīsēide**: Briseis was the concubine of Achilles. Her appropriation by Agamemnon provoked the "wrath of Achilles" on which the *Iliad* hinges. *Brīsēide* is ablative singular; for the forms of Greek nouns in the third declension, see AG §81. *in* + abl., here "over/because of/in the matter of." **dum licet**: Achilles' anger about his loss of Briseis led him to withdraw from the fighting, allowing the Trojans their best chance of defeating the Greek army. **Argēās** < *Argēus, -a, -um* "Argive, of Argos," used (as in Homer) as an equivalent of "Greek." **Trōes**: "Trojans, men of Troy"; vocative. **opēs**: "military strength, troops."

Fig. 19 Achilles surrendering Briseis, Fresco from the House of the Tragic Poet, Pompeii. Naples, National Archaeological Museum. Wikimedia, https://commons.wikimedia.org/wiki/File:Achilles_Briseis_MAN_Napoli_Inv9105_n01.jpg

35–36: Andromachēs: Greek genitive singular. Andromache was the wife of Hector; for their famous farewell see *Iliad* 6.369–502. **complexibus**: "embrace." **galeam**: "helmet"; Hector's helmet figures prominently in his parting from Andromache, when its plume frightens their little boy Astyanax. *galeam capitī ... daret* = "put the helmet on his head." **quae**: "she who," postponed to emphasize *galeam*. **uxor erat**: "was his wife."

Fig. 20 Hector saying farewell to Andromache and Astyanax. Detail from an Apulian red-figure crater, c. 370–360 BC. Ruvo di Pugilia (Bari), Museo Nazionale, Palazzo Jatta. Wikimedia, https://commons.wikimedia.org/wiki/File:Hector_Astyanax_MN_Jatta.jpg

37–38: **summa ducum**: "head of the leaders"; Agamemnon was the paramount Greek king. **Atrīdēs** < *Atrīdēs, -ae* m. "son of Atreus" (patronymic), Agamemnon. **Priamēide** < *Priamēis, -idos* f. "daughter of Priam" (patronymic), Cassandra, see on 1.7.17 above. For the forms of Greek nouns in the third declension, see AG §81. **fertur**: "is said." *ferō* is often used, especially in the passive, to mean "relate, tell." **Maenadis**: Cassandra was actually not a Maenad, but since her hair was always messy she is compared to one of the Maenads, who were notoriously unkempt. **obstipuisse**: "to have been stunned at" + dat.

39–40: **Mars quoque**: Hephaestus (Vulcan) made a snare (*fabrīlia vincula*) and caught Ares (Mars) in the act of adultery with his wife Aphrodite (Venus) (*Odyssey* 8.266–366). **nōtior in caelō fābula nulla fuit**: Hephaestus (Vulcan) then summoned all the Olympian gods to laugh at the captured adulterers.

Fig. 21 Vulcan surprising Venus and Mars, before the Assembly of the Gods. By Johann Heiss (1697). Sotheby's. Wikimedia, https://commons.wikimedia.org/wiki/File:JOHANN_HEISS_VULCAN_SURPRISING_VENUS_AND_MARS.jpg

41–42: discinctaque in ōtia: "for easygoing leisure." *discinctus* means "wearing a tunic without a belt, wearing loose clothes," hence "easygoing, undisciplined." *discincta ōtia* is a striking phrase (transferred epithet), since logically the adjective applies to *ipse ego*, not *ōtia*. **lectus et umbra** = *lectus umbrōsus* (hendiadys, on which see 1.4.53).

43–44: ignāvum: understand *mē*. **fōrmōsae cūra puellae:** "love of a beautiful girl" but Ryan and Perkins note also a military allusion, since *cūra* could also mean "command" (of an army, see OLD 7). **puellae:** objective genitive (AG §348). **iussit et** = *et iussit*. **merēre:** supply *mē* as the subject. **in castrīs ... suīs:** "in her camp," the same metaphor as in line 1. **aera:** "(military) pay."

45–46: vidēs: understand *mē* as direct object; remember that the poem is an address to Atticus (line 2). **agilem** < *agilis, e* here "energetic, busy." **dēsidiōsus:** "idle, lazy." The final point is perhaps a sexual one: in British English "get busy" can refer to sex.

16. *Amores* 1.10: Love for sale

This poem is conspicuously manipulative. We are led to expect a love poem, with the poet comparing his girlfriend to three legendary beauties. But we quickly learn that the poet is in fact angry, because his girl has asked for presents. The poet then shifts into his rhetorical mode, and argues elaborately that women should not charge for sex. Or if they do (the poet apparently changes his mind on this point), a man should pay with poetry, not cash.

The first six lines, with three mythological exempla in as many couplets, is one of Ovid's most sustained and obvious allusions to his predecessor Propertius. Propertius 1.3 begins with a comparison of his sleeping girlfriend Cynthia to three sleeping heroines, in three couplets:

> Qualis Thesea iacuit cedente carina
>> languida desertis Cnosia litoribus;
>
> qualis et accubuit primo Cepheïa somno
>> libera iam duris cotibus Andromede;
>
> nec minus assiduis Edonis fessa choreis
>> qualis in herboso concidit Apidano:
>
> talis…

"Like the maiden of Knossos [Ariadne], who lay exhausted on the deserted shore while Theseus' ship was sailing away; like the daughter of Cepheus, Andromeda, when she lay in her first sleep after her rescue from the hard rock; and like a girl [a Bacchant] exhausted from intense Thracian dances, who has collapsed beside the grassy Apidanus: so…."

© William Turpin, CC BY   http://dx.doi.org/10.11647/OBP.0067.15

In the Propertius poem, too, the relationship between the poet-lover and his girlfriend turns out to be more difficult than that suggested by the idyllic (and sexual) opening comparisons. But in Ovid the reversal is even more dramatic. Ovid's three heroines are cited not because they are in a specific situation (asleep), but simply because they are spectacularly beautiful: Helen of Troy, Leda, and Amymone (lines 1–6). Now, although the poet *had* been possessive about his gorgeous girlfriend (lines 7–8), that's all over: he has decided that she's not attractive at all (lines 9–10). The reason for this change, we learn, is that she has asked for presents (*munera*, line 11). The poet realizes, now, that there's something wrong with what we might call her personality (*animus, mens*), and that apparently means her beauty isn't beauty at all.

We may pause here to reflect briefly on whether or not this is plausible. A disillusioned lover might well conclude that a woman's moral flaws made her beauty irrelevant. He might even say, perhaps, that it made her beauty non-existent, at least to him. But that latter formulation, in this case, seems hard to accept as genuine: this girl is not just good-looking, she's in the Helen of Troy league. The poet, then, can hardly be sincere: he's trying to convince the girl, and perhaps himself, that there's no physical attraction any more, but he's protesting far too much to be convincing. We get a sense of his desperation, perhaps, in his odd arrangement of mythological *exempla*: he starts out with the glibbest of glib comparisons, to Helen, but then moves, through Leda, to the far more obscure Amymone. Is he not working just a little too hard to make his point?

Our poet's long attack on the buying and selling of love is self-consciously rhetorical. The fictional audience changes from one particular girl (note the singulars in lines 7 and 10), to women in general (see the 2nd person plural at line 17 and subsequently). This is a standard rhetorical move, even in modern discourse: a single instance of something mildly offensive can provoke a harangue full of generalizations addressed to an entire class of likely culprits. But it is an overreaction: asking for a present does not actually make a woman a prostitute (see McKeown's note on lines 17–18).

The most conspicuous feature of his "speech" is its variety, reflecting the age-old debating technique of trying out argument after argument in hopes of finding one that will work. And indeed, as he proceeds, our speaker seems to get more and more desperate to find a valid argument. His first point is the light-hearted one that neither Cupid nor Venus, as portrayed in literature, have any interest in money (lines 15–20). He then moves to the opposite end of the emotional spectrum and compares girls who ask for presents to common prostitutes (lines 21–24). This is followed by the equally insulting observation that female farm animals, unlike some women, require no payment for sex (lines 25–32). Less insulting, though equally carnal, is the argument that payment makes no sense, since sex is pleasurable for women too (lines 33–36). The next argument is even more obviously flawed: since it is immoral for a witness, juror, or lawyer to accept payment, it must be wrong for a woman to profit from her love affair (lines 37–42). The final argument is perhaps almost as weak: paying for favors dissolves any sense of gratitude (lines 43–46). The attack concludes with a flat assertion: nothing good ever comes of women trading sex for presents. The claim is supported by the examples of Tarpeia, who betrayed Rome to the Gauls for gold, and Eriphyle, who betrayed her husband in return for a necklace (lines 47–52). But of course just because deals sometimes go wrong is no proof that they always do.

At this point our speaker apparently contradicts everything he has said so far: it is acceptable, he says, for a girl to ask for gifts when her lover is rich (lines 53–56). It helps a little if we see this as a *refutatio* (here an "answer" to a question like "Are there *any* circumstances in which a girl should accept presents?") But certainly we now have to re-evaluate. The mention of *wealthy* givers of gifts leads to the subject closest to our speaker's heart, the question of what a *poor* man has to offer: love and devotion, certainly, but also poetry, which is better than fancy clothes and jewelry (lines 57–62). As we learned in *Amores* 1.3, poetry can make a girl immortal.

The final couplet adds a final twist: it's not payment (*pretium*, line 63) that the poet objects to, it's being asked. The girl will in fact get what she wants, but it has to be a surprise (*desine velle*, line 64). Her request for a present has not in fact led the poet to end the relationship, and we remember, now, that the girl is (supposedly) one of the great beauties of all time. The crisis has been averted, and the relationship looks solid after all.

But there is one slight problem. The girl surely did not ask for a poem; that would make nonsense of the poet's reaction. But that is what she gets: the poet uses the future (*dabo*, line 64), but of course the poem is already there. We might wonder if that's going to be enough.

Moreover, it is hard to forget the bitterness of the attack on mercenary women. The point, perhaps, is similar to that of a famous story told about George Bernard Shaw (and others). A society lady jokingly agreed that she would probably sleep with Shaw for a million pounds, but when he suggested five pounds she asked, indignantly: "What do you think I am?" Shaw's answer was not chivalrous: "We've already established what you are, ma'am. Now we're just haggling over the price."

Suggested reading

Curran, L. C. "Ovid, *Amores* 1.10," *Phoenix* 18 (1964): 70–87. http://dx.doi.org/10.2307/1086365

Amores 1.10

Quālis ab Eurōtā Phrygiīs āvecta carīnīs
    coniugibus bellī causa duōbus erat,
quālis erat Lēdē, quam plūmīs abditus albīs
    callidus in falsā lūsit adulter ave,
quālis Amȳmōnē siccīs errāvit in Argīs,   5
    cum premeret summī verticis urna comās,
tālis erās: aquilamque in tē taurumque timēbam
    et quicquid magnō dē Iove fēcit Amor.
nunc timor omnis abest animīque resānuit error,
    nec faciēs oculōs iam capit ista meōs.   10
cūr sim mūtātus quaeris? quia mūnera poscis:
    haec tē nōn patitur causa placēre mihi.
dōnec erās simplex, animum cum corpore amāvī;
    nunc mentis vitiō laesa figūra tua est.
et puer est et nūdus Amor: sine sordibus annōs   15
    et nullās vestēs, ut sit apertus, habet.
quid puerum Veneris pretiō prostāre iubētis?
    quō pretium condat, nōn habet ille sinum.
nec Venus apta ferīs Veneris nec fīlius armīs:
    nōn decet imbellēs aera merēre deōs.   20
stat meretrix certō cuivīs mercābilis aere
    et miserās iussō corpore quaerit opēs;
dēvovet imperium tamen haec lēnōnis avārī
    et, quod vōs facitis sponte, coacta facit.
sūmite in exemplum pecudēs ratiōne carentēs: 25
    turpe erit, ingenium mītius esse ferīs.

nōn equa mūnus equum, nōn taurum vacca poposcit,
    nōn ariēs placitam mūnere captat ovem.
sōla virō mulier spoliīs exultat ademptīs,
    sōla locat noctēs, sōla licenda venit   30
et vendit, quod utrumque iuvat, quod uterque petēbat,
    et pretium, quantī gaudeat ipsa, facit.
quae Venus ex aequō ventūra est grāta duōbus,
    altera cūr illam vendit et alter emit?
cūr mihi sit damnō, tibi sit lucrōsa voluptās,   35
    quam sociō mōtū fēmina virque ferunt?
nec bene conductī vendunt periūria testēs
    nec bene sēlectī iūdicis arca patet:
turpe reōs emptā miserōs dēfendere linguā;
    quod faciat magnās, turpe tribūnal, opēs;   40
turpe torī reditū censūs augēre paternōs,
    et faciem lucrō prostituisse suam.
grātia prō rēbus meritō dēbētur inemptīs;
    prō male conductō grātia nulla torō.
omnia conductor solvit mercēde solūtā;   45
    nōn manet officiō dēbitor ille tuō.
parcite, formōsae, pretium prō nocte pacisci:
    nōn habet ēventūs sordida praeda bonōs.
nōn fuit armillās tantī pepigisse Sabīnās
    ut premerent sacrae virginis arma caput;   50
ē quibus exierat, trāiēcit viscera ferrō
    fīlius, et poenae causa monīle fuit.

nec tamen indignum est ā dīvite praemia poscī:

    mūnera poscentī quod dare possit habet;

carpite dē plēnīs pendentēs vītibus ūvās,   55

    praebeat Alcinoī pōma benignus ager.

officium pauper numeret studiumque fidemque;

    quod quis habet, dominae cōnferat omne suae.

est quoque carminibus meritās celebrāre puellās

    dōs mea: quam voluī, nōta fit arte meā.   60

scindentur vestēs, gemmae frangentur et aurum;

    carmina quam tribuent, fāma perennis erit.

nec dare, sed pretium poscī dēdignor et ōdī;

    quod nego poscentī, dēsine velle, dabō.

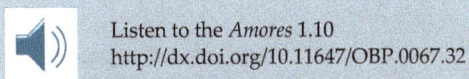

Listen to the *Amores* 1.10
http://dx.doi.org/10.11647/OBP.0067.32

Notes on *Amores* 1.10

1–2: Quālis: understand *ea*. The poet begins by comparing his *puella* to three beautiful heroines, concluding with *tālis erās* in line 7: "Just as *x*, *y*, and *z* were… such (i.e., so beautiful) were you." **Eurōtā** < *Eurōtās, -ae* f. the Eurotas river,[1] the river of Sparta. **Phrygiīs** < *Phrygius, -a, -um* "Phrygian," a territory in Asia Minor,[2] hence "Trojan." **āvecta**: "she who was carried away," a reference to Helen. **coniugibus … duōbus**: "for her two spouses," Menelaus and Paris.

---

1   http://pleiades.stoa.org/places/570248
2   http://pleiades.stoa.org/places/609502

3–4: **Lēdē**: alternative form of *Lēda*, raped by Jupiter in the form of a swan (*in falsā ... ave*). **callidus ... adulter**: Jupiter, renowned for his many sexual dalliances with mortals. **in**: "in the guise of" + abl. **lūsit**: here *lūdō* means primarily "deceive," but it retains its erotic meaning of "sport amorously" and "be promiscuous" (see on 1.8.43 above).

5–6: **Amȳmōnē** < *Amȳmōnē, -ēs*, f. Amymone was one of the fifty daughters of Danaus, king of Argos. When Danaus came with his family to Argos, Poseidon blighted the city with drought. Danaus sent his daughters to look for water, but Amymone was attacked by a satyr. The satyr was driven off by Poseidon, who both successfully seduced Amymone and produced a spring. **Argīs** < *Argī, Argōrum*, m. pl. "Argos" (an important city of the northern Peloponnese). **premeret**: *premō* can mean "be on top of, cover"; Amymone was carrying the jar on her head.

Fig. 22 Neptune (Poseidon) and Amymone. Mosaic from the House of Dionysus. 2nd Century CE. Paphos Archaeological Park, Cyprus. Wikimedia, https://commons.wikimedia.org/wiki/File:Paphos_Haus_des_Dionysos_-_Poseidon_und_Amymone_1_cropped.jpg

7–8: **tālis ... timēbam**: the scansion of this line is unusual, especially in Ovid. Instead of a caesura in the third foot there is an elision (*aquilamq(ue) in tē*); the elision is combined with caesuras in the second and fourth feet: *tālis erās | aquilamq(ue) in tē | taurumque timēbam*. **tālis erās**: the narrator is addressing his *puella* and placing her in the same category with these three women of myth. **aquilamque**: Jupiter took the form of an eagle to abduct Ganymede. **in tē**: "for you"; *in* + accusative can indicate the person towards whom feelings are directed. **taurumque**: Jupiter took the form of a bull to abduct Europa. **quicquid**: "whatever," i.e., whatever other shape, like that of eagle or bull, was adopted by Jupiter in pursuit of his love affairs. **magnō dē Iove**: "out of great Jupiter"; *dē* here is perhaps used humorously to indicate the material from which a thing is made.

9–10: **timor omnis**: the fear that she too, like Helen, Leda, Amymone, Europa, and Ganymede, would be abducted. **animīque resānuit error**: his "mistake" was being in love. **faciēs ... ista**: either "that well-known face of yours" or "that well-known beauty"; in either case *ista* ("well-known, notorious") indicates contempt. **capit**: "captivates/captures."

11–12: note the slow, heavy pace of the spondees that make up the question, then the light rapidity of the dactyls that form the response.

13–14: **simplex**: "artless, naïve, lacking guile."

15–16: **nūdus**: "naked, exposed" and "devoid of wealth" (OLD 10). **annōs**: object of *habet*; the point is that Amor is a child, uninterested in money or possessions. **sordibus** < *sordēs, sordis* f. usually "filth," but here "greed." **ut sit apertus**: "so that he is open in his ways" (Barsby); result clause (AG §537).

17–18: **quid** = *cur*. **puerum Veneris** = *fīlium Veneris*, i.e. Cupid. **pretiō**: ablative of price (AG §416). **prostāre**: "to offer oneself for sale," used specifically of prostitutes. **iubētis**: the plural indicates that the poet is now addressing a more general audience, of women in particular. **quō**: "where." **condat** < *condō, condere, condidī, conditum* "to put away"; subjunctive in a relative clause of purpose (AG §531.2). **sinum**: *sinus, ūs*, m. here a fold in clothing used as a pocket. Cupid doesn't have a *sinus* because he is *nūdus*.

19–20: **apta**: governs not only *Venus* but also *fīlius*. An adjective modifying two or more nouns is usually plural, but it can be singular, and agree in gender with the nearest of the nouns (AG §286); supply *est*. **ferīs**: construe with *armīs*. **aera merēre**: "serve for money" or perhaps "serve as mercenaries"; there is an untranslatable pun here, since *mereō* is used for the activities of prostitutes, and (esp. with *stīpendium*) can mean simply "serve in the army."

21–22: **certō ... aere**: "at a set charge" (ablative of price, AG §416). **cuivīs**: "by anyone"; dative of agent with *mercābilis* (AG §375). **mercābilis**: "purchasable" (rare); she can be bought. **iussō corpore**: that is, by being forced to sell her body; ablative absolute (AG §420).

23–24: **dēvovet ... avarī**: "even so she (*haec*, the prostitute) curses the power of the greedy pimp." **facitis sponte, coacta facit**: the contrast between the willing *puella* and the unwilling *meretrix* is underscored by the reversed order of words (chiasmus).

25–26: **in exemplum**: *in* + acc., "for the sake of." **ratiōne**: ablative of separation with *carentēs* (AG §400). **turpe ... ferīs**: "It will be disgraceful for beasts to have a nature more gentle (than you)." **mītius**: comparative adjective modifying *ingenium*, "a gentler nature"; supply *quam vōbīs*. **ferīs** < *ferus, ferī*, m. "beast, animal" (not necessarily *wild* animal); dative of possession (AG §373).

27–28: **poposcit**: gnomic perfect (AG §475); note that *poscō* takes a double accusative ("ask X for Y"). **placitam**: "pleasing to him." **captat** < *captō* (1) "try to catch (a lover)" (OLD 7d).

29–30: **ademptīs** < *adimō, adimere, adēmī, ademptum* "to remove"; take with *virō*, dative of disadvantage, "taken away from a man." **locat noctēs**: supply *sē*, "hires herself out for the night." **licenda** < *liceor, licērī*, "to bid for"; the gerundive indicates purpose: "comes to be bid upon."

31–32: **quod**: "that which." **pretium ... facit**: "sets her fee." **quantī gaudeat ipsa**: "for as much as she herself would like." *quantī* is genitive to express indefinite value (AG §417). *gaudeat* is potential subjunctive (AG §447.3).

33–34: **quae ... duōbus** = *Venus quae ventūra est grāta ex aequō duōbus*. **Venus**: here not the goddess, but sex itself. Note the word play on *Venus ... ventūra ... / ... vendit*. **ex aequō**: "equally, to an equal extent." **ventūra est**: for the future active periphrastic, constructed from the future active participle and forms of *sum*, see AG §195. **illam**: i.e. *Venerem*.

35–36: **damnō**: "(a cause of) financial loss"; dative of purpose or end, also called the double dative construction in combination with the dative of reference (*mihi*); it indicates that for which a thing serves or what it accomplishes (AG §382). **lucrōsa** < *lucrōsus, -a, -um* "lucrative, profitable" (rare). **sociō** < *socius, -a, -um*, "shared, common," but the legal and political meanings of *socius, -iī* ("partner, ally") are also relevant; *sociō motū* = sex, with an emphasis on mutuality.

37–38: **nec bene ...**/ **nec bene** = *male* (litotes), "unethically"; other forms of unethical behavior are underscored by the anaphora. **conductī**: "hired." **sēlectī iūdicis**: Roman trials, both civil and criminal, were decided by judges (*iūdicēs*) chosen (*sēlectī*) by the *praetor urbānus* for inclusion on a list of potential jurors. **arca** < *arca, -ae* f. "chest," especially "money box." *arca patet*: i.e., the chest is open to receive bribes.

39–40: **turpe**: understand *est*. **emptā ... linguā**: ablative absolute (AG §420). It was illegal for lawyers to receive payment for their services; they were supposed to speak as a personal favor when, in theory, they were convinced of the justice of the litigant's cause. **dēfendere**: subjective infinitive. **quod faciat magnās, turpe tribūnal, opēs** = *tribūnal turpe est, quod faciat magnās opēs; faciat* is subjunctive in a relative clause of characteristic (AG §534–5). **tribūnal**: *tribūnal, -ālis*, n. "tribunal," the platform on which a magistrate sat while judging cases.

41–42: **reditū** < *reditus, -ūs*, m. "revenue, return," here of money made in bed (*torī*). **faciem**: a part representing the whole. **lucrō**: "profit"; ablative of price (AG §416). **prostituisse**: either a gnomic perfect (AG §475) or an aoristic use of the perfect (indicating that the action has occurred but making no statement about when, AG §473). The poets often use perfect forms with this aoristic meaning as metrically convenient substitutes for the present tense.

43–44: **meritō**: "with good cause, deservedly." **prō ... torō** = *nulla grātia (dēbētur) prō male conductō torō*. **male**: "with base intent," i.e., in the exchange of sex for money.

45–46: **conductor**: "one who hires (someone else) for wages," i.e. the man who employs a prostitute, the "john" (UK, "punter"). **omnia solvit**: "has paid off everything"; < *solvō, solvere, solvī, solūtum*, here "discharge the cost of, pay" (OLD 19); i.e. there are no strings attached. **mercēde solūtā**: ablative absolute (AG §420); "after the payment has been made in full." **nōn manet officiō dēbitor ille tuō** = *ille nōn manet dēbitor officiō tuō. officiō tuō* is probably dative, "under any obligation to you."

47–48: **parcite** = *nōlīte*.

49–50: **nōn fuit armillās tantī pepigisse Sabīnās** = *nōn fuit tantī pepigisse armillās Sabīnās*. **pepigisse** < *pangō, pangere, pepigī, pactum* "fix; strike a bargain (for)." The reference is to Tarpeia, the Vestal Virgin who betrayed Rome to the Sabines because they promised her the golden bracelets they wore on their arms. They fulfilled their promise by crushing her with their shields (also worn on the arm). **nōn fuit tantī**: "it wasn't of much value," i.e. "it wasn't worth it." Certain adjectives, including *tantus*, are used in the genitive to express indefinite value (AG §417). **ut**: "with only this result"; for the use of a result clause in a restrictive sense, see AG §537b.

Fig. 23 Denarius of L. Titurius L. f. Sabinus, 89 BC. Obverse: head of King Tatius. Reverse: Tarpeia between two soldiers about to crush her with their shields. Wikimedia, http://commons.wikimedia.org/wiki/File:Tarpeia_coins.jpg

51–52: **ē quibus exierat, trāiēcit viscera ferrō / fīlius** = *fīlius ferrō trāiēcit viscera ē quibus exierat*. Alcmaeon killed his mother Eriphyle, to whom Polynices had given a golden necklace in return for persuading her husband Amphiaraus to join the expedition against Thebes, where he was killed. **monīle**: emphatic: "and a *necklace* was the cause."

53–54: **mūnera poscentī quod dare possit habet** = *habet (id) quod possit dare poscentī mūnera*. The subject is the *dīves* mentioned in line 53.

55–56: **praebeat**: hortatory subjunctive. **Alcinoī** < *Alcinous, -ī*, m. Alcinous was king of the Phaeacians. His rich orchards welcomed Odysseus after his escape from Calypso and shipwreck.

57–58: **pauper numeret**: "let the poor man pay" (+ acc.). **quod quis haberet**: "that which each man possesses." *quis* is an indefinite pronoun, which can be used in generalizations.

59–60: **est quoque … dōs mea**: "it is my gift (literally 'dowry') also." **quam** = *ea fēmina quam*. **voluī**: understand *celebrāre*.

61–62: **carmina quam tribuent, fāma perennis erit** = *fāma quam carmina tribuent perennis erit*. The emphatic word is placed first.

63–64: **nec dare, sed pretium poscī**: objects of *dēdignor* and *ōdī*. **dēdignor** < *dēdignor, -ārī, -ātus*, "to refuse scornfully" (+ infinitive). **poscentī** = *tibi poscentī*. **dēsine velle** = *sī dēsieris velle*.

17. *Amores* 1.11: Sending a message

This poem and the one after it form a matching pair, much like the writing tablets (*tabellae*) that are central to each poem. The *tabella* was the normal medium in Rome for taking notes. It consisted of a wooden board with a frame on each side, and within each frame was a layer of hardened wax (*cera*); the *tabella* looked a little like an iPad, except that we should imagine a "screen" and frame on both sides. Writing was done with a sharp stylus, and the end of the stylus provided a flat blade for rubbing out mistakes. *Tabellae* could be bound together, typically in pairs, with the outside surfaces exposed and the inside surfaces private.

Fig. 24 A tabula, with stylus. Wikimedia, https://commons.wikimedia.org/wiki/File:Table_with_was_and_stylus_Roman_times.jpg

For our poem two functions of *tabellae* are important. In the first place, a *tabella* was an obvious medium for sending a simple message. But it was also a medium used regularly by poets, who would typically write drafts (not necessary *rough* drafts) on such *tabellae*. This would allow the poems to circulate in a more informal mode than would be expected in a *liber*, typically a roll of papyrus used when books were "published" formally. The relationship between *tabella* and *liber* is perhaps analogous to the relationship (in pre-computer days) to the relationship between a poet's spiral notebook and a published volume.

The nature and poetic functions of *tabellae* are central to an understanding of *Amores* 1.11 and 1.12. At the most immediate level, the *tabellae* in question are simply the medium for our poet to send a note to his girlfriend, and for her to reply. But scholars have suggested that we are also supposed to think of the *tabellae* that poets would typically use for their poetry: what our poet offers in *Amores* 1.11, and what gets rejected in 1.12, are poems.

In *Amores* 1.11 the poet begins by flattering Nape, Corinna's hairdresser, and asking to take *tabellae* that he wrote that morning (lines 1–8). Nape has had a love life of her own, and so she should be sympathetic (lines 9–12). The poet then gives detailed instructions: Nape should give Corinna a message in person, but the *tabellae* will say most of what needs to be said (lines 13–14). Nape should observe Corinna's reaction, and insist (*iubeto*) that she write a long message in reply (lines 15–22). But no, why should she bother: all Corinna has to say is, "Come!" (lines 23–24). If that happens the poet will dedicate the *tabellae* to Venus, in thanksgiving, complete with dedicatory inscription (lines 25–28).

There are a number of inconsistencies in all this. Why *two* messages, oral and in writing? Why does the poet need to be *told* about Corinna's reaction? How can Nape really give her mistress *orders*? And why does the poet change his mind about what she should write? But this simply enhances our picture of the poet; he is so excited that he talks nonsense (see McKeown on lines 17–18 and 19–20).

The problem with this poem, in my view, is that it is hard to see anything more. The poet's excitement is perhaps endearing, and so perhaps is his imagined success. But those things are only preliminaries to the disappointment of *Amores* 1.12, whereas we want the poem to be successful as a poem in its own right. Moreover, the conclusion of *Amores* 1.11 seems flat: dedicating a writing tablet to Venus is a striking conceit, perhaps, but we want more. The final couplet is devoted to the poet's inscription, but it doesn't seem to add much: he dedicates the *tabellae* to Venus, because they were loyal helpers in his love-affair, but they used to be just cheap maplewood.

The solution, I suggest, lies in that ambiguity about *tabellae*. What the poet is sending to Corinna is not just a message, but a poem. He just wrote it that morning (line 7), and the situation is urgent (line 15). Of course that urgency could simply be the ardor of youth, but we might wonder if there is not a more specific reason. In *Amores* 1.10 the poet, after that insulting tirade against mercenary women, concluded that he would give her a *poem*. And the *tabellae* of *Amores* 1.11 contain precisely that, the poem to win her back.

We can imagine, too, that the earlier poem, complete with tirade, was also written on *tabellae*. And when we remember that one feature of *tabellae* is that they could be used more than once, we have an interesting possibility for reading the final couplet. It isn't just the maplewood of the *tabellae* that until recently (*nuper*) was *vilis*. It is also the previous poem, inscribed on these same *tabellae*, that the poet now insists was "worthless."

Fig. 25 Relief from the tomb of a scribe, with stylus and writing tablets. Early 4th century AD. From Flavia Solva (ancient Noricum, modern Austria). Graz, Archaeological Museum. Wikimedia, https://commons.wikimedia.org/wiki/File:Scribe_tomb_relief_Flavia_Solva.jpg

Suggested reading

Meyer, E. "Wooden Wit: *Tabellae* in Latin Poetry," in *Essays in Honor of Gordon Williams: Twenty-Five Years at Yale*, eds. E. Tylawski and C. Weiss, 201–212. New Haven: Henry R. Schwab, 2001.

Amores 1.11

Colligere incertōs et in ordine pōnere crīnēs
    docta neque ancillās inter habenda Napē
inque ministeriīs furtīvae cognita noctis
    ūtilis et dandīs ingeniōsa notīs,
saepe venīre ad mē dubitantem hortāta Corinnam,   5
    saepe labōrantī fīda reperta mihi,
accipe et ad dominam perarātās māne tabellās
    perfer et obstantēs sēdula pelle morās.
nec silicum vēnae nec dūrum in pectore ferrum
    nec tibi simplicitās ōrdine maior adest;   10
crēdibile est et tē sēnsisse Cupīdinis arcūs:
    in mē mīlitiae signa tuēre tuae.
sī quaeret quid agam, spē noctis vīvere dīcēs;
    cētera fert blandā cēra notāta manū.
dum loquor, hōra fugit: vacuae bene redde tabellās,   15
    vērum continuō fac tamen illa legat.
aspiciās oculōs mandō frontemque legentis:
    et tacitō vultū scīre futūra licet.
nec mora, perlectīs rescrībat multa iubētō:
    ōdī, cum lātē splendida cēra vacat.   20
comprimat ōrdinibus versūs, oculōsque morētur
    margine in extrēmō littera rāsa meōs.
quid digitōs opus est graphiō lassāre tenendō?
    hoc habeat scriptum tōta tabella "venī."

nōn ego victrīcēs laurō redimīre tabellās 25
nec Veneris mediā pōnere in aede morer.
subscrībam VENERĪ FĪDĀS SIBI NĀSO MINISTRĀS
DĒDICAT. AT NŪPER VĪLE FUISTIS ACER.

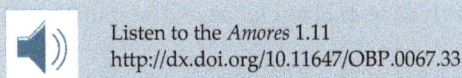 Listen to the *Amores* 1.11
http://dx.doi.org/10.11647/OBP.0067.33

Notes on *Amores* 1.11

1–2: colligere ... pōnere: the infinitives depend on *docta* in line 2, "taught to gather up ... and to arrange," i.e. skilled in hairdressing. Nape was Corinna's *ornātrix*. **incertōs**: "disarrayed, errant, wayward." **docta neque ... habenda**: vocatives; the gerundive shows necessity or worthiness; "(you who) should not be considered." **ancillās inter** = *inter ancillās* (anastrophe, the inversion of the usual word order), "among (ordinary) maidservants"; i.e., Nape stands out from the throng of normal maids. **Napē**: the name of the servant means "woodland glen" in Greek; vocative. Several grave inscriptions survive for Roman slave hairdressers.

3–6: the next two couplets indicate that hairdressing is not Nape's only skill; she is also adept at serving as a go-between for her mistress and her secret lover. *cognita, ūtilis, ingeniōsa, hortāta*, and *reperta* are vocative.

3–4: furtīvae: transferred epithet; though in agreement with *noctis*, it more properly describes the *ministeriīs*. **ūtilis**: predicate adjective (*esse* understood), with *cognita* in line 3, "known (to be) useful." **dandīs ... notīs**: "at giving signs." For this meaning of *nota* see OLD 8; the dative can be used with adjectives (here, *ingeniōsa*) to indicate "that to which the given quality is directed" (AG §383).

5–6: saepe venīre ... hortāta Corinnam = *saepe hortāta Corinnam, dubitantem ad mē venīre, ut venīret*. In poetry *hortor* can take an accusative and infinitive instead of an indirect command. **dubitantem**: the participle has a concessive force, "even though she may be hesitant." **labōrantī ... mihi**: dative of reference with *fīda*. *labōrantī* means "anxious, in trouble, having difficulty." **fīda reperta**: supply *esse*; *fīda* is a predicate nominative with *reperta*.

7–8: **perarātās**: "incised" with a stylus. **māne**: "in the morning"; adverb. Construe with *perarātās*. **perfer**: "carry straight through, deliver." **sēdula**: vocative; an adjective translated with adverbial force, "carefully, cautiously."

9–10: **vēnae ... ferrum**: understand *tibi sunt* (dative of possession). **silicum** < *silex, icis*, m.(f.) "flint"; genitive of material (AG §344). **nec tibi simplicitās ōrdine maior adest** = *nec simplicitās, maior simplicitāte ordinis (tuī), adest tibi*, i.e., "you're no more unsophisticated than the average *ancilla*." **maior**: the a is long by position (as with *maius* at *Amores* 1.7.30); see AG §11d: "a syllable whose vowel is a, e, or or u, followed by the consonant i, is long whether the vowel itself is long or short." *ordō* here means "rank, station, social standing," and is ablative of comparison (AG §406).

11–12: **arcūs**: more logically, *sagittās*, but that would not fit the metrical requirements of the line. **in mē**: "for me, on my account," i.e., by helping me. **signa**: here "legionary standards." For the use of military imagery in erotic contexts see *Amores* 1.9. **tuēre**: imperative, "protect" (especially in a military sense). The point is that Nape has also been in love, so she should fight on the poet's side.

13–14: **quaeret**: supply *Corinna* as the subject. **quid agam**: "how I'm doing"; indirect question. **spē noctis vīvere**: understand *me* as the subject of *vīvere*: Nape will say that the only thing keeping the poet going is the anticipation of a night with Corinna. **dīcēs**: the future indicative can be used as the equivalent of an imperative (AG §449b). **fert**: "reports, tells"; its direct object is *cētera* (n. pl.). **blandā ... manū**: transferred epithet, with *blandā* more logically describing the tablet's wax (*cēra*).

15–16: **vacuae**: dative; understand *dominae*; *vacuus* here means "free from other occupations," "at leisure"; for the dative with a verb implying motion see AG §363.2. **bene**: construe with *vacuae*. **redde** < *reddō, reddere, reddidī, redditum*: here "hand over, deliver" (see OLD 12). **vērum**: "but, however"; as at 1.4.65. **continuō**: "forthwith, immediately"; adverb. Construe with *legat*. **fac ... illa legat**: for the omission of *ut* with verbs of commanding, see AG §565.

1.11: Sending a message

17–18: aspiciās ... mandō: *ut* is again omitted with a verb of commanding. **legentis:** "of her as she reads." **et:** "even." **tacitō vultū:** ablative of source (AG §403) or cause (AG §404).

19–20: nec mora: supply *sit* as a jussive subjunctive, "let there be no delay, let no time be lost." The expression is used parenthetically. **perlectīs:** understand *tabellīs*; ablative absolute (AG §420). **rescrībat ... iubētō:** "tell her to write back" *iubētō* is future imperative (AG §449). **lātē splendida cēra:** "broadly shining wax," i.e., the wax of the *tabella* is shiny and bright on its entire surface because nothing has been written on it.

21–22: comprimat: jussive subjunctive, with the softer form of command now directed to Corinna, understood as the subject. **ōrdinibus:** "in lines" (ablative of place where, AG §421). **littera:** singular for plural. "Let letters inscribed on the edge of the margin detain my eyes" (Barsby). **meōs:** modifies *oculōs* in the preceding line. The distance between the words emphasizes the way his eyes will linger (*morētur*) over the message.

23–24: quid ... opus est: "what need is there." **graphiō** < *graphium, (i)ī*, "stylus." **lassāre** < *lassō* (1) "tire out, wear out." The infinitive is the subject of *opus est*. **venī:** imperative, in apposition to *hoc*.

Fig. 26 Portrait of a young woman with stylus and writing tablets. Fresco from Pompeii, c. 50 AD. Naples, National Archaeological Museum. Wikimedia, https://commons.wikimedia.org/wiki/File:Herkulaneischer_Meister_002b.jpg

25–26: redimīre < *redimiō, redimīre, redimiī, redimītum* "to encircle" (with a garland). Roman generals announced victories by sending to Rome dispatches wreathed with laurel (*litterae laureātae*). *Redimīre* and *pōnere* (26) are both infinitives with *nec morer* (26). **Veneris ... in aede:** inscribed votive tablets were often placed in the temple of a deity as a thank offering. Here, of course, the deity is Venus, the goddess of love. **nec morer**: potential subjunctive, "I would not delay (to)."

27–28: **subscrībam**: future. **VENERĪ**: dative with *DĒDICAT*. **FĪDĀS ... MINISTRĀS**: earlier in the poem (line 6) the narrator referred to Nape as a loyal servant; now he makes the same assertion, only in reference to the *tabellae*. **SIBI**: dative with *FĪDĀS*. **NĀSO**: the poet himself, P. Ovidius Naso. The final o of *NĀSO* is short, by "systole," a rarely used kind of poetic licence. **FUISTIS**: 2nd person plural, addressed to the *tabellae*. **acer**: *acer, acris,* n. "maple"; both the scansion and agreement with *vīle* distinguish this word from *ācer*, "harsh."

18. *Amores* 1.12: Shooting messengers

This poem, as we have said, forms a pair with *Amores* 1.11. In the first poem we learned about the *tabellae* the poet sent to his girl, and in this one we learn that he has failed.

The most immediate point of the poem is to show that the poet takes this rejection hard. We are treated to a display of invective, humorously directed at the innocent vehicles of this communication, with particular attention to the *tabellae* themselves. The poet attacks the hairdresser Nape for letting him down; she seems now to be a drunkard, like Dipsas in *Amores* 1.8 (lines 3–6). He then directs his wrath at the *tabellae* themselves, which he hopes will come to a disgraceful end (lines 7–14). He supplements this with an attack on the man who cut the wood for the *tabellae* (lines 15–16) and on the tree that produced the wood (lines 17–20). He was, in fact, crazy to entrust his *amores* to *tabellae*, which are really only suitable for legal and financial documents (lines 21–26). The *tabellae* are "two-faced," in both senses of the word (lines 27–28). And he hopes they will grow old and gray, and waste away.

It is human nature to curse an inanimate object when we lose our temper, and the literary version of such an attack was a recognized form of literary humor, exemplified most famously in Latin in Horace's *Ode* 2.13, attacking a tree. (Horace's poem, along with Propertius 3.23 on *tabellae*, are two important predecessors for Ovid's poem.) But this does not mean that our poet is being reasonable. The girl has turned him down, and instead of facing facts he lashes out at innocent intermediaries.

It is also worth suggesting that, as with *Amores* 1.11, the *tabellae* refer not just to simple messages, but also to poetry. The poet tells us, after all, that the *tabellae* have been entrusted with "his *amores*" (line 21); even if this is not quite his *Amores*, the word had been associated with love poems from the time of Cornelius Gallus (for the title of Ovid's collections see McKeown vol. 1, 103–107).

Moreover, this double sense of *tabellae* provides, again, a much-needed point to the final couplet. On the face of it, the poem ends simply with a final curse: I want you, *tabellae*, to be ground down with a burdensome old age, and I want your wax to whiten with an ugly disuse (Dipsas was cursed in similar terms, *Amores* 1.8.113–114). The personification is striking, but is not in itself enough to provide the poem with much punch. But if the *tabellae* refer to poetry, things get more interesting. The poet relied on his poetry to work its magic on the girl: poetry could bestow immortality on a poet and his girlfriend because good poetry is immortal. That was the premise of *Amores* 1.3, and the poet reverted to it in *Amores* 1.10; the girl *could* reasonably ask for a poem. In *Amores* 1.11 the poet has sent her *tabellae*: a note, but also a poem. We now see why the poet is so upset: the poem he sent didn't actually do the job, because it wasn't good enough. Far from claiming that it will be immortal, the poet in the final couplet says the opposite: he wants it to disappear without a trace.

Amores 1.12

Flēte meōs cāsūs: tristēs rediēre tabellae;
    infēlix hodiē littera posse negat.
ōmina sunt aliquid: modo cum discēdere vellet,
    ad līmen digitōs restitit icta Napē.
missa forās iterum līmen transīre mementō   5
    cautius atque altē sobria ferre pedem.
īte hinc, difficilēs, fūnebria ligna, tabellae,
    tūque negātūrīs cēra referta notīs,
quam, puto, dē longae collectam flōre cicūtae
    melle sub infāmī Corsica mīsit apis.   10
at tamquam miniō penitus medicāta rubēbās:
    ille color vērē sanguinulentus erat.
prōiectae triviīs iaceātis, inūtile lignum,
    vōsque rotae frangat praetereuntis onus.
illum etiam, quī vōs ex arbore vertit in ūsum,   15
    convincam pūrās nōn habuisse manūs.
praebuit illa arbor miserō suspendia collō,
    carnificī dīrās praebuit illa crucēs;
illa dedit turpēs raucīs būbōnibus umbrās,
    volturis in rāmīs et strigis ōva tulit.   20
hīs ego commīsī nostrōs insānus amōrēs
    molliaque ad dominam verba ferenda dedī?
aptius hae capiant vadimōnia garrula cērae,
    quās aliquis dūrō cognitor ōre legat;
inter ephēmeridas melius tabulāsque iacērent,   25
    in quibus absumptās flēret avārus opēs.

ergō ego vōs rēbus duplicēs prō nōmine sēnsī:

auspiciī numerus nōn erat ipse bonī.

quid precer īrātus, nisi vōs cariōsa senectus

rōdat, et immundō cēra sit alba sitū?

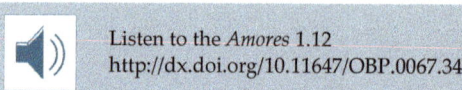
Listen to the *Amores* 1.12
http://dx.doi.org/10.11647/OBP.0067.34

Notes on *Amores* 1.12

1–2: tristēs: "unhappy in their outcome," "grim," because they have failed in their mission. The *tabellae* are personified with this modifier. **rediēre** = *rediērunt*, perfect tense. **infēlix**: "ill-fated"; again, this adjective personifies the *littera*. **littera**: singular for plural. **posse negat**: "says that she cannot" (meet).

3–4: ōmina < *ōmen, inis*, n. "omen, augury." **aliquid**: "something important"; the omens mean something and must be given due consideration. **modo**: "only recently, just now." **discēdere vellet** = *discessūra esset*. **digitōs ... īcta**: "having been struck with respect to her toes," i.e., having stubbed her toe; *digitōs* is accusative of part affected (Greek accusative, AG §397b). The Romans believed that stumbling over a threshold portended misfortune.

5–6: mementō: "remember to"; future imperative, regular with this verb. **sobria**: the poet apparently believes that Nape has been drinking.

7–8: hinc: "hence, from here"; adverb. **difficilēs**: *difficilis* can be used of persons (here of a personified object) to mean "difficult, obstinate." **fūnebria ligna**: vocative, in apposition to *difficilēs ... tabellae*. **negātūrīs ... notīs**: ablative of means with *referta*; the future active participle *negātūrīs* indicates intention ("intending to deny"). **referta** < *refertus, a, um* "crammed, crammed full with."

9–10: quam: the antecedent is *cēra* in the preceding line; object of *mīsit*. **puto**: from the time of Ovid onwards a final *ō* of a verb is often shortened, as here, for metrical convenience; see AG §604g, and Raven, *Latin Metre*,

p. 13. **longae ... cicūtae** < *cicūta, ae,* f. "hemlock," a long stalked plant from which was derived poison. **melle sub infāmī** = *sub infāmī melle*. Wax in the ancient world was usually beeswax, made from the honeycomb; in this case the honey was Corsican and famously bitter. Thus the wax had been gathered from "underneath the notorious honey." **Corsica mīsit apis**: i.e. the wax had been sent to Rome by "the Corsican bee."

11–12: **tamquam miniō penitus medicāta**: "as if deeply dyed with cinnabar." *minium, -(i)ī,* n. "cinnabar" (sulphide of mercury, which produces a bright red pigment). **rubēbās**: the poet continues speaking directly to the wax of the tablet. **ille color**: i.e. the color of the wax in the writing tablet. **sanguinulentus**: in this case the wax was clearly red, seen now as ill-omened.

13–14: **triviīs**: "in crossroads," i.e. "in the gutter." **iaceātis**: hortatory subjunctive (AG §439). **inūtile lignum**: vocative. **vōs**: the 2nd person plural pronoun refers back to the plural addressee *tabellae* (line 7). **onus**: "weight" of a cart or other passing vehicle.

15–16: **illum**: accusative subject of the infinitive *habuisse* (16) in an indirect statement. **vōs ... vertit in ūsum**: "converted you into an object of use" (Barsby). *vertō* can mean "transform" or "undergo physical change," here in the perfect tense. **convincam**: "I will prove that," governing an indirect statement. The tone is legalistic. **pūrās ... manūs**: "clean hands," i.e., the craftsman himself must have done something to bring this "bad mojo" to the wood of the *tabellae*.

17–18: **praebuit**: "supplied." **suspendia** < *suspendium, -(i)ī,* n. "the act of hanging oneself, a hanging," here "gallows"; plural for singular (unless *miserō ... collō* is singular for plural). **dīrās ... crucēs**: "terrifying crosses": for crucifixion.

19-20: **būbōnibus** < *būbō, -ōnis,* m./f. "owl"; specifically the horned or eagle owl, a bird of ill omen. **volturis** < *vultur (voltur), vulturis,* m. "vultur." **strigis** < *strix, strigis,* f. "screech-owl," also ill-omened.

21–22: **hīs**: i.e. *hīs tabellīs;* dative indirect object with *commīsī*. **commīsī** < *committō, committere, commīsī, commissum* here "entrust" (see OLD 14). **insānus**: adjective used adverbially: "was I insane enough to?" **ferenda**: gerundive expressing purpose or intention, "words to be delivered."

23–25: **aptius** .../ **melius**: comparative degree adverbs; the narrator suggests ways in which the *tabellae* could be used "more appropriately" and "better" than as a love missive.

23–24: **capiant**: "would contain"; potential subjunctive. The present subjunctive means that the reference is to the future (AG §447.3). **vadimōnia**: "guarantees"; the *vadimōnium* was a written agreement to appear in court for trial, and (like many legal documents) was typically written on wax tablets. **garrula** < *garrulus -a -um*, "talkative, chatty, babbling." Legal documents such as *vadimōnia* typically seemed wordy. **cērae** = *tabellae*. **dūrō ... ōre**: ablative of manner; "with an unfeeling expression." **cognitor**: "attorney, learned counsel." **legat**: subjunctive in a relative purpose clause (AG §531.2) or characteristic (AG §535).

25–26: **ephēmeridas** < *ephēmeris, -idis* or *-idōs*, f., Greek accusative plural; "day-book, account-book." **tabulāsque**: *tabula* is regularly used in plural to mean "account-books, ledgers." **iacērent**: potential subjunctive; the imperfect subjunctive means that the reference is to present (AG §447.3). **flēret**: "would be weeping over" (+ acc.), another relative purpose clause or clause of characteristic; the *avārus* weeps (supposedly) whenever he has to spend money. Wax tablets are well-attested in business contexts, especially from Pompeii, where a famous set of 153 tablets was found documenting the business affairs of the banker Lucius Caecilius Iucundus.

27–28: **ergō ... sensī**: "And so, I have realized (*sēnsī*) from the circumstances (*rēbus*) that you are 'double' in fact (*rēbus*) as well as in accordance with your name." **rēbus**: "circumstances, the march of events," see OLD *rēs* 17b. **duplicēs**: wax tablets were typically bound in pairs. *duplex, duplicis* has precisely the same double meaning as our "two-faced." **auspiciī ... bonī**: "was not of good omen"; genitive of quality (AG §345). **numerus ... ipse** = *duo*.

29–30: **nisi** = *nisi ut*. **vos**: accusative. **cariōsa** < *cariōsus, -a, -um*, "decayed," though the original meaning of "rotten" (used of wood etc.) is also important. **senectus**: the *tabellae* are personified as going through the ravages of old age. **alba**: white (with age). **sitū** < *situs, sitūs*, m. "neglect" or "physical deterioration."

19. *Amores* 1.13: Oh how I hate to get up in the morning

This poem is appealing in a number of ways, though marred by a momentary brush with Roman racism. The poet's situation is one that is easy to sympathize with: dawn is coming, he is in bed, and he has company. He hates the thought of getting up, so he complains to Aurora, goddess of the dawn, and becomes increasingly personal and vicious. In the final couplet we find out whether he has made an impact.

The poet begins by trying to persuade. He is comfortably in bed with his girlfriend, so there's no need for Aurora to hurry (lines 1–10). Ever the rhetorician, the poet produces a series of arguments: people from very different walks of life all have to get up at dawn, and they hate it (lines 11–24). Normally a poem (or prayer) to a goddess would give a list of the *good* things for which she is responsible; here we get the exact opposite, because all this early rising is Aurora's *fault*.

All these arguments merely support the point important to the poet: the person harmed most by Aurora is the man who's got a woman in bed with him (lines 25–26). The poet, it turns out, has been in this situation often, and he has often wished that something would keep Aurora away. He has fantasized (absurdly) about changes in the cosmos, and about a heavenly chariot accident (lines 28–30).

At this point things turn nasty, with the poet getting more pointedly personal: Aurora, he says, does what she does out of sheer spite. She is as black-hearted as her son is black-skinned (Memnon was an Aethiopian prince). If the poet were to tell her husband what's going on, her reputation would be destroyed. Tithonus, her husband, was incredibly old (Aurora had asked that he be made immortal but forgot to mention eternal youth),

© William Turpin, CC BY   http://dx.doi.org/10.11647/OBP.0067.18

and so Aurora can't wait to get away from him; a young man would make her want to slow night down. (Aurora supposedly had a fair number of lovers; the suggestion here may be that she leaves Tithonus to go out looking for them). But none of that is the poet's fault (lines 31–42).

At this point we get another one of those leaps of logic best explained as a rhetorician's *refutatio* (see Elliott, 130). There is an imaginary objection: "But nobody can change the natural order of things." And mythology offers two responses: Luna put Endymion to sleep forever, and (a much better example) Jupiter doubled the length of the night he spent with Alcumena (lines 43–46). The basic proposition remains: Aurora is bringing in the day out of spite, because her own love life is a mess.

The final couplet brings the poem to an amusing and satisfying conclusion. There is no reason to spoil the joke by explaining it here. But it is important to be aware that the Romans saw blushing as the expected response to *insults*, as well as to embarrassment.

Suggested reading

Elliott, Alison G. "*Amores* 1.13: Ovid's Art," *Classical Journal* 69 (1973–74): 127–132.

Amores 1.13

Iam super ōceanum venit ā seniōre marītō
    flāva pruīnōsō quae vehit axe diem.
quō properās, Aurōra? manē: sīc Memnonis umbrīs
    annua sollemnī caede parentet avis.
nunc iuvat in tenerīs dominae iacuisse lacertīs;   5
    sī quandō, laterī nunc bene iūncta meō est.
nunc etiam somnī pinguēs et frīgidus āēr,
    et liquidum tenuī gutture cantat avis.
quō properās ingrāta virīs, ingrāta puellīs?
    roscida purpureā supprime lōra manū.   10
ante tuōs ortūs melius sua sīdera servat
    nāvita nec mediā nescius errat aquā.
tē surgit quamvīs lassus veniente viātor
    et mīles saevās aptat ad arma manūs.
prīma bidente vidēs onerātōs arva colentēs,   15
    prīma vocās tardōs sub iuga panda bovēs.
tū puerōs somnō fraudās trādisque magistrīs,
    ut subeant tenerae verbera saeva manūs,
atque eadem sponsum †cultōs† ante ātria mittis,
    ūnius ut verbī grandia damna ferant.   20
nec tū consultō nec tū iūcunda disertō:
    cōgitur ad lītēs surgere uterque novās.
tū, cum fēmineī possint cessāre labōrēs,
    lānificam revocās ad sua pensa manum.

omnia perpeterer; sed surgere māne puellās 25
 quis, nisi cui nōn est ulla puella, ferat?
optāvī quotiens nē nox tibi cēdere vellet,
 nē fugerent vultūs sīdera mōta tuōs!
optāvī quotiens aut ventus frangeret axem
 aut caderet spissā nūbe retentus equus! 30
invida, quō properās? quod erat tibi fīlius āter, 33
 māternī fuerat pectoris ille color. 34
Tīthōnō vellem dē tē nārrāre licēret 35
 fēmina nōn caelō turpior ulla foret.
illum dum refugis, longō quia grandior aevō,
 surgis ad invīsās ā sene māne rotās;
at sī quem manibus Cephalum complexa tenērēs,
 clāmārēs "lentē currite, noctis equī." 40
cūr ego plectar amans, sī vir tibi marcet ab annīs?
 num mē nupsistī conciliante senī?
aspice quot somnōs iuvenī dōnārit amātō
 Lūna, neque illīus fōrma secunda tuae.
ipse deum genitor, nē tē tam saepe vidēret, 45
 commīsit noctēs in sua vōta duās.
iurgia fīnieram. scīrēs audisse: rubēbat,
 nec tamen adsuētō tardius orta diēs.

 Listen to the *Amores* 1.13
http://dx.doi.org/10.11647/OBP.0067.35

Notes on *Amores* 1.13

1–2: super ōceanum: note that the ocean was, for the ancients, the body of water circling the known world, very different from sea. **venit**: notice the scansion, and thus the tense: "is coming." **seniōre marītō**: the husband of Aurora (Dawn) was Tithonus, an Ethiopian prince. Aurora had obtained the gift of immortality for him, but forgot to ask that he also be granted eternal youth, with the result that he got very old while she stayed young. **flāva**: "the golden [female] one." Aurora is not named until line 3, but the description here makes it clear whom the poem is about. **pruīnōsō … diem** = *quae vehit diem pruīnōsō axe*. **axe** = *currū* (synecdoche, with a part representing the whole).

3–4: quō: "why" or "where to." **manē**: the *a* is short, so this is the imperative of *maneō*, not *māne* = "early" (see line 25). **sīc … avis**: "so to the shades of Memnon may his birds make their annual offering" (Barsby). Memnon, prince of Ethiopia, was the son of Aurora and Tithonus, killed by Achilles in the Trojan War. Each year, according to legend, Memnon's grave was visited by birds born from his ashes, who then fought among themselves. The blood they shed was thus a sort of offering to their "parent." **sīc**: see on 1.6.25. In this case the speaker is hoping that Aurora will do as he orders when he says *manē*. He says that in that case (*sīc*) he hopes that the grave of Memnon shall continue to receive its annual sacrifice. **annua**: either an internal accusative, translated as an adverb, "annually," or feminine singular nominative modifying *avis*. **sollemnī** < *sollemnis, -e*, "customary." **parentet** < *parentō -āre*, "to make memorial offerings for one's parents," + dative (*umbrīs*) and ablative (*sollemnī caede*). **avis**: singular for plural.

5–6: iuvat: impersonal; supply *mē*. **iacuisse**: perfect infinitive with *iuvat*, used aoristically (the aorist use of the perfect indicates that the action has occurred but makes no statement about when, see AG §473). The poets often use perfect forms with this aoristic meaning as metrically convenient substitutes for the present tense. **sī quandō**: "if ever," i.e., *sī quandō laterī meō puella bene iuncta est*.

7–8: somnī < *somnus, ī*, m. "sleep"; plural for singular. **pinguēs**: "lazy" or "comfortable"; predicate nominative (understand *sunt*). **frīgidus**: predicate nominative (understand *est*). **liquidum**: "clearly, melodiously."

Fig. 27 The "Memnon pieta": Eos lifting up the body of her son Memnon. Interior from an Attic red-figure cup, ca. 490–480 BC. From Capua, Italy. Paris, The Louvre. Wikimedia, https://commons.wikimedia.org/wiki/File:Eos_Memnon_Louvre_G115.jpg

9–10: **ingrāta virīs, ingrāta puellīs**: the adjective *ingrāta* takes the dative. Aurora is criticized instead of praised, a reversal of the traditional hymn of praise to a deity. **roscida ... manū**: a "golden line": adjective A, adjective B, verb, substantive A, substantive B. **supprime**: "hold back, check."

11–12: **ante tuōs ortūs**: "before your risings," i.e., before you rise. **servat**: "keeps under observation, watches." **nāvita**: a poetic word for *nauta*. **mediā ... aquā**: ablative of place where (AG §421). **errat**: *errō* can mean "go astray, wander." The point is that sailors can navigate better when they can see the stars; this does not mean that they actually get lost in the daytime.

13–14: **tē ... veniente**: ablative absolute, "when you come," "as you arrive." **surgit quamvīs lassus ... viātor**: Ryan and Perkins note the sexual overtones in the language of arousal.

15–16: **prīma ... vidēs**: "you are the first to see." **bidente** < *bidens, -entis* m., "mattock, hoe"; ablative with *onerātōs*. **arva colentēs**: "those tilling the fields," an elegant periphrasis for *agricolae*. **panda** < *pandus -a -um*, "bent, crooked, curved." Ryan and Perkins see sexual overtones in language used for the soldier and and farmer.

17–18: **fraudās**: "you cheat of, deprive of" + abl. of separation (AG §400). **trādisque**: "and hand them over to." Whacks on the hands were the main memory Roman adults had from primary school.

19–20: **eadem**: feminine singular, "it is you, the same (female) who." **sponsum** < *spondeō, spondēre, spopondī, sponsum* "to make a solemn promise";

supine with verb of motion to indicate purpose (AG §509). "It is also you who send men into court to pledge themselves, so that they may suffer severe losses which attach to a single word" (Barsby). To initiate a civil suit a litigant had to pledge a certain amount of money (hence *sponsum*), which he would forfeit if his case was judged to be without merit; making that pledge required just one word, *spondeō*. †**cultōs**†: the daggers (*obeli*) mean that editors cannot make good sense of the manuscript readings, and are reluctant to commit themselves to emendations. Some scholars do accept *cultōs*, given in the manuscripts, understanding it as "well-groomed, neat in appearance." Romans often complained about having to wear the uncomfortable toga on formal occasions, such as a visit to the law courts. Others prefer the emendation *incautōs*: it was well-known that litigation could be ruinous for the unwary. **ātria**: "the courts." The reference here is probably to the *ātrium* of the Temple of Vesta in the Forum, where lawsuits were typically conducted.

21–22: **nec tū … nec tū**: understand *es*. **consultō … disertō**: these terms refer to the two kinds of lawyers in the Roman world: a *iūris consultus* would give advice on the substance of the law, while a rhetor (= *disertus*) would offer his skill in speaking. The distinction is analogous to that of the English legal system, where solicitors do the paperwork and barristers (often called "advocates") argue in court. Both nouns are dative with the adjective *iūcunda*. **uterque**: "each one," i.e. the rhetor and the *iūris consultus*. The *iūris consultus* did not have to be present in court, and thus did not really have to get up early.

23–24: **possint**: potential subjunctive in a temporal *cum* clause. **cessāre**: "be idle, rest." **lānificam … manum**: "the wool-working hand," i.e., women spinning wool, a grand and poetic phrase for a humble, everyday activity. **pensa** < *pensum, -ī*, n. "wool" (a pile of unworked wool for spinning or weaving).

25–26: **omnia perpeterer**: "I would be able to bear all that"; imperfect subjunctive expressing potential in the present. **surgere**: objective infinitive dependent on *ferat* in line 26. Its subject is *puellās*: "Who would endure that girls get up?" **māne**: note the long a: "early in the morning"; adverb. **cui** = *alicui*, dative of possession with *non est*, "someone for whom there is not," i.e., "who does not have."

27–28: tibi: the dawn. **nē fugerent ... mōta**: "that they would not move and flee," literally, "that they, having been set in motion, would not flee." **vultūs ... tuōs**: plural for singular; the "countenance" of Aurora is the rising sun.

29–30: frangeret: *optō* can take a subordinate clause with the subjunctive, without *ut*. **axem** = *currum* as in line 2. **spissā nūbe**: "by a thick cloud"; abl. with *retentus*. **retentus**: from *retineō*, "to keep back." Either the horse as a whole is kept back (blinded?) by the cloud and therefore falls, or his foot is kept back so that he trips.

33–34: lines 31–32 are not printed in the text, since they are seen as a later interpolation. They read: *quid sī nōn cephalī quondam flāgrāsset amōre/an putat ignōtam nēquitiam esse suam*. **invida**: supply *Aurora*; vocative. **quod**: "because." **fīlius āter**: Memnon, Aurora's son, was Ethiopian. The Romans were not particularly prone to color prejudice, but they certainly made jokes about physical characteristics. **fuerat**: notice the tense: she had been that way before giving birth to Memnon.

35–36: Tīthōnō vellem ... licēret = *vellem ut Tīthōnō licēret*. For the omission of *ut* from a substantive clause of purpose with *volō*, see AG §565. *Tīthōnō* is dative because governed by *licēret*. (It is tempting to take *Tīthōnō* as dative with *dē tē nārrāre*: "I could wish it were permitted (for me) to tell Tithonus about you." But the story was that Aurora kept Tithonus prisoner; see McKeown *ad loc*.) **caelō**: ablative of place where. **nōn ... turpior ulla foret**: the point is that if Tithonus heard about what Aurora was doing, he would spread the tale and thus ruin her reputation. *foret* is a regular alternative to *esset* (AG §170a).

37–38: grandior: understand *ille*, i.e. Tithonus, who was much older than his wife (see on line 1 above). **aevō**: ablative of degree of difference (AG §414) or cause (AG §404). **ad invīsās ... rotās**: *rotās* = *currum*. Aurora's chariot is hated by Tithonus (because he hates it when she leaves), or by all humankind (who hate it when she arrives). **ā sene**: "from the old man," or "by the old man."

39–40: sī ... tenērēs/clāmārēs: present contrary to fact condition, "if you were holding ... you would shout." **quem ... Cephalum**: "some Cephalus, someone like Cephalus." For the use of indefinite *quis, quid* with *sī nisi, nē,* and *num*, see AG §310a. Cephalus was a handsome young man, married to Procris, with whom Aurora fell in love. **manibus** = *bracchiīs*. **noctis equī**:

better printed *Noctis equī*, since the owner of the horses is the goddess Nox. Several artists have protrayed Aurora in the throes of passionate desire for the young and handsome Cephalus, who makes such a contrast with her aged husband Tithonus.

Fig. 28 Aurora departing from Tithonus. By Giovanni da San Giovanni (1592–1636). Florence, Museo Bardini. Wikimedia, https://commons.wikimedia.org/wiki/File:Giovanni_Da_San_Giovanni_-_Aurora_and_Tithonus_-_WGA09419.jpg

Fig. 29 *Cephalus and Aurora*, by Nicolas Poussin (1594–1665). London, National Gallery. Wikimedia, http://commons.wikimedia.org/wiki/File:Nicolas_Poussin_-_Cephalus_and_Aurora_-_Google_Art_Project.jpg

41–42: **cūr ego plectar**: "why should I be punished?"; deliberative subjunctive. A question implying doubt or indignation can become a simple exclamation (AG §444a). **vir tibi**: "your husband," literally, "the husband for you." **nupsistī ... senī**: *nūbō* is the normal word for marriage by a *woman*; it takes a dative. **conciliante** < *conciliō -āre*, "to advise"; *mē ... conciliante* is ablative absolute, "with me advising," i.e., "I wasn't the one who advised you to marry an old man!"

43–44: **somnōs**: "(nights of) sleep." **dōnārit** = *dōnāverit* (perfect subjunctive in an indirect question). For the contracted perfect forms, see AG §181a. *dōnō* is stronger than *dō*, and means "present, make a present of, reward someone with." **Lūna** = Selene, who fell in love with Endymion, while he was asleep on a hillside. She caused him to sleep forever, so that she could always admire his beauty. The poet is suggesting that Aurora, too, could reasonably change the natural order of things if she had a handsome young lover. Roman sarcophagi often depict Selene and the sleeping Endymion. **neque ... tuae** = *neque fōrma illīus (= fōrma Lūnae) secunda est (fōrmae) tuae*.

Fig. 30 Fragment of a sarcophagus, with Endymion greeting Luna (Selene). 2nd century CE. Berlin, Altes Museum. Wikimedia, https://commons.wikimedia.org/wiki/File:-0175_Endymion_empfängt_Selene_Altes_Museum_anagoria.JPG

45–46: **ipse deum genitor**: *deum* = *deōrum* (AG §49g). The phrase is intended to remind us of the formulaic description of Zeus/Jupiter in Homer and Vergil. The reference in this couplet is to Jupiter's rape of Alcmene, the wife of Amphitryon, by assuming the features of her husband. In order to take full advantage of this trick, he ordered that the night be doubled in length. **commīsit**: "joined together, made continuous." **in sua vōta**: "for his desires"; *in* + acc. expresses purpose.

47–48: **iurgia fīnieram**: "I had finished my rant." **scīrēs**: potential subjunctive. The second person singular is probably indefinite ("one might know"); see AG §447.2 for this meaning of the second person singular subjunctive (present or imperfect) of verbs of saying, thinking, etc. **audisse** = syncopated form of *audīvisse* or *audiisse*; the understood subject is *eam* (= *Aurōram*). **rubēbat** < *rubeō, rubēre* "to be or become red" and/or "to blush," as a sign of shame or modesty. There is a pun here, and the whole poem depends on it: the arrival of Aurora makes everything pink. Note also the imperfect tense. **adsuētō tardius**: "later than the accustomed (time)"; ablative of comparison (G §406). **orta**: understand *est*.

20. *Amores* 1.14: Bad hair

This poem, like *Amores* 1.7, is hard to like. Here the poet is not violent, but he seems to be conspicuously unsympathetic. There are moments of wit and cleverness, but taken at face value the poem is unpleasant, and it is difficult to see any satisfactory point in the end. I will suggest a reading that makes the poem more appealing (perhaps), and reads the poet as a less (or at least differently) annoying character.

If we take the first couplet literally, we have to believe that the poet's girlfriend (we may assume she is Corinna) has, thanks to some combination of curling iron and dyes, lost all her hair. If so, we have to conclude that our poet is astonishingly heartless: a major cosmetic disaster of this sort is no time to be saying "I told you to leave it alone." But what if he's exaggerating? He didn't *want* her to get her hair done, and now that there's a *slight* problem she overreacts. Could it be that she simply got it cut shorter than either one of them had expected?

Our poet goes on to talk at length about how much he liked Corinna's hair in its natural state: very long, very delicate, with a beautiful color (lines 3–12). It was also easy to manage, needing no pins or combs, which could hurt anyone who messed with it (lines 13–18). In fact Corinna had looked wonderful with her hair left loose, like a Bacchante (lines 19–22). Again, if her hair really fell out, this is pretty tactless. But comparison with a Bacchante points in a very different direction: for a girl to have long and messy hair, as we saw with *Amores* 1.5 and 1.7, suggested that she was (or had been) ready for sex.

This leads to a more explicit discussion of the process that has done so much harm (lines 23–26). The emphasis is on the use of hot curling irons, which are perhaps the instruments most immediately responsible for any

© William Turpin, CC BY   http://dx.doi.org/10.11647/OBP.0067.19

hair loss. The poet had warned quite explicitly about their use, on the grounds that he liked Corinna's hair the way it was (lines 27–30). Tellingly, his interest in her turns out, again, to be sexual: her hair had been as nice as that of Apollo and Bacchus (Dionysus), but it was also as nice as that of the wet and naked Venus (lines 31–34).

At this point our poet returns to his initial and problematic proposition of "It's all your fault." There's no point in Corinna's complaining about the lost hair, and no point in her looking in the mirror. The only remedy is to forget about her appearance; indeed she should stop thinking about herself entirely (lines 35–38). Is this because she should be thinking about him?

Moreover, it wasn't some external force such as witchcraft or illness that caused the hair loss: Corinna put the "poison" on herself (lines 39–44). So now she has to wear a wig, and she feels sad when people praise her fake hair instead of the real thing (lines 45–50). In fact she's in tears (the poet is now sympathetic), just sitting there with the old hair on her lap (lines 51–54).

The poet ends with words of encouragement: everything will be alright in the end (lines 55–56). This makes sense, at some level, if we take the story at face value: hair usually *does* grow back, even if it all falls out. We can also, on this reading, see the final couplet as to some extent redeeming the poet: Corinna, he says, will look great when her real hair grows back, and, we infer, he will be supporting her during the long months before that happens.

But I want to suggest that the point is somewhat different. Corinna is sad because she doesn't like her new cut, and she will be wearing a wig to compensate. Her long messy hair had been sexy, and now it's shorter and covered up by a wig, and thus not sexy at all. But wigs are easy to remove, and he is hoping to remove it soon: *postmodo* (line 56) can mean "presently" as well as "later." She will be back in his bed, and her hair will still be the way he likes it: *nativa conspiciere coma* (line 56).

Suggested reading

Boyd, Barbara Weiden. *Ovid's Literary Loves*: *Influence and Innovation in the Amores*. Ann Arbor: University of Michigan Press, 1997. See pp. 117–122.

Amores 1.14

Dīcēbam "medicāre tuōs dēsiste capillōs";
  tingere quam possīs, iam tibi nulla coma est.
at sī passa forēs, quid erat spatiōsius illīs?
  contigerant īmum, quā patet, usque latus.
quid, quod erant tenuēs, et quōs ornāre timērēs, 5
  vēla colōrātī quālia Sēres habent,
vel pede quod gracilī dēdūcit arānea fīlum,
  cum leve dēsertā sub trabe nectit opus?
nec tamen āter erat neque erat tamen aureus ille,
  sed, quamvīs neuter, mixtus uterque color, 10
quālem clīvōsae madidīs in vallibus Īdae
  ardua dēreptō cortice cedrus habet.
adde quod et docilēs et centum flexibus aptī
  et tibi nullīus causa dolōris erant.
nōn acus abrūpit, nōn vallum pectinis illōs; 15
  ornātrix tūtō corpore semper erat;
ante meōs saepe est oculōs ōrnāta nec umquam
  bracchia dēreptā saucia fēcit acū.
saepe etiam nondum dīgestīs māne capillīs
  purpureō iacuit sēmisupīna torō; 20
tum quoque erat neglecta decens, ut Thrācia Bacchē,
  cum temerē in viridī grāmine lassa iacet.
cum gracilēs essent tamen et lānūginis instar,
  heu, mala vexātae quanta tulēre comae!

quam sē praebuerunt ferrō patienter et ignī, 25
    ut fieret tortō nexilis orbe sinus!
clāmābam: "scelus est istōs, scelus, ūrere crīnēs!
    sponte decent: capitī, ferrea, parce tuō.
vim procul hinc removē: nōn est, quī dēbeat ūrī;
    ērudit admōtās ipse capillus acūs." 30
fōrmōsae periēre comae, quās vellet Apollō,
    quās vellet capitī Bacchus inesse suō;
illīs contulerim, quās quondam nūda Diōnē
    pingitur ūmentī sustinuisse manū.
quid male dispositōs quereris periisse capillōs? 35
    quid speculum maestā pōnis, inepta, manū?
nōn bene consuētīs ā tē spectāris ocellīs:
    ut placeās, dēbēs immemor esse tuī.
nōn tē cantātae laesērunt paelicis herbae,
    nōn anus Haemoniā perfida lāvit aquā, 40
nec tibi vīs morbī nocuit (procul ōmen abestō),
    nec minuit densās invida lingua comās:
facta manū culpāque tuā dispendia sentīs;
    ipsa dabās capitī mixta venēna tuō.
nunc tibi captīvōs mittet Germānia crīnēs; 45
    tūta triumphātae mūnere gentis eris.
ō quam saepe comās aliquō mīrante rubēbis
    et dīcēs "emptā nunc ego merce probor.
nescioquam prō mē laudat nunc iste Sygambram;
    fāma tamen meminī cum fuit ista mea." 50

mē miserum! lacrimās male continet, ōraque dextrā
   prōtegit ingenuās picta rubōre genās;
sustinet antīquōs gremiō spectatque capillōs,
   ei mihi, nōn illō mūnera digna locō.
collige cum vultū mentem: reparābile damnum est;   55
   postmodo nātīvā conspiciēre comā.

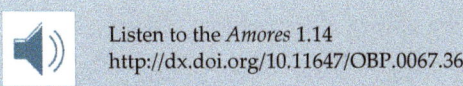

Listen to the *Amores* 1.14
http://dx.doi.org/10.11647/OBP.0067.36

Notes on *Amores* 1.14

1–2: dīcēbam: notice the tense: the poet kept saying it, but she didn't listen. Now he has his opportunity to say "I told you so!" **medicāre tuōs dēsiste capillōs**: Roman love elegists seem to prefer the "natural look" in their mistresses, complaining of their reliance on makeup, perfumes, dyes, overly elaborate hair ornamentations, and the like. Ovid follows in this tradition by demanding that his *puella* stop dying her hair. **possīs**: potential subjunctive (AG §445–447). **tibi**: dative of possession.

3–4: passa forēs < *patior, patī, passus*, "leave alone, let be"; *passa forēs* is a poetic equivalent of *passa essēs* (AG §170a). **erat**: a mixed condition (AG §517b): in the apodosis of a contrary to fact condition, the use of an imperfect indicative instead of the imperfect subjunctive expresses that the action was intended to happen, likely to happen, or already begun. Cf. *eram* (6.34). **illīs**: *capillīs*. **contigerant ... latus** = *(capillī) contigerant usque latus īmum, quā patet*: "your hair had reached all the way the bottom of your side, where it widens out," i.e. it reached all the way to her hips. **īmum** < *īmus -a -um*, "the lowest part of." **quā** = "where." **patet** < *pateō patēre, patuī* here "extends in space" (OLD 7a). *latus* is singular for plural.

5–6: quid, quod: "what of the fact that"; an idiomatic expression, short for *quid dē hōc dīcendum est quod*. **erant tenuēs**: understand *capillī* as the subject. **quōs ... timērēs**: relative clause of characteristic, "the sort (of hair) you would be afraid to...." **vēla colōrātī quālia Sēres habent**: "like the fabrics that the colored Chinese wear," i.e., like silk; the Chinese are *colōrātī* because they produce brightly colored silks (transferred epithet).

7–8: **vel ... quod ... fīlum**: "or the filament which"; the odd word order allows for the placing of *filum* in last position for emphasis.

9–10: **ille**: clarified by *color* in line 10. **mixtus**: supply *erat*.

11–12: **quālem**: supply *colōrem*, "the sort of color which." **Īdae** < *Īda, -ae*. f. "Mt. Ida."[1] There are two mountains named Ida, the one in Crete on which Jupiter was born, and the one near Troy on which the Judgment of Paris took place; Ovid is probably referring to the Trojan one. **dēreptō cortice**: "when its bark has been stripped." Cedars do not grow on Mt. Ida near Troy, so the tree in question here is probably in fact the juniper, which when stripped of its bark reveals an auburn wood. Dark-haired Roman women seemed to favor a reddish tint, achieved in early times through a concoction of ashes and later through dyes from Gaul and Germany (Barsby).

13–14: **adde quod**: "not to mention the fact that..." **docilēs**: "teachable," "responsive (to styling)," with *capillī* (understood). **flexibus**: "curls" (literally the "act of bending or curling"). **nullīus ... dolōris**: objective genitive; your hair never caused you any distress.

Fig. 31 Roman hairpins, from Chichester, Sussex. Wikimedia, https://commons.wikimedia.org/wiki/File:Chichester_hair_pins.jpg

---

1   http://pleiades.stoa.org/places/550592

15–16: **acus** < *acus, -ūs*, f., "hairpin." **vallum pectinis**: "the palisade of the comb," a humorously grand phrase for a humble object. The *vallum* was a fortification made of sharpened stakes and placed on top of an earthwork; *acus* and *vallum* are both subjects of the verb, *abrūpit*. **ōrnātrix** < *ornātrix, -īcis* f. "hairdresser, lady's maid" (rare); literally a female slave who assisted her mistress in getting dressed and adorned. **tūtō corpore**: ablative of description, used predicatively. The *ornātrix* was safe because the hair of her mistress did not get badly tangled, and thus did not provoke an angry response.

17–18: **est … ōrnāta**: "she had her hair done." **bracchia**: understand *ornātricis*. **dēreptā … acū**: "with a snatched hairpin," i.e., snatched out of the hand of the *ōrnātrix*.

19–20: **nondum digestīs … capillīs**: ablative absolute. The poet recalls with admiration the times when his mistress lay half-reclined in bed early in the morning before her hair had been done up. He found this to be quite becoming (*decens*, 21).

21–22: **Bacchē**: "a Bacchante"; a Greek nominative singular. The Bacchantes were particularly famous for their wild hair. **temerē**: "at random, casually."

23–24: **cum … essent tamen**: "nevertheless, though they were"; a concessive *cum* clause. **lānūginis instar**: "like down." *instar* is a neuter noun, found only in the nominative and the accusative singular, meaning "the equivalent" or "just like"; it often takes a genitive. **heu, mala vexātae quanta tulēre comae!** mock-tragic in tone. "Alas! What great evils your troubled hair has endured!"

25–26: **quam**: with *patienter*, "how patiently." **sē praebuerunt**: "they submitted (themselves) to"; the second e should be long (*praebuērunt*) but is shortened for the sake of the meter. **ferrō … et ignī**: the reference here is to the use of hot curling irons, although more frequently these nouns are used in a military context to describe destruction by fire and sword. **ut … sinus**: "so that tight ringlets in coiled spirals might be created." *sinus* can mean merely something that is curved. *nexilis -e* = "plaited, intertwined." *tortō* means "twisted" (< *torqueō*), but with the nuance "tortured." Many busts of Roman women depict the type of hairstyle alluded to here, especially those with rows of little curls piled up high and encircling the face.

Fig. 32 Bust of Agrippina the Younger (15–59 AD). Pula, Croatia, Archaeological Museum. Wikimedia, https://commons.wikimedia.org/wiki/File:Agrippina_(1),_Pula_archeological_museum.JPG

27–28: **clāmābam**: note the tense, suggesting repeated action. **ūrere**: subjective infinitive. **sponte decent**: "they are appealing in their natural form," literally "of their own free will." **capitī ... tuō**: dative object of the verb *parce*. **ferrea**: vocative case, addressed to Corinna, who is hard-hearted like iron because she does not have compassion for her hair.

29–30: **vim**: *vīs* here means "violence." **nōn est, quī** = *nōn est (capillus) quī*, "It is not the kind of hair that should be burned"; relative clause of characteristic. **ērudit ... acūs**: "the hair itself instructs the hairpins that have been applied to it." The conceit is that her hair's natural inclinations (*sponte*, 28) are better than any hairdresser.

31–32: **Apollō / ... Bacchus**: both Apollo and Bacchus (Dionysus) were famous for their beautiful long hair. **periēre** = *periērunt*. **vellet / ... vellet**: potential subjunctive; "hair that Apollo, (and) that Bacchus would want." **capitī ... suō**: dative with the compound verb *inesse*.

33–34: **illīs contulerim, quās**: "I would compare them to those (hairs) which." *contulerim* is potential subjunctive (perfect tense), see AG §447.1, used in first person singular expressions of cautiously saying, thinking or wishing. **Diōnē** < *Diōnē, -ēs*, f. Dione was the mother of Aphrodite, but the name is often used for Aphrodite/Venus herself. **pingitur**: the 4th-century Greek painter Apelles painted a famous picture of "Aphrodite Anadyomene" ("Aphrodite Rising from the Sea"), which showed her wringing sea water out of her hair; the painting was brought to Rome by Augustus (Pliny, *Natural History* 35.36.91). Aphrodite Anadyomene was often depicted in sculpture as well. **sustinuisse**: the infinitive depends on *pingitur*, treated as a verb of speaking: "which naked Dione was painted as having held up."

Fig. 33 Venus Anadyomene ("Venus Rising from the Seas") copy of a lost original by Apelles (4th century BC), 3rd–4th century AD. Paris, The Louvre. Wikimedia, https://commons.wikimedia.org/wiki/File:P1230246_Louvre_venus_anadyomene_Ma3537_rwk.jpg

35–36: **quid** = *cūr*. **male dispositōs**: "(which you considered to be) badly ordered"; it is the *puella* who had this opinion of her lost hair; Ovid seems to have liked the messiness. **maestā**: transferred epithet; though the adjective agrees with *manū*, it more logically describes the *puella* who has just looked at herself in the mirror. **pōnis**: "lay aside, put down." **inepta**: "foolish"; here the adjective is best translated as an adverb.

37–38: **nōn bene … ocellīs**: "it's wrong for you to be looked at by yourself with your usual eyes." i.e. it's a bad idea to look at yourself with eyes accustomed to the way you looked before this disaster. The grammatical awkwardness makes sense once we realize that the poet is talking about an image in a mirror. **ut placeās**: supply *tibi*. **tuī**: objective genitive (AG §348); "of your (former) self."

39–40: **cantātae**: "bewitched"; modifies *herbae*. **paelicis** < *paelex, -icis*, f., a mistress who was a rival to a wife or lover. **lāvit**: "has washed up." **Haemoniā** < *Haemonius, -a, -um* "Haemonian, Thessalian"; Thessaly[2] was traditionally associated with witchcraft.

41–42: **tibi**: dative with the verb *nocuit*. **procul ōmen abestō**: "may ill-omen be far away," "may ill-omen not attend my words." *Abestō* is future imperative, third person singular; the form is typical of formal prayers. **invida lingua**: "jealous tongue," i.e., a curse or evil spell.

43–44: **facta**: supply *esse* for a perfect passive infinitive in indirect discourse, "you perceive that your loss was produced." **venēna** < *venēnum, -ī*, n. "magic potion" or "poison." When modified by certain proper adjectives the word can also mean "dye."

45–46: **captīvōs mittet Germānia crīnēs**: wigs made from hair imported from Germany[3] were particularly desirable; the military imagery is appropriate in view of the Germans' custom of cutting their hair as a sign of surrender. **mūnere**: "thanks to the gift"; ablative of means or cause.

47–48: **emptā ... merce**: *merce* < *merx, -cis*, f. "a commodity"; ablative of cause (AG §404). **probor**: "I will be approved of" i.e. "people will think well of me." The point is that this approval will come not from Corinna's natural beauty, but because of something she has bought.

49–50: **nescioquam**: modifies *Sygambram*, "some Sygambrian woman, I know not who"; note the bracketing of the line with the adjective and its modified noun. **iste**: the male admirer of line 47. **Sygambram** < *Sygamber, -bra, -brum* "of the Sygambri" (a tribe of Germans recently subjugated by Augustus); here a woman of that tribe. **fāma ... cum fuit ista mea**: "when that glory was my own."

---

2 http://pleiades.stoa.org/places/991374
3 http://pleiades.stoa.org/places/20468

51–52: mē miserum: accusative of exclamation (AG §397d). **lacrimās male continet**: "she scarcely contains her tears." This and the gestures that follow are signs of Corinna's regret and shame, as if she has taken Ovid's words to heart. **ōraque** < *ōs, ōris,* n. here "face" as often; plural for singular, object of *prōtegit*. **dextrā**: supply *manū*; ablative of means. **ingenuās picta rubōre genās**: "painted with redness in respect to her delicate cheeks" i.e. she is blushing. **picta**: nominative femine singular, agreeing with the subject of *continet*. The metaphor of painting is unusual. McKeown suspects an allusion to the fact that barbarians, especially Britons, used warpaint, but the allusion could perhaps be to women's makeup generally: Corinna is "painting her face" with her blushes. **ingenuās ... genās**: the so-called Greek accusative (also called accusative of part affected, accusative of specification, and accusative of respect), AG §397b; *ingenuus* here means "tender, delicate" (cf. *Amores* 1.7.50) but also "free-born," i.e. authentically Roman, unlike the German wig. **rubōre** < *rubor, -ōris,* m. here perhaps both "redness of face" and "a feeling of shame."

53–54: sustinet: "holds up." **gremiō** < *gremium, -(i)ī,* n. "lap"; ablative of place means or ablative of place where; in poetry prepositions with the ablative of place where can be omitted (AG §429.4). **nōn illō mūnera digna locō**: "a gift that does not deserve that place"; in apposition to *antīquōs ... capillōs* in the preceding line. **ei mihi**: "woe is me!"; *ei* (a monosyllable) is an interjection, followed by a dative of reference (AG §379a). **nōn illō mūnera digna locō**: "gifts that do not deserve that place"; in apposition to *antīquōs ... capillōs* in the preceding line.

55–56: collige cum vultū mentem: "compose your mind along with your face"; zeugma, in which the verb *collige* applies to both nouns but has different meanings in respect to each. **postmodo** "later, presently"; adverb. **nātīvā ... comā**: i.e., your natural-born hair; it was taken for granted by the erotic poets that a girl's natural beauty was preferable to artifice; there may also be an implied contrast between "home-grown" hair and that imported from Germany (see on line 45 above). **conspiciēre** = *conspiciēris* (future tense, 2nd singular passive); *conspiciō* here means "to notice, attract attention"; "you will soon catch the eye" (Barsby).

21. *Amores* 1.15: Poetic immortality

The final poem of a Greek or Roman poetry book typically offered some kind of closure (for details see McKeown's discussion of this poem). A *sphragis* (Greek for "seal") would say something about who the poet was (Propertius 1.22), or about the nature of the poetry (Horace, *Odes* 3.30). Such poems were typically short—more epilogues than formal conclusions—but they did not have to be. And such poems often proclaimed that the poetry in question would survive long after the poet's own death: in *Odes* 3.30 Horace claims that he "built a memorial" (*exegi monumentum*), which would survive as long as Rome did.

Ovid's readers would have come to this poem with the sphragis and its various possibilities in mind. They might, at first, have thought the poem was going to be about who the poet is and how he leads his life. The poem begins with an address to a personified *Livor* ("envy, malice, spite"), who has supposedly been complaining about his avoidance of more patriotic careers, specifically the army, jurisprudence, and (closer to poetry) public speaking (lines 1–6). But at lines 7–8 it becomes clear that the focus is on poetry and immortality.

The bulk of the poem consists of a long list of poets, Greek and Roman, who have achieved immortality (lines 9–30). The conclusion is simple: things of this world are impermanent (lines 31–34), and they are valued only by the common crowd (*vulgus*). But our poet has been favored by Apollo, will wear (as a love poet) a garland of myrtle, and will be read by lovers in difficulty (lines 35–38). *Livor* operates only on the living; when people die they receive their just deserts, so *Livor* is no longer possible (lines 39–40). And so our poet will live on even after his body is burned on his funeral pyre, and a large part of him (*parsque ... multa*) will survive (lines 41–42).

© William Turpin, CC BY   http://dx.doi.org/10.11647/OBP.0067.20

One reaction, reading these lines some 2000 years after they were written, might be simply to note that what they say is true, at least so far. But should we encounter similar claims by a contemporary poet, even a successful one, we might be more skeptical. It is true that *Amores* 1.15 dials the claim down a little: we end up with Tibullus and Gallus, to whom even the youthful Ovid could probably be compared favorably, but that long list of poets, from Homer down to Ovid's own day, is surely meant to seem excessive (see Vessey 1981). We might also wonder if it is not supposed to be conspicuously pedestrian. Pleasant though they are, those twenty lines on other poets lack much of the verve of Ovid's preceding fourteen poems, which makes the claim for immortality all the more jarring. Our poet, in short, has delusions of grandeur.

On top of that, our poet is (again) strikingly self-absorbed. This is the only poem in the book that is not about the poet's relationship with his *puella*. Of course a shift to the poet's identity and output is exactly what we would expect in a *sphragis*. But the focus on the immortality of the poet himself, alone, contrasts sharply with his insistence, especially in *Amores* 1.3, that his poems will bestow immortality on the *puella*. Thus the poet's focus on himself seems downright inconsistent (*in toto semper ut in orbe canar*, line 8), or at least forgetful. And it is at least tactless to end his long list of immortal poets with the claim that it is one of their *girlfriends*, Gallus' famous Lycoris, who will be famous (line 30). In *Amores* 1.1 the poet ended up promising a garland of myrtle (sacred to Venus) to his muse, his inspiration, his Corinna. Here, selfishly, he's planning to wear it himself (line 37). Lovers will be reading about *him*, not her (line 38).

Even if we read the poem as self-mockery, the final couplet at first seems disappointing, merely summing up the basic proposition about poetic immortality. But it is worth suggesting that there is a literary joke at work here, consistent with our picture of a poet at once self-important and self-absorbed. The two poets most conspicuously absent from the list of immortals are Horace and Propertius, older contemporaries who had an enormous influence on Ovid. And both poets are invoked, I suggest, in the final couplet. When Ovid speaks of the funeral pyre that will finally consume him (*cum me supremus adederit ignis*, line 41) we are to remember that Propertius was obsessed with his own funeral and his own ashes, and obsessed with the contrast of his ashes with the immortality of his poems (e.g. Prop. 3.1.35–36: "Rome will praise me among its later generations, and I predict that that day will come after my ashes"). And Ovid's last line alludes unmistakably to Horace's famous poem about his own poetic immortality (Hor. *Carm.* 1.30.6–7): "I will not die completely (*non omnis moriar*) and a large part of me (*multaque pars mei*) will escape Death."

This, I argue, is self-mockery with a vengeance. Our poet has made a pretentious claim for the immortality of his own poetry, comparing himself to a long list of poets that omits two of his most immediate influences. But the last couplet shows that it is the poetry of Propertius and Horace that will survive, despite Ovid's clumsy attempt to write them out of his story, prompted by none other than *Līvor edax*. We wonder whether Ovid's poetry will be equally resilient.

Suggested reading

Vessey, D. W. T. "Elegy Eternal: Ovid, *Amores* 1.15," *Latomus* 40 (1981): 607–617.

Amores 1.15

Quid mihi, Līvor edax, ignāvōs obicis annōs
    ingeniīque vocās carmen inertis opus,
nōn mē, mōre patrum, dum strēnua sustinet aetās,
    praemia mīlitiae pulverulenta sequī
nec mē verbōsās lēgēs ēdiscere nec mē   5
    ingrātō vōcem prostituisse forō?
mortāle est, quod quaeris, opus; mihi fāma perennis
    quaeritur, in tōtō semper ut orbe canar.
vīvet Maeonidēs, Tenedos dum stābit et Īdē,
    dum rapidās Simoīs in mare volvet aquās;   10
vīvet et Ascraeus, dum mustīs ūva tumēbit,
    dum cadet incurvā falce resecta Cerēs.
Battiadēs semper tōtō cantābitur orbe:
    quamvīs ingeniō nōn valet, arte valet.
nulla Sophocleō veniet iactūra cothurnō;   15
    cum sōle et lūnā semper Arātus erit.
dum fallax servus, dūrus pater, improba lēna
    vīvent et meretrix blanda, Menandros erit.
Ennius arte carens animōsīque Accius ōris
    cāsūrum nullō tempore nōmen habent.   20
Varrōnem prīmamque ratem quae nesciet aetās,
    aureaque Aesoniō terga petīta ducī?
carmina sublīmis tunc sunt peritūra Lucrētī,
    exitiō terrās cum dabit ūna diēs.
Tītyrus et frūgēs Aenēiaque arma legentur,   25
    Rōma triumphātī dum caput orbis erit.

dōnec erunt ignēs arcūsque Cupīdinis arma,
  discentur numerī, culte Tibulle, tuī.
Gallus et Hesperiīs et Gallus nōtus Eōīs,
  et sua cum Gallō nōta Lycōris erit. 30
ergō, cum silicēs, cum dens patientis arātrī
  dēpereant aevō, carmina morte carent:
cēdant carminibus rēgēs rēgumque triumphī,
  cēdat et auriferī rīpa benigna Tagī.
vīlia mīrētur vulgus; mihi flāvus Apollō 35
  pōcula Castaliā plēna ministret aquā,
sustineamque comā metuentem frīgora myrtum
  atque ā sollicitō multus amante legar.
pascitur in vīvīs Līvor; post fāta quiescit,
  cum suus ex meritō quemque tuētur honōs. 40
ergō etiam cum mē suprēmus adēderit ignis,
  vīvam, parsque meī multa superstes erit.

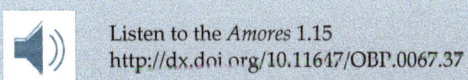
Listen to the *Amores* 1.15
http://dx.doi.org/10.11647/OBP.0067.37

Notes on *Amores* 1.15

1–2: Quid = *Cūr*. **mihi ... obicis**: "bring up as criticism for me," "throw in my teeth" the o is long by position (*obicis* = *objicis*). **Līvor** < *līvor, -ōris*, m. "envy." The personification is a purely literary device; there was no Roman cult of *Līvor*. Ovid views Envy as signifying criticism of poetry as an unworthy pursuit. **edax** < *edax, -ācis*, adj. "voracious, greedy."

3–4: mē ... sequī: indirect statement, dependent on *obicis* in line 1; "that I do not follow." **mōre patrum**: "like my ancestors"; for the idiom see OLD *mōs* 7b) **strēnua** < *strēnuus, a, um* "vigorous." **sustinet** < *sustineō, sustinēre, sustinuī*, here "support, keep from failing" (see OLD 3).

5–6: **mē ... ēdiscere ... mē ... prostituisse**: also indirect statement dependent on *obicis* in line 1. The references are to the two forms of specialist legal activity, that of the *iūris consultus* who studied the substance of the law (*verbōsās lēgēs*) and that of the *rhētor* who made speeches in court (*forō*); see on 1.13.21. **prostituisse**: aorist (AG §473); *prostituō* is a strong word, having much of the flavor that "to prostitute" a talent has in English.

7–8: **mihi**: dative of agent.

9–10: **Maeonides** < *Maeonidēs, -ae*, m., patronymic for "Homer," Maeon reputedly being his father's name; Maeonia was also the Homeric name for **Lydia**,[1] one of the poet's possible birthplaces; "the Lydian." **Tenedos** < *Tenedos, -ī*, f. **Tenedos**[2] is the small island that lies off the Trojan shore where the Greek fleet infamously anchored immediately before the sack of Troy. **Īdē**: *Īdē, Īdēs* is an alternate form for *Īda, -ae*. f. As in 1.14.11, the reference is to the **Mt. Ida**[3] overlooking the plains of Troy, where the Judgment of Paris took place. Both *Tenedos* and *Īdē* are part of the setting of Homer's great work, the *Iliad*. **Simoīs** < *Simoīs, -entis*, m., a small river[4] near Troy, flowing into the Scamander.

Fig. 34 Portrait of Homer. Roman copy, from Baiae, after a 2nd century BC, Greek original. London, British Museum. Wikimedia, http://commons.wikimedia.org/wiki/File:Bust_Homer_BM_1825.jpg

---

1   http://pleiades.stoa.org/places/991385
2   http://pleiades.stoa.org/places/550912
3   http://pleiades.stoa.org/places/550592
4   http://pleiades.stoa.org/places/550883

11–12: **Ascraeus** < *Ascraeus, -a, -um* "belonging to Ascra"; **Ascra**,[5] a village in Boeotia, was the birthplace of the poet Hesiod, here associated with his didactic poem *Works and Days* about the farmer's year and about justice. In it he discusses wine (*ūva*, 11) and the harvesting of grain (*Cerēs*, 12). **mustīs** < *mustum, -ī*, n. "must," new and unfermented wine; ablative of source or material (AG §403). **incurvā falce**: "with the *curved* sickle." **Cerēs** < *Cerēs, -eris*, f., "wheat."

13–14: **Battiadēs** < *Battiadēs, -ae*, m. "son of Battus," the founder of **Cyrene**,[6] i.e., "the Cyrenian," referring to the third-century B.C. Hellenistic poet Callimachus; his poetry had a significant influence on later Roman poets, and for this reason Ovid elevated him to a prominent position, third only to Homer and Hesiod. **ingeniō nōn valet, arte valet**: Callimachus, like the Alexandrian poets in general, laid great stress on the need for poetic technique (*ars*) as well as natural talent or inspiration (*ingenium*). Ovid points to Callimachus' polished artistry (*arte valet*), but says that when it comes to inspiration Callimachus was not as strong.

15–16: **Sophocleō** < *Sophoclēus -a -um*, "Sophoclean, of Sophocles," the fifth-century B.C. Greek tragedian. **iactūra**: *iactūra, ae*, f. "loss" (see OLD 4); the loss is one of prestige. **cothurnō** < *cot(h)urnus, -ī*, m. "buskin," a special kind of high, thick-soled boot worn by actors in tragedy to increase their height on stage. *Cothurnus* commonly serves as a metonymy for "tragedy." Note the golden line (adjective A, adjective B, verb, substantive A, substantive B) emphasizing Sophoclean grandeur. **Arātus** < *Arātus, -ī*, m. Aratus of Soli was the 3rd century Hellenistic author of an extant poem in Greek on astronomy, the *Phaenomena*. It was widely read in the ancient world, rivaling Homer's epics in popularity; it was translated by (among others) Ovid himself, thought the translation does not survive. **erit**: "will be (associated with)."

17–18: **fallax servus ... meretrix blanda**: the deceitful slave, the stern father, the nasty brothel-keeper, and the lovable prostitute were all stock figures of Attic New Comedy, of which Menander (342–291 BC) was the most famous exponent. **Menandros** = *Menander*, a Greek nominative masculine singular form.

---

5   http://pleiades.stoa.org/places/540670
6   http://pleiades.stoa.org/places/373778

19-20: Ennius: Q. Ennius (239–169 BC) was a famous early writer of Latin historical epic. **arte carens:** "lacking artifice"; *arte* is ablative of separation (AG §400). Ennius wrote verse that was later seen as awkward and unsophisticated, but here that roughness is seen as a positive quality. **animōsī ... ōris:** "of the spirited tongue" (Barsby); genitive of quality(AG §345). **Accius:** L. Accius (b. 170 BC) was the most famous of the Latin tragedians of the Republic; his style was later considered high-flown and bombastic (*animōsī ... ōris*, 19). **cāsūrum:** "(that is) going to fall (into oblivion)"; < *cadō, cadere, cecidī, cāsum*, "fall."

21-22: Varrōnem < *Varrō, Varrōnis* m. Varro of Atax (b. 82 BC, not the better known Marcus Terentius Varro), who wrote a lost Latin translation of the *Argonautica* (the story of Jason and the Argonauts) of Apollonius Rhodius. **prīmamque ratem** < *ratis, -is,* f., "ship"; according to Greek legend the first ship was the Argo. **Aesoniō ... ducī:** periphrasis for Jason, < *Aesonius -a –um,* "of or descended from Aeson" (Aeson was the father of Jason); dative of agent. **terga** < *tergum, -ī,* n., "skin, hide" referring to the Golden Fleece; plural for singular.

23-24: Lucrētī < *Lucrētius, -a, -um*. The philosopher-poet Titus Lucretius (b. 94 BC) wrote his didactic poem *De Rerum Natura*, based on Epicurean philosophy, to prove that the gods were a dangerous illusion and that all things were composed of atoms and would sooner or later decompose into atoms. **exitiō ... dabit ūna diēs:** i.e., when the world comes to an end. This is a quotation from Lucretius, 5.95).

25-26: these lines allude to the great Roman epic poet Vergil. Ovid mentions neither his name nor patronymic nor place of birth (as he has done with the previous poets), but makes brief reference only to his three great works: the *Eclogues*, the *Georgics*, and the *Aeneid*. **Tītyrus:** one of the shepherds in Virgil's *Eclogues* and actually the first word of *Eclogue* 1. **frūgēs:** the reference is to Virgil's *Georgics*, written in praise of farming. **Aenēiaque** < *Aenēius, -a, -um* (four syllables), "of Aeneas." **arma:** famously, the first word in the *Aeneid*. **triumphātī** is a more vivid equivalent of *victī*. **dum caput orbis erit:** "as long as Rome is the capital"; for *dum* + future indicative = "as long as," see OLD 1a.

27-28: dōnec: "as long as." **ignēs arcūsque Cupīdinis arma:** "torches and bows, the weapons of Cupid," i.e. as long as love and lovers exist. *arma* could also be predicate nominative (Ryan and Perkins), i.e. "as long as torches and bows are the weapons of Cupid." **numerī**: "verses." **culte Tibulle**: apostrophe; Albius Tibullus, along with Propertius and Gallus, was a famous elegist of the generation preceding Ovid.

Fig. 35 Aeneas and Dido in the cave, an illustration of *Aeneid* IV from the "Roman Vergil" (Vergilius Romanus), a 5th century AD illustrated manuscript of the *Eclogues*, *Georgics*, and *Aeneid*. Vatican City, Biblioteca Apostolica, Cod. Vat. lat. 3867, folio 108v. Wikimedia, https://commons.wikimedia.org/wiki/File:RomanVirgilFolio108vAeneasDidoCave.jpg

29–30: **Gallus**: i.e. C. Cornelius Gallus (born c. 70 BC), whose elegies are almost entirely lost. **nōtus**: supply *est*. **Hesperiīs … Eōīs**: both words are dative masculine plural ("those dwelling in"); Ovid is probably alluding to a line from Gallus himself, as at *Ars Amātōria* 3.537: *Vesper et Eōae nōvēre Lycōrida terrae*. **sua**: reflexive, referring to *Gallō*. **Lycōris** < *Lycōris, -idis* or *-idos*, f. Lycoris is the poetic name Gallus gave to the lover who broke his heart; she was a well-known actress named Cytheris, and had been the mistress of (among others) Marc Antony.

31–32: **cum**: introduces a concessive clause. **silicēs** < *silex, -icis*, f. "flint" (actually any hard stone). **dēpereant** < *dēpereō, dēperīre, dēperiī*, "be completely destroyed." **aevō**: ablative of means or instrument (AG §409). **carmina morte carent**: this line has taken on a proverbial life of its own; "poetry is immortal." **morte** = ablative of separation (AG §400).

33–34: cēdant ... rēgēs: "let kings yield"; hortatory subjunctive, as are the verbs in the following lines. **Tagī** < *Tagus, -ī,* m. The river Tagus[7] (in Lusitania; Tajo in Spanish, Tejo in Portuguese) produced much gold and provided Rome with great wealth.

35–36: Castaliā < *Castalius, -a, -um* "Castalian," i.e., associated with the spring[8] on Mt. Parnassus, sacred to Apollo and the Muses, all metaphors for poetic inspiration. **aquā**: ablative of source and material (AG §403).

37–38: sustineamque: *ministret* in the preceding line suggests that this is present subjunctive, not future indicative. **comā**: ablative of means or place where; see on 1.14.53. **myrtum**: the myrtle was sacred to Venus, therefore more appropriate for a love poet than laurel; it is also intolerant of cold weather *(metuentem frīgora)*. **sollicitō** < *sollicitus, -a, -um* "troubled." **multus**: adverbial. **legar**: present subjunctive, like *sustineamque*.

39–40: pascitur in vīvīs Līvor: "Envy feeds on the living"; **pascitur** < *pascō, pascere, pāvī, pastum,* here "graze on, feed on" (passive in middle sense, OLD 6b). **fāta** < *fātum, -ī,* n., "death." **cum ... honōs**: "when each man's fame protects him as he deserves," "in accordance with what he deserves." Literally, "his own honor protects each man." For *cum* + indicative introducing a circumstance which supports the main verb ("seeing that"), see OLD 6a. **quemque** < *quisque, quaeque, quidque* "each."

41–42: adēderit < *adedō, adedere, adēdī, adēsum,* "to consume"; future perfect. **meī**: partitive genitive.

---

7 http://pleiades.stoa.org/places/256463
8 http://pleiades.stoa.org/places/203037083

Full vocabulary for Ovid's *Amores*, Book 1

The frequency of each word in the *Amores*, Book 1 appears in parentheses.

— A —

ā ab abs: from, by (+abl.) (16)

abdō -dere -didī -ditum: put away, withdraw; conceal, cover (1)

abdūcō -dūcere -duxī -ductum: lead away, carry off (1)

abeō -īre -iī -itum: go away (4)

abiciō abicere abiēcī abiectum: throw down (1)

abrumpō -rumpere -rūpī -ruptum: break off, sever (1)

absum abesse āfuī: be away, absent (4)

absūmō -sūmere -sumpsī -sumptum: take away; use up, consume, waste (2)

accendō -cendere -cendī -censum: kindle, set afire; make hotter, intensify, aggravate (2)

accipiō -cipere -cēpī -ceptum: receive (4)

Accius -iī m.: Accius (1)

accumbō -cumbere -cubuī -cubitum: lie down; recline at dinner (1)

ācer ācris ācre: sharp, piercing (1)

acer -cris n.: maple tree (1)

acervus -ī m.: heap, pile (1)

Achillēs -is m.: Achilles (1)

acus -ūs m.: hairpin (3)

acūtus -a -um: sharp, piercing (1)

ad: to, up to, towards (+acc.) (18)

adaperiō -aperīre -aperuī -apertum: open fully (1)

addō -dere -didī -ditum: give to (3)

adedō -edere -ēdī -ēsum: consume (1)

adeō -īre -iī -itum: go to (1)

adfectō -āre: strive after, grasp at (1)

adimō -imere -ēmī -emptum: remove (1)

aditus -ūs m.: entrance, approach (1)

adiungō -iungere -iunxī -iunctum: join to, connect; yoke, harness (1)

adiuvō -iuvāre -iūvī -iūtum: help, assist (1)

admittō -mittere -mīsī -missum: send in; let in, allow (4)

admoveō -movēre -mōvī -mōtum: move to, apply to; (mil.) move up (into position) (1)

adsuētus -a -um: usual, customary (1)

adsum adesse affuī: be present (4)

adulter -erī m.: adulterer (2)

adveniō -īre -vēnī -ventum: come to, arrive at (1)

adversus -um: (adv. and prep.) facing, opposite, against, opposed (to) (1)

aedēs -is f.: building; (pl.) house (1)

aeger aegra aegrum: sick, (adv.) with difficulty (1)

Aenēās -ae m.: Aeneas (2)

Aenēius -a -um: of Aeneas (1)

aequus -a -um: equal (1)

āēr āeris m.: air (1)

aes aeris n.: copper, money, bronze, (military) pay, price (4)

Aesonius -a -um: of or descended from Aeson (1)

aestus -ūs m.: tide; heat (1)

aetās -tātis f.: age, time of life (4)

aevum -ī n.: eternity; lifetime, age (2)

afferō afferre attulī allātum: bring to (1)

ager agrī m.: field (2)

agilis -e: light, agile (1)

āgmen -minis n.: line of march (3)

agō agere ēgī actum: drive, do, act (3)

āiō: say, affirm, say yes; **ut āiunt**, as they say (1)

Ājax -ācis m.: Ajax, a Greek hero (1)

albus -a -um: white (5)

Alcinous -ī m.: Alcinous, king of the Phaecians (1)

āles -itis m./f.: large bird, bird of prey; rooster (2)

aliqui -qua -quod: some, any; **aliquis aliqua aliquid**: someone (3)

alter altera alterum: other of two (10)

altus -a -um: high, lofty; deep (1)

amātor -ōris m.: lover (5)

ambiguus -a -um: uncertain, ambiguous (1)

ambitiōsus -a -um: ambitious, eager (1)

ambō -ae -ō: both (2)

āmens, -ntis: out of one's mind, insane; distracted, frantic (1)

amīcus -a -um: friendly; (as subst.) friend (3)

amnis -is m.: river, torrent (1)

amō -āre: love; **amans -ntis m./f.**: lover (25)

amor -ōris m.: love, lover (23)

Amȳmōnē -ēs f.: Amymone, one of the fifty daughters of Danaus (1)

an: or (in questions); **utrum ... an**: whether ... or (6)

ancilla -ae f.: female slave (2)

Andromachē -ēs f.: Andromache, wife of Hector (1)

anīlis -e: old woman (1)

animōsus -a -um: bold, spirited (1)

animus -ī m.: spirit, mind (6)

annus -ī m.: year (5)

annuus -a -um: of the year, yearly (1)

ante: before, in front of (adv. and prep. + acc.) (12)

antequam: before (1)

antīquus -a -um: ancient, old-time, former (2)

ānulus -ī m.: ring (1)

anus -ūs f.: old woman, hag; sorceress (2)

Āonius -a -um: of Aonia, Boeotian (1)

apertus -a -um: open, exposed; free (1)

apis -is f.: bee (1)

Apollō -inis m.: Apollo (2)

appōnō -pōnere -posuī -positum: place near; appoint (2)

aptō -āre: fit to, adapt to (1)

aptus -a -um: fit, suitable (11)

aqua -ae f.: water (9)

aquila -ae f.: eagle (1)

arānea -ae f.: spider's web; spider (1)

arātrum -ī n: plough (3)

Arātus -ī m.: Aratus (1)

arbor arboris f.: tree (2)

arca -ae f.: chest; money box (1)

arcānus -a -um: secret, mysterious, hidden (1)

arcus arcūs m.: bow; arch, arc (6)

ardeō ardēre arsī arsum: blaze, glow; be eager (1)

arduus -a -um: towering, lofty (1)

Argēus -a -um: Argive, of Argos (1)

Argī -ōrum m.: Argos (a city in the Peloponnese) (1)

arguō arguere arguī argūtum: accuse, charge; reveal, prove (1)

ariēs -etis m.: ram (1)

arma -ōrum n. pl.: arms, weapons (17)

armilla -ae f.: bracelet (1)

armō -āre: equip, arm (1)

ars artis f.: skill (7)

artus -ūs m.: joint; limb (1)

arvum -ī n.: ploughed land, field (3)

Ascraeus -a -um: belonging to Ascra (1)

asper -era -erum: rough, harsh; wild, uncultivated (1)

aspiciō -ere -spexī -spectum: look to or at, behold (7)

assiduus -a -um: continual, constant (1)

astō -stāre -stitī: stand by; stand still (1)

at: but, but yet (16)

atavus -ī m: grandfather (1)

āter -tra -trum: dark, black (2)

atque: and in addition, and also, and; (after comparatives) than; **simul atque**, as soon as; → **ac** (4)

Ātrax -acis m.: Atrax (1)

Atrīdēs -ae m.: son of Atreus, Agamemnon (1)

ātrium -ī n.: atrium (2)

attenuō -āre: make thin; weaken (1)

Atticus -ī m.: Atticus (1)

auctor -ōris m.: originator, founder (2)

audeō audēre ausus sum: dare, be eager (1)

audiō -īre -īvī/-iī -ītum: hear, listen to (6)

augeō augēre auxī auctum: increase (1)

aura -ae f.: breeze (3)

aurātus -a -um: golden (1)

aureus -a -um: golden; splendid (4)

aurifer -era -erum: gold-bearing (1)

auris -is f.: ear (2)

Aurōra -ae f.: Aurora (1)

aurum –ī n.: gold (1)

auspicium -ī n.: omen, sign (1)

aut: or (11)

avārus -a -um: greedy, miserly (2)

āvehō -vehere -vehexī -vectum: carry off, bear away (1)

avis -is f.: bird (5)

avus -ī m.: grandfather, forefather (1)

axis -is m.: axle; chariot (3)

— B —

Bacchē -ae f.: a Bacchante (1)

Bacchus -ī m.: Bacchus (2)

barbarus -a -um: foreign, strange, savage (1)

Battiadēs -ae m.: son of Battus, the founder of Cyrene (1)

beātus -a -um: happy, blessed, prosperous, fortunate (1)

bellum -ī n.: war (6)

bellus -a -um: pretty (1)

bene: well (14)

benignus -a -um: kind, generous (2)

bibō bibere bibī: drink (6)

bidens -ntis: mattock, hoe (1)

blandior -īrī -ītus sum: flatter (2)

blanditia -ae f.: flattery, endearment (often pl. with sg. meaning) (2)

blandus -a -um: flattering, charming, pleasant; attractive (3)

bonus -a -um: good (7)

Boreās -ae m.: the god of the North Wind (1)

bōs bovis m.: ox (gen. pl. **boum**) (2)

bracchium -ī n.: the forearm (elbow to hand), arm (3)

Brīsēis -idos f.: Briseis, daughter of Breses (1)

būbō -ōnis m.: owl (1)

— C —

cadō cadere cecidī cāsum: fall, be killed (7)

caecus -a -um: blind, unseeing; dark, obscure (2)

caedēs -is f.: killing, slaughter (2)

caedō caedere cecīdī caesum: strike, kill, cut down; quarry (stone) (2)

caelum -ī n.: sky, heavens (3)

Caesar -aris m.: Caesar (1)

callidus -a -um: clever, crafty, cunning (2)

campus -ī m.: plain, field (1)

candidus -a -um: white, fair (3)

cānescō -ere: become white or hoary; become old (1)

canis -is m./f.: dog (1)

canō canere cecinī cantum: sing (3)

cantō -āre: sing (4)

capillus -ī m.: hair (12)

capiō capere cēpī captum: seize (7)

captīvus -a -um: captured, captive (3)

captō -āre: woo, court (1)

caput capitis n.: head (10)

carcer -eris m.: prison (1)

cardō -inis m.: hinge (2)

careō -ēre -uī -itum: lack (+ abl.) (5)

carīna -ae f.: keel; ship (1)

cariōsus -a -um: decayed, rotten (1)

carmen -inis n.: song (13)

carnifex -icis m.: executioner (1)

carpō carpere carpsī carptum: pluck, harvest, despoil, fleece (2)

cārus -a -um: dear (1)

Cassandra -ae f.: Cassandra, a daughter of Priam (1)

Castalius -a -um: Castalian (1)

castīgātus -a -um: checked, restrained (1)

castrum -ī n.: fortress (regularly plural; **castra**, camp) (3)

castus -a -um: pure, spotless, chaste (2)

cāsus -ūs m.: a fall; chance, accident (1)

catēna -ae f.: chain, fetter (4)

caterva -ae f.: crowd, troop (1)

causa -ae f.: cause, reason; **causā** (+ preceding gen.), for the sake of (8)

causor -ārī: plead, pretend, blame (1)

cautus -a -um: cautious, careful, prudent (1)

caveō cavēre cāvī cautum: be on guard, beware (2)

cēdō cēdere cessī cessum: go, move; yield (6)

cedrus -ī f.: cedar (1)

celebrō -āre: frequent, throng, crowd (1)

celer -is -e: swift (1)

celō -āre: hide, conceal; cover; keep in the dark, deceive (2)

cēna -ae f.: dinner (1)

census -ūs m.: census, wealth (1)

centum: one hundred (1)

Cephalus -ī m.: Cephalus (1)

cēra -ae f.: wax portrait bust (6)

Cerēs -eris f.: Ceres (2)

certus -a -um: sure, fixed (6)

cessō -āre: cease, leave off (2)

cēterus -a -um: the others, the rest (2)

cibus -ī m.: food (1)

cicūta -ae f.: hemlock (1)

cingō cingere cinxī cinctum: encircle, surround, gird (2)

circā: around (adv. and prep. +acc.) (1)

circum: around (adv. and prep. + acc) (1)

citus -a -um: swift; **citō**, swiftly (1)

clam: (adv.) secretly (1)

clāmō -āre: shout, call (4)

claudō claudere clausī clausum: close, shut (2)

claustrum -ī n.: bolt, bar (1)

clipeus -ī m.: round shield (1)

clīvōsus -a -um: steep, hilly (1)

coepī coepisse coeptum: begin (1)

cognātus -a -um: related by birth (1)

cognitor –ōris m.: attorney, learned counsel (1)

cognoscō -gnoscere -gnōvī -gnitum: learn, understand (4)

cōgō cōgere coēgī coactum: drive together; compel (5)

cohaereō -haerēre -haesī -haesum: cling to, adhere to (2)

colligō -ere -lēgī -lectum: gather together, collect (4)

collum -ī n.: neck (6)

colō colere coluī cultum: cultivate, tend; worship (2)

color -ōris m.: color (3)

colōrātus -a -um: colored (1)

columba -ae f.: pigeon, dove (1)

coma -ae f.: hair, tresses (19)

comes comitis m./f.: companion, comrade; attendant, follower (2)

comitō -āre: accompany, follow (1)

comitor -ārī: accompany, follow (1)

commendō -āre: commit, commend, recommend (1)

committō -mittere -mīsī -missum: join, entrust to (+ dat.); perform, do (3)

commodō -āre: adapt, accommodate; lend, provide (2)

commodum -ī n.: advantage, benefit, (pl.) assets (1)

cōmō cōmere compsī comptum: make beautiful, adorn; dress, arrange, comb (1)

comparō -āre: get ready, provide; compare (1)

complector -plectī -plexus sum: embrace, clasp (1)

complexus -ūs m.: embrace (1)

compōnō -pōnere posuī positum: build, construct, arrange (1)

comprimō -primere -pressī -pressum: compress; embrace (1)

conciliō -āre: advise (1)

concitō -āre: stir up, excite (1)

concutiō -cutere -cussī -cussum: shake, strike, shatter (2)

condō -dere -didī -ditum: build, found; store up; hide, conceal (1)

condūcō -dūcere -duxī -ductum: lead together, unite; hire; bribe (2)

conductor -ōris m.: contractor (1)

conferō conferre contulī collātum: collect, bring to (2)

confiteor confitērī confessus sum: admit (a fact), confess (a crime); reveal, disclose (1)

congerō -gerere -gessī -gestum: gather together, collect; pile up (1)

coniunx coniugis m./f.: spouse, husband, wife (1)

conscius -a -um: having common knowledge with another; conspiratorial, conspiring; aware (1)

conserva -ae f.: fellow-slave (female) (1)

consilium -ī n.: plan; council, group of advisors (1)

consonus -a -um: harmonious (1)

conspiciō -spicere -spexī -spectum: notice, attract attention, catch the eye of (1)

constō -stāre -stitī: agree; **constat**, it is established that (+ acc. and infin.) (3)

consuētus -a -um: accustomed, usual (1)

consultus -ī m.: jurist, consult, lawyer (1)

consūmō -sūmere -sumpsī -sumptum: to use up, consume (1)

contineō -tinēre -tinuī -tentum: contain, restrain (2)

contingō -tingere -tigī -tactum: touch, border on; happen, come to pass (2)

continuō: (adv.) forthwith, immediately (1)

contrārius -a -um: opposite, opposed (1)

contundō -tundere -tudī -tūsum: crush, bruise, break (1)

conveniō -venīre -vēnī -ventum: assemble, meet; agree (2)

convīcium -ī n.: clamor, uproar; insulting talk, abuse, mockery (1)

convincō -vincere -vīcī -victum: overcome; prove; convict (1)

convīva -ae m.: guest, table-companion (1)

cor cordis n.: heart; **cordī est**, it is pleasing to (+ dat.) (1)

Corinna -ae f.: Corinna (2)

corneus -a -um: made of horn (1)

cornū -ūs n.: horn (2)

corōna -ae f.: garland, crown (2)

corpus corporis n.: body (9)

Corsicus -a -um: Corsican (1)

cortex -icis m.: bark, shell (1)

cothurnus -ī m.: high boot, buskin (1)

crās: tomorrow (1)

crēdibilis -e: believable, credible (1)

crēdō crēdere crēdidī crēditum: believe (3)

crepusculum -ī n.: evening, twilight (1)

crescō crescere crēvī crētum: grow, increase (1)

Cressa -ae f.: Cretan woman (1)

crīmen -inis n.: verdict, accusation (3)

crīnis -is m.: lock of hair; (pl. or collective sg.) hair (4)

crūdēlis -e: cruel, merciless (1)

crūs -ūris n.: shin, leg (1)

crux -ucis f.: a cross (1)

cubō cubāre cubuī cubitum: lie down, recline (1)

culpa -ae f.: guilt, fault, blame (3)

cultus -a -um: elegant, polished, sophisticated; cultivated (3)

cum: with (prep. + abl.); when, since, although (conj. +subj.) (45)

Cupīdō -inis m.: Cupid (6)

cupiō -ere -īvī -ītum: desire (2)

cūr: why? (7)

cūra -ae f.: care, concern (3)

currō currere cucurrī cursum: run (1)

currus -ūs m.: chariot (4)

cuspis -idis f.: sharp point, tip (esp. of a spear) (1)

custōs custōdis m.: guardian (2)

Cytherēa -ae f.: Venus (1)

— D —

damnō -āre: condemn (1)

damnum -ī n.: damage, injury (2)

dē: down from, about, concerning (+ abl.) (12)

dēbeō dēbēre dēbuī dēbitum: owe, be obliged (5)

decens decentis: becoming, seemly, attractive (1)

decet decēre decuīt: it is right, proper, fitting (+acc. +infin.) (5)

dēcipiō -cipere -cēpī -ceptum: catch; cheat, deceive (1)

dēdecet -ēre -uit: be unsuitable for or unbecoming to (+acc.) (1)

dēdicō -āre: dedicate, consecrate (1)

dēdignor -ārī: refuse scornfully (1)

dēdūcō -dūcere -duxī -ductum: launch, lead away (1)

dēfendō -fendere -fendī -fensum: defend, ward off (1)

dēficiō -ficere -fēcī -fectum: fail, give out; revolt from (1)

dēfungor -fungī -functus sum: perform, discharge, finish; die (1)

dēiciō -icere -iēcī -iectum: cast down (1)

dēmens -ntis: out of one's mind, insane, senseless (1)

dēmō dēmere dempsī demptum: take away, subtract (3)

dēnique: finally (1)

dens -ntis m.: tooth (2)

densus -a -um: thick, dense; frequent (2)

dēpereō -perīre -periī: destroy completely (1)

dēpre(he)ndō -pre(he)ndere -pre(he)ndī -pre(he)nsum: catch, seize, trap (2)

dērigō -rigere -rexī -rectum: set straight, direct, guide (1)

dēripiō -ripere -ripuī -reptum: snatch away, tear down (3)

dēserō -serere -seruī -sertum: desert, abandon, leave (2)

dēserviō -servīre: serve, be devoted to (+dat.) (1)

dēsidia -ae f.: idleness, inactivity (1)

dēsidiōsus -a -um: slothful, idle, lazy (1)

dēsinō -sinere -siī -situm: leave off, cease (4)

dēsistō -sistere -stitī: stand away, withdraw; desist (1)

despiciō -spicere -spexī -spectum: look down on; be contemptuous of (1)

dēsultor -ōris m.: leaper, a circus rider who leaps from horse to horse (1)

dēsum -esse -fuī: be lacking (1)

dētractō -āre: decline, refuse (1)

dētrahō -trahere -traxī -tractum: strip off, remove (1)

deus -ī m.; dea -ae f.: god; goddess (8)

dēvoveō -vovēre -vōvī -vōtum: devote, consecrate; curse, execrate (1)

dexter -tra -trum: right; **dextera -ae f.**, right hand (1)

dīcō dīcere dixī dictum: say; **causam dīcere**, plead a case; **diem dīcere**, appoint a day (13)

dīdūcō -dūcere -duxī -ductum: draw apart, separate (1)

diēs diēī m./f.: day (7)

difficilis -e: not easy, hard, difficult (2)

dīgerō -gerere -gessī -gestum: separate, spread (2)

digitus -ī m.: finder; toe (5)

dignus -a -um: worthy (4)

dīligō -ligere -lexī -lectum: choose, cherish, love (1)

dīmittō -mittere -mīsī -missum: send away (1)

Diōnē -ēs f.: Dione, the mother of Aphrodite; often used for Aphrodite/Venus herself (1)

dipsas -adis f.: Dipsas; a kind of serpent whose bite causes violent thirst (1)

dīrus -a -um: fearful, dire (1)

discēdō -ere -cessī -cessum: go away, depart (1)

discinctus -a -um: wearing a tunic without a belt, wearing loose clothes; easygoing, undisciplined (1)

discō -ere didicī: learn (2)

disertus -a -um: eloquent, expressive (1)

dispendium -ī n.: loss (2)

dispōnō -pōnere -posuī -positum: arrange, put in place; (mil.) to post, station (1)

distrahō -trahere -traxī -tractum: pull apart, tear to pieces (1)

diū: for a long time (1)

dīves dīvitis: rich (poet. **dīs, dītis**) (3)

dīvidō -ere dīvīsī dīvīsum: divide, separate (1)

dīviduus -a -um: divided (1)

dō dare dedī datum: give (34)

doceō -ēre -uī doctum: teach (2)

docilis -e: teachable, responsive (to styling) (1)

doleō -ēre doluī dolitum: feel pain or grief, grieve (2)

dolor -ōris m.: pain, grief (3)

dominus -ī m.; domina -ae f.: household master, lord; mistress (14)

domō domāre domuī domitum: subdue, tame, conquer (1)

domus -ūs f.: house, home (2)

dōnec: until (2)

dōnō -āre: present with a gift (+acc. of person and abl. of thing) (4)

dōs dōtis f.: gift, endowment; dowry (1)

dubitō -āre: hesitate, doubt (2)

dubius -a -um: doubtful; **sine dubiō**, without a doubt, certainly (1)

dūcō dūcere duxī ductum: lead; **uxōrem dūcere**, marry (5)

dulcis -e: sweet (2)

dum: while (+indic.); until (+subj.); provided that (+subj.) (14)

dummodo: (conj.) provided that, if only, as long as (1)

duo duae duo: two (4)

duplex -icis: double, folded; deceitful, duplicitous (2)

duplicō -āre: fold over; double (2)

dūrō -āre: last, endure; harden (1)

dūrus -a -um: hard, tough, harsh (13)

dux ducis m./f.: leader, general (1)

— E —

ecce: behold! (2)

edax -ācis: voracious, greedy (1)

ēdiscō -discere -didicī: learn thoroughly, study (1)

ēdō ēdere ēdidī ēditum: put forth, state, explain; publish (1)

efficiō -ficere -fēcī -fectum: bring about, complete; render (+**ut** +subj.) (1)

effundō -fundere -fūdī -fūsum: pour out (2)

ego meī mihi mē: I, me (88)

ēloquium -ī n.: eloquence (1)

emō emere ēmī emptum: buy, purchase (6)

ēmodulor -ārī: measure out; put into meter (1)

ēn: lo! behold! (2)

Ennius -iī m.: Ennius (1)

eō īre iī/īvī itum: go (9)

Ēōus -a -um: of the east, of the dawn (1)

ephēmeris -idis f.: day-book, account-book (1)

epulae -ārum f. pl.: banquet, dinner party (1)

equa -ae f.: mare (2)

eques equitis m.: horseman, knight (5)

equus -ī m.: horse (3)

ergō: therefore (9)

errō -āre: go astray, wander (2)

error -ōris m.: error, mistake (2)

ērubescō -rubescere -rubuī: grow red, blush (1)

ērudiō -rudīre -rudiī -rudītum: to instruct, train; free from roughness (1)

et: and (102)

etiam: also, even (7)

Eurōtās -ae m.: the Eurotas river, the river of Sparta (1)

Eurus -ī m.: Southwest wind (2)

ēventus -ūs m.: consequence, outcome, event, occurrence (1)

ēvocō -āre: call out, summon (1)

ex ē: out of, from (+abl.) (6)

exanimis -e: scared stiff, frightened out of one's wits (1)

excipiō -cipere -cēpī -ceptum: take out (1)

excitō -āre: wake, rouse (1)

exclūdō -clūdere -clūsī -clūsum: shut out (2)

excubiae -ārum f. pl.: the keeping of a watch, a watch (1)

excutiō -cutere -cussī -cussum: shake out, throw off (7)

exemplum -ī n.: example, sample, copy (2)

exeō -īre -iī -itum: go forth (1)

exerceō -ercēre -ercuī -ercitum: train, exercise, carry on (2)

exigō -igere -ēgī -actum: drive out; collect (2)

exiguus -a -um: small, slight (1)

eximō -imere -ēmī -emptum: take out, remove (1)

exitium -ī n.: going out; destruction, death (2)

experiens -ntis: active, enterprising (1)

externus -a -um: external, outside; foreign (1)

exterō -terere -trīvī -trītum: rub out, wear away (1)

exterritus -a -um: badly frightened (1)

extrēmus -a -um: farthest, situated at the end or tip, extreme (2)

exultō -āre: exult, rejoice, triumph (1)

— F —

fabrīlis -e: skillfully made (1)

fābula -ae f.: account, tale, story (1)

faciō facere fēcī factum: do, make (35)

fallax -ācis: deceitful, treacherous, false (1)

fallō fallere fefellī falsum: deceive (4)

falsus -a -um: deceptive, false (1)

falx -cis f.: scythe, sickle (1)

fāma -ae f.: rumor, fame (4)

fateor fatērī fassus sum: admit, confess; profess, declare; assent, say yes (1)

fātum -ī n.: fate, death (2)

fēlix -īcis: lucky (3)

fēmina -ae f.: woman (2)

fēmineus -a -um: feminine (1)

femur -oris n.: thigh (3)

fenestra -ae f.: window (1)

ferē: almost (1)

ferō ferre tulī lātum: bear, carry, endure (22)

ferox -ōcis: fierce, savage, ferocious (1)

ferreus -a -um: made of iron; hard-hearted, cruel (4)

ferrum -ī n.: iron, iron weapon or implement (4)

ferus -a -um: wild, fierce; **fera -ae f.**, wild animal (5)

fervidus -a -um: intensely hot, blazing (1)

fidēs -eī f.: trust, faith (5)

fīdus -a -um: faithful, true (2)

figūra -ae f.: form, figure (1)

fīlia -ae f.; fīlius -ī m.: daughter; son (3)

fīlum -ī n.: thread, string (3)

findō findere fidī fissum: split apart (1)

fingō fingere finxī fictum: shape; invent (1)

fīniō -īre: limit, enclose; end, finish (1)

fīnis -is m.: end, boundary (1)

fīō fierī factus sum: become, happen, be done (7)

flāgitō -āre: ask for repeatedly (1)

flāmen -inis n.: gust, blast (of wind) (1)

flamma -ae f.: flame, fire (2)

flāvens -ntis: golden, yellow (1)

flāvus -a -um: golden; fair-haired, blonde (4)

fleō flēre flēvī flētum: weep (4)

flexus -ūs m.: curl, wave; the act of bending or curling (1)

flōs flōris m.: flower, bloom (1)

flūmen -inis n.: stream, river (1)

flūmineus -a -um: of a river (1)

fluō fluere fluxī fluxum: flow, stream, pour (1)

forās: outside, out of doors (1)

fore = futūrum esse (2)

foris foris f.: door (9)

fōrma -ae f.: shape; beauty (4)

formīdō -āre: fear, dread (1)

formōsus -a -um: shapely, beautiful (8)

fors fortis f.: chance (1)

forsitan: perhaps, perchance (2)

forte: by chance (1)

fortis -e: brave (5)

fortūna -ae f.: fortune (1)

forum -ī n.: market-place, forum (1)

foveō fovēre fōvī fōtum: warm; caress (1)

frangō frangere frēgī fractum: break, shatter (5)

fraudō -āre: cheat of, deprive of (1)

frēnum -ī n: bridle, reins (1)

fretum -ī n.: strait, (pl.) sea (1)

frīgidus -a -um: cold (1)

frīgus -oris n.: cold, coldness (2)

frons frontis f.: forehead, brow; front (3)

frux -ūgis f.: crops, fruits, grain (1)

fugiō fugere fūgī fugitum: flee, escape (4)

fulciō fulcīre fulsī fultum: strengthen, fortify, reinforce (1)

fulgeō fulgēre fulsī: shine brightly, flash (1)

fulmen -inis n.: thunderbolt; threat of destruction (1)

fulminō -āre: flash like lightning (1)

fūnebris -e: funereal (1)

furor -ōris m.: rage, fury (3)

furtim: (adv.) stealthily, secretly (2)

furtīvus -a -um: secret, furtive (2)

— G —

galea -ae f.: helmet (1)

Gallus -ī: Gallus (3)

Gangētis -idis: of the Ganges, Indian (1)

garrulus -a -um: talkative, chatty, babbling (1)

gaudeō gaudēre gāvīsus sum: rejoice (1)

geminus -a -um: twin, double (1)

gemma -ae f.: jewel, gem (3)

gena -ae f.: cheek (6)

genitor -ōris m.: father (1)

gēns gentis f.: family, clan (1)

genū -ūs n.: knee (1)

Germānia -ae f.: Germany (1)

gerō gerere gessī gestum: bear, manage; **bellum gerere**, wage war (1)

glomerō -āre: form into a ball; mass together (1)

gracilis -e: slender, thin (3)

grāmen -inis n.: herbs, especially magical ones (2)

grandis -e: great, large (3)

graphium -ī n.: stilus (1)

grātia -ae f.: favor, influence, gratitude (3)

grātus -a -um: pleasant; grateful (3)

gravis -e: heavy, serious (3)

gremium -ī n.: lap, bosom (2)

grex -egis m.: herd, flock (2)

guttur -uris n.: windpipe, throat (1)

gypsātus -a -um: whitened with gypsum (1)

— H —

habeō habēre habuī habitum: have, hold (26)

habilis -e: suited (1)

Haemonius -a -um: Haemonian, Thessalian (1)

haereō haerēre haesī haesitum: stick, adhere (2)

harundō -inis f.: reed (1)

Hector -oris m.: Hector (1)

Helicōnius -a -um: of Helicon (1)

herba -ae f.: herb (1)

here: (adv.) yesterday (1)

Hesperius -a -um: of the west, western (1)

heu: alas! (3)

hic haec hoc: this, these (26)

hīc: here; **hinc**, from here; **hūc**: to this place (3)

hiems hiemis f.: winter (1)

hodiē: today (1)

Homērus -ī m.: Homer (1)

homō hominis m.: human being (1)

honor -ōris m.: honor, glory; office, post; compliment (2)

hōra -ae f.: hour (3)

hortor hortārī hortātus sum: urge strongly, advise, exhort (1)

hostis -is m./f.: stranger, enemy (6)

humus -ī f.: earth (2)

— I —

iaciō iacere iēcī iactum: throw, hurl (8)

iactō -āre: throw, cast (1)

iactūra -ae f.: loss (of stature/prestige) (1)

iam: now; already (9)

iānitor -ōris m.: door-keeper (2)

iānua -ae f.: door, entrance (5)

ibi: there (1)

īciō īcere īcī ictum: strike (1)

Īda -ae f.: Mount Ida (1)

Īdē -ēs f.: Mount Ida (1)

īdem eadem idem: the same (2)

ignāvus -a -um: lazy, idle (2)

ignis -is m.: fire (5)

ille illa illud: that (55)

imbellis -e: unwarlike; peaceful (1)

imber -ris m.: rain, shower (1)

immemor -oris: unmindful, forgetful (1)

immītis -e: hard, harsh, cruel (1)

immundus -a -um: unclean, foul (2)

impellō -ere impulī impulsum: strike or beat against; push (2)

imperium -ī n.: command, power (1)

impius -a -um: impious, wicked (1)

impōnō -ere -posuī -positum: put in, put on, impose, levy upon (1)

imprimō -primere -pressī -pressum: apply with pressure, press onto, imprint (1)

improbus -a -um: inferior, bad; shameless (1)

in: in, on (+abl.), into, onto (+acc) (77)

inānis -e: empty, void; foolish, trifling (1)

inaurātus -a -um: gilt (1)

incertus -a -um: disarrayed, errant, wayward (1)

inclāmō -āre: shout abuse at (+dat.) (1)

inclūdo -clūdere -clūsī clūsum: shut in; confine (1)

incurvus -a -um: bent, curved (1)

inde: from there, from then (2)

indignus -a -um: unworthy, beneath one's dignity, shameful (2)

inemptus -a -um: un-bought (1)

ineptus -a -um: foolish (1)

inermis -e: unarmed, defenseless (2)

iners -tis: crude, lacking skill; lazy, idle (1)

infāmis -e: notorious, disreputable (1)

infēlix -īcis: ill-fated (1)

inferus -a -um: low; **inferior**, lower; **infimus** or **īmus**, lowest (2)

infestus -a -um: hostile, savage (1)

infirmus -a -um: weak, feeble (1)

ingeniōsus -a -um: talented, naturally clever (2)

ingenium -ī n.: disposition, ability, talent (4)

ingenuus -a -um: native, natural, indigenous, tender, delicate (2)

ingrātus -a -um: unpleasant, disagreeable (3)

iniciō -icere -iēcī -iectum: cast into, throw over (3)

innumerus -a -um: countless (1)

inoffensus -a -um: (esp. of feet) not striking against an obstacle, unhindered (1)

inops -pis: without means; poor, destitute (1)

insānus -a -um: mad, insane, senseless (1)

insignis -e: distinguished, remarkable, notable (1)

instar n.: the equivalent, just like (+gen.) (1)

instruō -struere -struxi -structum: equip, furnish; prepare, provide (1)

insum -esse -fuī: be in or on, be present (1)

inter: between, among; during (+acc.) (2)

intonō -tonāre -tonuī: thunder forth (1)

inūtilis -e: useless, unserviceable (1)

invādō -vādere -vāsī -vāsum: attack, assault, fall upon (1)

inveniō -venīre -vēnī -ventum: find; discover (2)

invidiōsus -a -um: envious, hateful (1)

invidus -a -um: envious, jealous (2)

invīsus -a -um: unseen, secret; hated (1)

invītus -a -um: unwilling (2)

iō: hurrah! oh! (3)

ipse ipsa ipsum: him- her- itself (24)

īra īrae f.: wrath, anger (4)

īrascor īrascī īrātus sum: grow angry; **īrātus -a -um**, angry (2)

is ea id: he, she, it (2)

Īsis -dis f.: Isis, an Egyptian goddess (1)

iste ista istud: that, that of yours; (adv.) **istīc** or **istūc**, over there; **istinc**, from over there (6)

ita: thus, so (1)

iterum: again (1)

iubeō iubēre iussī iussum: bid, order (6)

iūcundus -a -um: pleasant, agreeable, delightful (1)

iūdex iūdicis m.: judge, juror (1)

iugōsus -a -um: hilly, mountainous (1)

iugum -ī n.: yoke; ridge, chain of hills (3)

iungō iungere iunxī iunctum: join (4)

Iuppiter Iovis m.: Jupiter (2)

iurgium -ī n.: altercation, quarrel (1)

iūs iūris n.: right, justice, law (4)

iustus -a -um: right, just, fair (1)

iuvenālis -e: youthful (1)

iuvencus -ī m.: young bull, bullock (1)

iuvenis -is m.: youth (4)

iuvō iuvāre iūvī iūtum: help, assist; please, delight (7)

— L —

lābellum -ī n.: lip (1)

labor -ōris m.: toil, exertion (1)

lābor lābī lapsus sum: slip and fall; glide, drop; perish (3)

labōrō -āre: toil, work; be in trouble or distress (1)

lacertus -ī m.: the arm, esp. the upper arm (4)

lacrima -ae f.: tear (6)

lacrimō -āre: weep, shed tears (1)

lacrimōsus -a -um: tearful (1)

laedō laedere laesī laesum: injure by striking, hurt (7)

laetus -a -um: glad, joyful (2)

Lāis -idis or -idos f.: Lais, the name of two famous Greek courtesans (1)

lānificus -a -um: wool-working, spinning (1)

laniō -āre: tear to pieces, mangle, lacerate (1)

lānūgō -inis f.: soft hair, down (1)

Lār Laris m.: Lar, household god (1)

lascīvia -ae f.: playfulness; wantonness, licentiousness (2)

lassō -āre: tire out, wear out (1)

lassus -a -um: tired, weary (4)

latebra -ae f.: hiding place, concealment (1)

lateō latēre latuī: lie hidden, be hidden (2)

latus -eris n.: side, flank; physical strength (4)

lātus -a -um: broad, wide (2)

laudābilis -e: praiseworthy, laudable (1)

laudō -āre: praise (1)

laurus -ī f.: laurel (2)

laus laudis f.: praise, glory (1)

lavō lavāre lāvī lautum: wash, bathe (1)

laxus -a -um: wide, loose, spacious (1)

lectus -ī m.: couch, bed (2)

Lēdē -ēs f.: Leda (1)

legō legere lēgī lectum: gather, choose, read (10)

lēna -ae f.: brothel-keeper, madam, procuress, go-between (2)

lēnis -e: gentle, kind, mild (2)

lēnō -ōnis m.: pimp (1)

lentē: (adv.) slowly, leisurely (1)

lentus -a -um: yielding, pliant, supple, unbreakable (3)

levis -e: light, trivial (6)

levō -āre: lighten, relieve (1)

lex lēgis f.: law (3)

libellus -ī m.: little book (1)

Līber Līberī m.: Bacchus, Dionysus (1)

lībō -āre: nibble, sip, touch (1)

lībum -ī n.: cake (1)

liceor licērī licitus: bid for (1)

licet licēre licuit licitum est: although, even if (6)

līcium -ī n.: thrum, end of a thread; a thread (1)

lignum -ī n.: wood (3)

līmen līminis n.: threshold (6)

lingua -ae f.: tongue; language (5)

liquidus -a -um: clear, liquid (2)

līs lītis f.: lawsuit; quarrel (1)

lītoreus -a -um: of the seashore (1)

littera -ae f.: letter, (pl.) literature (2)

līveō -ēre: be livid, be black and blue with bruises (1)

līvidus -a -um: bluish; envious (1)

līvor -ōris m.: envy (2)

locō -āre: place, position, set; hire out (1)

locus -ī m.: place; **loca**, (n. pl.) region (2)

longus -a -um: long, far (12)

loquax loquācis: talkative, loquacious; (1)

loquor loquī locūtus sum: speak, say (2)

lōrum -ī n.: strap, (pl.) reins, bridle (1)

Lūcifer -ferī m.: Lucifer; the morning star (1)

Lucrētius -iī m.: Lucretius (1)

lucrōsus -a -um: lucrative, profitable (1)

lucrum -ī n.: profit (1)

luctor -ārī: wrestle, struggle, strive (1)

lūdō lūdere lūsī lūsum: play, mock (3)

lūmen lūminis n.: light (3)

lūna -ae f.: moon (3)

lūnō -āre: bend like a half-moon (1)

lupa -ae f.: she-wolf, prostitute (1)

lupātī ōrum n. pl.: jagged bit (for horses) (1)

lūsus -ūs m.: play, game (1)

lux lūcis f.: light (of day) (3)

Lycōris -idis f.: Lycoris (1)

lyra -ae f.: lyre (3)

— M —

madeō -ēre: be wet, be damp (2)

madidus -a -um: moist, wet; drunk (1)

Maenalius -a -um: of Mount Maenalus (1)

Maenas -adis f.: Maenad, priestess of Bacchus (1)

Maeonidēs -ae m.: Homer (1)

maestus -a -um: sad, sorrowful; depressing (2)

magister magistrī m.: master, chief (1)

magnificus -a -um: grand, splendid, magnificent (2)

magnus -a -um: great (10)

magus -a -um: magical (1)

male: (adv.) badly (5)

malignus -a -um: malignant, wicked, malicious (1)

malus -a -um: bad, evil (4)

mandō -āre: order, command, bid (1)

māne: (in the) morning (5)

maneō manēre mansī mansum: remain (2)

manifestus -a -um: clear, evident, manifest (1)

mānō -āre: flow (1)

manus -ūs f.: hand; band of men (29)

marceō -ēre: wither, droop, be feeble (1)

mare -is n.: sea (1)

margō -inis m.: rim; border, edge; margin (1)

marītus -ī m.: husband (2)

Mars Martis m.: Mars (6)

māter mātris f.: mother (4)

māteria -ae f.: material, subject matter; timber, lumber (2)

māteriēs māteriēī f.: material (1)

māternus -a -um: maternal (2)

medicō -āre: treat, medicate (with); dye (with) (2)

medius -a -um: middle, central (10)

mel mellis n.: honey (2)

membrum -ī m.: limb, member of the body (5)

meminī meminisse: remember, recollect (3)

Memnōn -onis m.: Memnon (2)

memor memoris: mindful, un-forgetting (2)

Menandros -drī m.: Menander (1)

menda -ae f.: fault, defect, blemish (1)

mens mentis f.: mind (6)

mensa -ae f.: table (1)

mercābilis -e: purchasable (1)

mercēs mercēdis f.: price (2)

mereō merēre meruī meritum: deserve, merit; serve as a soldier (5)

meretrix meretrīcis f.: prostitute (2)

meritō: (adv.) deservedly, justly (1)

meritum -ī n.: meritorious action, service (1)

meritus -a -um: deserving, meriting (1)

merum -ī n.: wine; wine unmixed with water (2)

merx mercis f.: commodity (1)

metuō metuere metuī metūtum: to fear, to dread (2)

metus -ūs m.: fear, dread (3)

meus -a -um: my (39)

mīles -itis m.: soldier (8)

mīlitia -ae f.: military service, warfare (2)

mīlitō -āre: to serve as a soldier (2)

mille (pl.) mīlia: thousand (2)

minae -ārum f. pl.: threats (2)

ministerium -ī n.: service, ministry (1)

ministra -ae f.: servant, attendant (2)

ministrō -āre: serve, attend to, take care of (1)

minium -ī n.: cinnabar (1)

minuō minuere minuī minūtum: make smaller, lessen, diminish (2)

Minerva -ae f.: Minerva (3)

mīror mīrārī mīrātus sum: wonder at, marvel at (+acc.) (4)

misceō miscēre miscuī mixtum: mix (4)

miser misera miserum: wretched, pitiable (10)

mītis -e: mild, soft, ripe (2)

mittō mittere mīsī missum: send, let go (7)

moderābilis -e: controllable (1)

modestus -a -um: moderate, respectful, unassuming (1)

modicus -a -um: moderate, limited (1)

modo: just, just now; **modo ... modo**; now ... now, at one moment ... at another, sometimes ... sometimes (5)

modus -ī m.: measure, manner, kind (2)

mōlior mōlīrī mōlītus sum: set in motion, stir; toil, struggle (2)

molliō mollīre mollīvī mollītum: make pliable, soften, weaken (1)

mollis -e: soft, yielding, gentle (3)

moneō monēre monuī monitum: warn, advise (2)

monīle -is n.: necklace (1)

monimentum (monumentum) -ī n.: reminder, example (1)

mons montis m.: mountain (1)

monstrō -āre: show, point out; show (how to) (+infin.) (1)

mora -ae f.: delay, hindrance (3)

morbus -ī m.: sickness, disease (1)

morior morī mortuus sum: die (2)

moror morārī morātus sum: delay (3)

mors mortis f.: death (1)

mortālis -e: liable to death, mortal (1)

mōs mōris m.: custom, habit; (pl.) character (3)

mōtus -ūs m.: motion, movement (1)

moveō -ēre mōvī mōtum: move (9)

mox: soon (1)

mulier -eris f.: woman (1)

multus -a -um: much, many; **multō**, by far (16)

mūnīmen -inis n.: protection, defence, fortification (1)

mūnus mūneris n.: gift, offering; duty, obligation; (pl.) gladiatorial show (9)

Mūsa -ae f.: a Muse, one of the goddesses of inspiration of poetry and the arts and sciences (1)

mustum -ī n.: unfermented grape juice, must (1)

mūtō -āre: change (1)

myrtus -ī f.: myrtle (3)

— N —

nam or namque: for, indeed, really (2)

Napē -ēs f.: Nape, 'woodland glen' in Greek (2)

narrō -āre: relate, recount (1)

nascor nascī nātus sum: be born (1)

Nāsō -ōnis m.: Naso (2)

nātālis -is m.: a birthday (1)

nātīvus -a -um: native, natural (1)

nāvita -ae m.: sailor, mariner (1)

nē: lest, that not (9)

nec or neque: and not, nor; **nec ... nec**, neither ... nor (60)

nectō nectere nexī nexum: tie, bind, connect, weave (2)

neglegō -legere -lexī -lectum: neglect, disregard (1)

negō -āre: deny, refuse (6)

nēmō: no one (gen. **nullīus**, dat. **nullī**, abl. **nullō** or **nullā, nullus -a -um**) (2)

nempe: certainly (1)

nēquīquam: to no avail (1)

nervus -ī m.: muscle, tendon; cord, string (1)

nesciō -scīre: not know, be ignorant (3)

nescius -a -um: unknowing, ignorant, unaware (1)

neuter -tra -trum: neither (1)

nēve or neu: and not, nor, and that not, and lest (2)

nexilis -e: plaited, intertwined (1)

niger nigra nigrum: black (1)

nihil or nīl: nothing; not at all (5)

nimbus -ī m.: rain-cloud, cloud-burst, downpour (1)

nimis or nimium: excessively (4)

nisi or nī: if not, unless (5)

niteō nitēre nituī: shine, sparkle (1)

nix nivis f.: snow (3)

nocens, nocentis: guilty (1)

noceō nocēre nocuī: harm (9)

nocturnus -a -um: by night, nocturnal (2)

nōlō nolle nōluī: be unwilling (3)

nōmen -inis n.: name (7)

nōn: not (50)

nondum: not yet (1)

nonne: (adv.) surely (1)

nonnumquam: (adv.) sometimes (1)

nōs nostrum/nostrī nōbīs nōs: we (8)

noscō noscere nōvī nōtum: learn, (in perfect tenses) know (4)

noster nostra nostrum: our (6)

nota -ae f.: mark; sign; brand (4)

notō -āre: mark, write (4)

Notus -ī m.: south wind (3)

nōtus -a -um: well-known (3)

novem: (indecl.) nine (1)

novus -a -um: new (6)

nox noctis f.: night (25)

nūbēs -is f.: cloud (1)

nūbilum -ī n.: darkness; cloud (1)

nūbō nūbere nupsī nuptum: cover, veil; be married to (1)

nūdus -a -um: naked, bare (5)

nullus -a -um: not any, no one (16)

num: interrogative particle implying negative answer (1)

nūmen -inis n.: divine will, deity (3)

numerō -āre: count; count out as payment (1)

numerus -ī m.: number, amount; poetic meter (3)

numquam: never (2)

nunc: now (14)

nūper: adv. not long ago, lately (2)

nusquam: (adv.) nowhere (2)

nūtrix -īcis f.: nurse (1)

nūtus -ūs m.: nod, command (1)

– O –

ō: oh! (2)

obiciō -icere -iēcī -iectum: throw in the way, reproach; charge, accuse (1)

oblīquus -a -um: slanting, indirect, covert (1)

oborior -orīrī -ortus sum: arise, appear (1)

obsideō -sidēre -sēdī -sessum: sit down near, blockade, besiege (2)

obstō -stāre -stitī -stātum: stand before, obstruct, hinder (2)

obsum -esse -fuī: be in the way, hinder, be against (2)

obvius -a -um: in the way, meeting (1)

occulō -culere -culuī -cultum: conceal (1)

occultē: (adv.) without being noticed (1)

ōceanus -ī m.: the ocean (1)

ocellus -ī m.: a (little) eye (2)

oculus -ī m.: eye (9)

ōdī ōdisse ōdōsum: hate (2)

officium -ī n.: service, duty (3)

Olympus -ī m.: Olympus (1)

ōmen -inis n.: omen, augury (2)

omnis -e: all, every, as a whole (11)

onerō -āre: weigh down, burden (1)

onus oneris n.: load, burden (2)

oppositus -a -um: hostile, opposed (1)

ops opis f.: assistance, resources (6)

optō -āre: choose, select (5)

opus operis n.: work (12)

ōra ōrae f.: edge. border (1)

orbis -is m.: circle; **orbis terrārum**, world (7)

ordō -inis m.: order, rank (3)

Orestēs -is or -ae m.: Orestes, a Greek hero (1)

orior orīrī ortus sum: arise, begin (3)

Ōrīthyia -ae f.: Orithyia, a daughter of Erechtheus (1)

ornātrix -īcis f.: hairdresser, lady's maid (1)

ornō -āre: decorate, beautify; arrange (hair); equip (2)

ōrō -āre: pray (2)

os ossis n.: bone (11)

osculum -ī n.: kiss (5)

ōtium -ī n.: leisure (1)

ovis -is n.: sheep (1)

ōvum -ī n.: egg (1)

— P —

paciscor paciscī pactus sum: negotiate, seek through bargaining (1)

paelex -icis f.: a mistress who was a rival to a wife or lover (1)

pāgina -ae f.: page (1)

palla -ae f.: cloak (1)

pallium -ī n.: coverlet, mantle (3)

pandō pandere pandi pansum or passum: spread out; open up; reveal (1)

pandus -a -um: bent, curved, crooked (1)

pangō pangere pepigī pactum: fasten, fix; settle for, agree upon, contract for (1)

papilla -ae f.: nipple, breast (2)

pār paris: equal (2)

parātus -a -um: prepared, ready (1)

parcō parcere pepercī parsum: spare, be sparing of (+dat.) (4)

parcus -a -um: thrifty, frugal (2)

parens -ntis m./f.: parent (4)

parentō -āre: make memorial offerings for one's parents (1)

Parius -a -um: of Paros (1)

parō -āre: prepare, acquire (2)

pars partis f.: part (8)

parum: too little (1)

parvus -a -um: small (5)

pascō pascere pāvī pātum: feed, nourish (1)

pateō patēre patuī: lie open, extend; be evident or obvious (2)

pater patris m.: father, ancestor (3)

paternus -a -um: of a father, paternal; ancestral (1)

patiens -ntis: long-suffering, patient; hardy (1)

patienter: (adv.) patiently (1)

patior patī passus sum: permit, endure (4)

paucus -a -um: small, few; **paucī -ae –a (pl)**: a little, a few (4)

pauper -eris: poor, lowly (3)

pavidus -a -um: trembling, quaking, fearful (1)

pax pācis f.: peace (2)

pecten -inis m.: comb (1)

pectus -oris n.: chest, breast (6)

pecus -oris n.: cattle, sheep/beast, animal, herd (1)

pellō pellere pepulī pulsum: strike, beat, push, drive (2)

pendō pendere pependī pensum: weigh, hang, suspend; pay (2)

Pēnelopē -ēs f.: Penelope (1)

penitus: (adv.) utterly, deeply (1)

pensum -ī n.: wool (1)

per: through (+acc.) (8)

peragō -agere -ēgī -actum: pass through; chase; complete (2)

perarō -āre: incise (1)

percellō -cellere -culī -culsum: strike down, overturn, shatter (1)

perdō -dere -didī -ditum: destroy (3)

perennis -e: continual, perpetual (3)

pereō -īre -iī -itum: perish, be lost (3)

perferō -ferre -tulī -lātum: carry through, deliver (2)

perfidus -a -um: faithless, treacherous, false (1)

periūrium (pēiūrium) -ī n.: false oath, lie (1)

periūrō (pēierō) -āre: swear a false oath (2)

perlegō -legere -lēgī -lectum: read through (1)

perpetior -petī -pessus sum: bear to the end, endure (1)

perpetuus -a -um: unbroken, perpetual (2)

pervigil -ilis: keeping watch all night, awake (1)

pervigilō -āre: keep vigil (1)

pēs pedis m.: foot (10)

petō petere petīvī petītum: seek, aim at (6)

pharetra -ae f.: quiver (1)

pharetrātus -a -um: wearing a quiver (1)

Phoebus -ī m.: Apollo (4)

Phrygius -a -um: Phrygian, a territory in Asia minor; Trojan (1)

Pīeris -idos f.: daughter of Pierus, i.e. a Muse (1)

pingō pingere pinxī pictum: paint, dye (2)

pinguis -e: lazy; comfortable (1)

pinna -ae f.: feather, wing (1)

placeō placēre placuī placitum: please (7)

plānus -a -um: flat, level (1)

plaudō plaudere plausī plausum: clap, applaud (for) (+dat.) (1)

plebs plēbis f.: the common people (1)

plectō –ere -xī -ctum: beat; punish (2)

plēnus -a -um: full (3)

plūma -ae f.: feather, down (2)

plūs plūris: more (2)

pōculum -ī n.: drinking-cup, goblet (2)

poena -ae f.: penalty, punishment (3)

pollex -icis m.: thumb (1)

pompa -ae f.: procession, parade (1)

pōmum -ī n.: fruit tree, fruit (1)

pondus -eris n.: weight (1)

pōnō pōnere posuī positum: put, place; put aside (8)

pontus -ī m.: the open sea, the deep (1)

pōpuleus -a -um: of the poplar tree (1)

populus -ī m.: people (1)

porrigō -rigere -rexī -rectum: stretch out, reach, extend (1)

porta -ae f.: gate (2)

portō -āre: carry a load; bear, carry, convey (1)

poscō poscere poposcī: demand, claim; inquire into (10)

possideō -sidēre -sēdī -sessum: have in one's control, possess, hold (1)

possum posse potuī: be able (18)

post: after (adv. and prep. +acc.) (2)

postis -is m.: doorjamb; door (7)

postmodo: (adv.) later, presently (2)

potens potentis: able, powerful (1)

praebeō -ēre -uī -itum: furnish, supply, render (7)

praecipiō -cipere -cēpī -ceptum: anticipate, advise, warn (1)

praecipuē: (adv.) especially, particularly (2)

praeda -ae f.: booty, prey (6)

praedor -ārī -ātus: plunder, rob (1)

praeferō -ferre -tulī -lātum: bear before or in front; prefer (1)

praegustō -āre: taste before (1)

praemium -ī n.: bounty, reward (2)

praeripiō -ere -uī -eptum: snatch, carry off (1)

praestō -stāre -stitī -stitum or -stātum: excel, exhibit (1)

praeter: by, along, past; besides, except (+acc.) (1)

praetereō -īre -iī -itum: go by, pass by (2)

precor -ārī -ātus: pray, invoke (5)

premō premere pressī pressum: press, pursue, overwhelm (7)

prendō -ere prendī prensum: to lay hold of, grasp, snatch (1)

pretium -ī n.: price, worth, reward; **pretium operae**, a reward for trouble, something worthwhile (6)

prex precis f.: prayers, entreaties (3)

Priamēis -idos f.: daughter of Priam, Cassandra (1)

prīmum: at first, firstly (1)

prīmus -a -um: first (8)

prior prius: earlier, preceding (1)

prō: for, on behalf of, in proportion to (+abl.) (8)

proavus -ī m.: great-grandfather; ancestor (1)

probō -āre: approve, prove; convince one (dat.) of a thing (acc.) (2)

procul: at a distance (2)

prōcumbō -cumbere -cubuī -cubitum: to fall forwards, sink down, fall prostrate (2)

prōditiō -ōnis f.: betrayal, abandonment (of a cause) (1)

prōdō prōdere prōdidī prōditus: project, thrust forward; bring forth, produce, give birth to (1)

proelium -ī n.: battle (1)

profiteor -fitērī -fessus sum: declare, claim, acknowledge (1)

prōiciō -icere iēcī -iectum: cast forth, throw out, fling to the ground (2)

prōmittō -mittere -mīsī -missum: send forth, offer (1)

properō -āre: hasten, speed (4)

prōpōnō -pōnere -posuī -positum: put forth, propose, present (1)

prōsequor -sequī -secūtus sum: follow, accompany, attend (1)

prostituō -stituere -stituī -stitūtum: prostitute, put to an unworthy use (1)

prostō -stāre -stitī -stitum: offer oneself for sale (2)

prōsum prodesse profuī: be of use, do good, help (+dat.) (5)

prōtegō -tegere -texī -tectum: cover, conceal; protect (2)

protervē: (adv.) boldly, impudently (1)

prōtinus: at once, forthwith (2)

prōveniō -venīre -vēnī -ventum: come forth; come about (2)

proximus: nearest, next, immediately following (1)

pruīnōsus -a -um: full of frost, frosty (2)

pudīcus -a -um: modest, chaste, virtuous (1)

pudor -ōris m.: sense of shame, modesty, propriety (5)

puella -ae f.: girl, girl-friend (16)

puer puerī m.: boy; slave (8)

pugnō -āre: fight (2)

pulcher -chra -chrum: beautiful (1)

pulverulentus -a- um: covered with dust, dusty (1)

pūpula -ae f.: the pupil (of the eye) (1)

purpureus -a -um: purple (5)

pūrus -a -um: clean, pure, innocent (3)

putō -āre: think, suppose (3)

– Q –

quā: where, how (2)

quaerō -rere -sīvī -sītum: seek, inquire (7)

quālis -e: of what kind? what? (12)

quāliscumque quālecumque: whatever kind, whatever sort (1)

quam: how?; (after comparative) than (11)

quamlibet: (adv.) however, in whatever degree (1)

quamvīs: however you like; although (3)

quandō: when?; since; **sī quandō**, at any time, at some time, if ever (1)

quantum: (adv.) how much? how greatly? how much! how greatly! as much as (1)

quantus -a -um: (interr.) how great? (rel.) of what size, amount, etc. (4)

quasi: as if (1)

-que: and (98)

queror querī questus sum: complain of, lament (3)

quī quae quod: who, which, what (94)

quia: because (4)

quīcumque quaecumque quodcumque: whoever, whatever (3)

quīdam quaedam quoddam: a certain one, someone (2)

quidem: certainly, at least (1)

quiescō quiescere quiēvī quiētum: keep quiet; sleep (1)

quīn: (adv.) indeed, in fact; (conj.) so that ... not (+subj.) (2)

quinque: (indecl.) five (2)

Quirīs -ītis m.: the formal term for a Roman citizen (1)

quis quid: who? what? which? (35)

quisque quaeque quidque: each one, everyone (3)

quisquis quidquid: whoever, whichever, whatever, anyone, anything (4)

quod: because (1)

quondam: formerly, once (3)

quoque: also, too (14)

quot: how many, as many as, every time (1)

quotiens: how many times? (2)

— R —

rādō rādere rāsī rāsum: scratch; inscribe (1)

rāmus -ī m.: branch (1)

rapidus -a -um: swift, tearing (1)

rapīna -ae f.: robbery, plundering, pillage (1)

rapiō rapere rapuī raptum: seize, tear away (2)

rārus -a -um: wide apart, loose, thin; rare, seldom (2)

ratiō -ōnis f.: method, plan, reason (1)

ratis -is f.: ship (1)

raucus -a -um: harsh-sounding, noisy (2)

recens -ntis: fresh, new (1)

recingō -cingere -cinxī -cinctum: ungird, loosen (1)

recipiō -cipere -cēpī -ceptum: take back, receive; **sē recipere**, betake oneself, go back, return (2)

recompōnō -pōnere -posuī -positum: put back together; readjust, rearrange (1)

recurvō -āre: bend back; curve backwards (1)

reddō -dere -didī -ditum: return, give back (5)

redeō -īre -iī -itum: go back, return (1)

redimiō -imīre -imiī -imītum: encircle (with a garland) (2)

reditus -ūs m.: return, revenue (1)

referō referre rettulī relātum: bring back; report (2)

refertus -a -um: crammed, bursting with (1)

refugiō -fugere -fūgī: flee back, run away (1)

regnō -āre: be king, rule (4)

regnum -ī n.: kingdom, kingship (1)

rēiciō -icere -iēcī -iectum: throw back or away; reject with scorn, spurn (1)

relaxō -āre: loosen, open (1)

relentescō -ere: slacken; become less ardent (1)

relevō -āre: lighten, relieve (1)

religō -āre: tie up, bind fast (1)

relinquō -linquere -līquī -lictum: abandon (2)

removeō -movēre -mōvī -mōtum: move back, withdraw, remove (1)

renovō -āre: restore, refresh, renew (1)

reparābilis -e: reparable, recoverable (1)

repellō repellere reppulī repulsum: drive back, repel (3)

rependō -pendere -pendī -pensum: make up for; balance (1)

reperiō -perīre -pperī -pertum: find, find out (1)

repertor -ōris m.: discoverer, inventor (1)

requiescō - quiescere -quiēvī -quiētum: rest, repose (3)

rēs reī f.: thing (6)

resānescō -sānescere -sānuī: be healed (1)

rescrībō -scrībere -scripsī -scriptum: write back, respond (1)

resecō -secāre -secuī -sectum: cut, cut back (1)

resīdō -sīdere -sēdī: sit down, sink down, shrink (1)

resistō -ere -stitī: stand still, halt, stop short (1)

respicio -ere -spexī -spectum: look back, regard, consider (1)

resurgō -surgere -surrexī -surrectum: rise again, reappear (1)

rēte -tis n.: net, trap (1)

retineō -tinēre -tinuī -tentum: hold back, keep (2)

retorqueō -torquēre -torsī -tortum: twist back, bend back (1)

reus -ī m.: defendant (1)

revocō -āre: call back, recall (1)

rex rēgis m.: king (2)

Rhēsus -ī m.: Rhesus (1)

rhombus -ī m.: a wooden object which, when attached to a string and twirled in the air, produced a loud hissing sound (1)

rīdeō -ēre rīsī rīsum: laugh, laugh at (2)

rigeō -ēre: be stiff, stiffen (1)

rigidus -a -um: hard, rigid (3)

rīpa -ae f.: bank of a river (1)

rītū: (+gen.) in the manner of, like (1)

rīvālis -is m.: rival (2)

rōbur -oris n.: oak (1)

rōdō rōdere rōsī rōsum: gnaw, eat away, erode (1)

rogō -āre: ask (9)

Rōma -ae f.: Rome (1)

rōs -ōris m.: dew (1)

rosa -ae f.: rose (1)

roscidus -a -um: bedewed, dewy (1)

roseus -a -um: rosy (1)

rota -ae f.: wheel (3)

rubeō -ēre: redden, blush (3)

rubor -ōris m.: redness of face, a feeling of shame (1)

rūga -ae f.: wrinkle (2)

rūgōsus -a -um: wrinkled (1)

rusticitās -ātis f.: lack of sophistication (1)

— S —

Sabīnus -a -um: Sabine (2)

sacer sacra sacrum: holy, sacred (3)

sacrilegus -a -um: guilty of impiety, sacrilegious (1)

saepe: often (14)

saevus -a -um: fierce, raging, wrathful (7)

sagitta -ae f.: arrow (3)

Samīramis -idis f.: the legendary queen of Assyria (1)

sanctus -a -um: sacred, inviolable (1)

sanguinulentus -a -um: bloodied; blood-red (1)

sanguis -inis m.: blood (5)

sapiō sapere sapīvī: be wise, be sensible (1)

satis sat: enough, sufficiently (3)

saucius -a -um: wounded (1)

saxum -ī n.: rock, cliff, crag (1)

scelus -eris n.: crime, sin (5)

Schoenēis -idos f.: the daughter of Schoenius, Atalanta (1)

scindō scindere scidī scissum: cut, rend, tear asunder (1)

sciō -īre -īvī/-iī -ītum: know (4)

scrībō scrībere scripsī scriptum: write (1)

sē/sēsē sui sibi: him- her- itself, themselves (6)

secundus -a -um: following; favorable (2)

sēcūrus -a -um: free from care, tranquil; careless (1)

sed: but (11)

sedeō sedēre sēdī sessum: sit (1)

sēdulus -a -um: careful, cautious (1)

segnis -e: slow, slothful (1)

sēligō -ligere -lēgī -lectum: choose, select (1)

sēmiadapertus -a -um: half-open (1)

sēmisupīnus -a -um: half-supine, half-reclining on one's back (1)

semper: always, ever (7)

senecta -ae f.: old age (1)

senectūs -ūtis f.: old age (1)

senescō senescere senuī: grow old, deteriorate (1)

senex -is m.: old man, elder; senior, older (4)

senīlis -e: of an old man, senile (1)

sentiō sentīre sensī sensum: perceive, feel, hear, see (8)

sēparō -āre: sever, separate (1)

septemplex -icis: sevenfold (1)

sepulcrum -ī n.: place of burial, tomb, grave (1)

sequor sequī secūtus sum: follow (5)

sera -ae f.: bar, bolt (5)

Sēres -um m.: Chinese (1)

sermō -ōnis m.: conversation, discourse (1)

servitium -ī n.: slavery, servitude (1)

servō -āre: save, watch over (3)

servus -ī m.: slave (2)

servus -a -um: of slavery, servile (1)

sex: six (1)

sī: if (36)

sīc: in this manner, thus; **sīc ... ut**, in the same way as (9)

siccus -a -um: dry, desiccated (1)

sīdus -eris n.: star, constellation (5)

signum -ī n.: sign, standard, mark (4)

sileō silēre siluī: be still, be silent (2)

silex -icis m.: flint; any hard stone (2)

silva -ae f.: forest, grove (3)

similis -e: like, similar (1)

Simoīs -oentis m.: a small river near Troy, flowing into the Scamander (1)

simplex -icis: artless, naïve, lacking guile (1)

simplicitās -ātis f.: simplicity; lack of sophistication, ignorance (2)

simulācrum -ī n.: image, effigy, apparition (1)

simulō -āre: pretend; produce, simulate, feign (3)

simultās -ātis f.: a state of animosity, a feud (1)

sine: without (+abl.) (5)

singulī -ae -a: one each (1)

sinō sinere sīvī situm: allow, let go (3)

sinuōsus -a -um: full of windings; sinuous (1)

sinus -ūs m.: fold of a garment; lap, bay, gulf (4)

sitis -is f.: thirst (1)

situs -ūs m.: site, position; neglect, disuse; rot, mold (2)

sōbrius -a -um: sober, moderate (2)

socius -a -um: friendly, allied; **socius -ī m.**, partner, comrade (2)

sōl sōlis m.: sun (1)

soleō -ēre -uī -itum: be accustomed (2)

solidus -a -um: dense, firm, solid (1)

sollemnis -e: customary (1)

sollers -rtis: clever, skilled (1)

sollicitō -āre: associated with trouble, troubling (2)

sollicitus -a -um: troubled (1)

sōlus -a -um: only, alone (4)

solvō solvere solvī solūtum: release, set sail (3)

somnus -ī m.: sleep, slumber; (pl.) dreams (7)

sonō sonāre sonuī sonitum: sound, resound (1)

Sophoclēus -a -um: Sophoclean, of Sophocles (1)

sōpiō sōpīre sōpīvī/iī sōpītum: put to sleep, lull to sleep (1)

sopōrō sopōrāre: lull to sleep (1)

sordēs -is f.: filth; greed (1)

sordidus -a -um: filthy, foul, tarnished by greed (1)

soror -ōris f.: sister (2)

sors sortis f.: lot, fate, destiny; oracle (2)

spargō spargere sparsī sparsum: scatter (1)

spatiōsus -a -um: wide, spacious, large (2)

spectābilis -e: visible, notable, remarkable (1)

spectō -āre: look at, consider (4)

speculātor -ōris m.: spy, sentinel, look-out, one employed to observe (1)

speculum -ī n.: mirror (1)

spērō -āre: to hope (1)

spēs speī f.: hope (2)

spīculum -ī n.: sharp point, sting, arrow (1)

spissus -a -um: close, dense, thick (1)

splendidus -a -um: shining, clear, brilliant, splendid (1)

spolium -ī n.: plunder, spoils (1)

spondeō -ēre spopondī sponsum: make a solemn promise (1)

sponte: (abl. sg. as adv.) naturally, by nature; voluntarily (2)

statiō -ōnis: position (1)

stella -ae f.: star (1)

sternō sternere strāvī strātum: spread out; strike down, lay low (1)

stillō -āre: drip with (1)

stipula -ae f.: stubble (1)

stō stāre stetī statum: stand (5)

strātum -ī n.: bedding, coverlet; (often in pl.) bed (1)

strēnuus -a -um: brisk, prompt, vigorous (2)

stringō stringere strinxī strictum: unsheathe (2)

strix strigis f.: screech owl (1)

studium -ī n.: eagerness, zeal (1)

suādeō suādēre suāsī suāsum: recommend, advise (1)

sub: under, close to (+acc. or abl.) (6)

subdūcō -dūcere -duxī -ductum: draw up, raise; remove, take away (1)

subeō -īre -iī -itum: go under; endure (4)

subiciō -icere -iēcī -iectum: throw under, place under, lift (1)

sublīmis -e: lofty, elevated (1)

sublūceō -lūcēre: shine faintly, glimmer, gleam (1)

subscrībō -scrībere -scripsī -scriptum: write under, write beneath (1)

succurrō -currere -currī -cursum: run quickly, come to mind (1)

sum esse fuī: be, exist (150)

summus -a -um: highest, uppermost; final (5)

sūmō sūmere sumpsī sumptum: take up (5)

super: over (adv. and prep. +acc.) (3)

superbus -a -um: overbearing, proud, haughty (1)

supercilium -ī n.: eyebrow (1)

superō -āre: overcome, surpass, defeat (1)

superstes -itis: surviving, remaining alive after death (1)

supersum -esse -fuī: remain, survive; be superfluous (to) (1)

supplex -icis: kneeling, supplicating, suppliant (1)

supprimō -primere -pressī -pressum: hold back, check (1)

suprēmus -a -um: highest, uppermost; final (1)

surdus -a -um: deaf (3)

surgō surgere surrexī surrectum: rise (8)

surripiō -ripere -ripuī -reptum: take away secretly, steal (1)

suspendium -ī n.: act of hanging oneself, a hanging; gallows (1)

suspendō -pendere -pendī -pensum: suspend, hold up, check, keep under control (1)

suspicor -ārī: suspect, suppose (2)

sustineō sustinēre sustinuī: hold up, sustain (7)

suus -a -um: his own, her own, its own (20)

Sygamber -bra -brum: of the Sygambri (1)

— T —

tabella -ae f.: flat board, tablet; (pl.) writing tablet (6)

tabula -ae f.: account-book, ledger (1)

taceō -ēre -uī -itum: be silent; **tacitus -a -um**, silent (4)

Tagus -ī m.: the river Tagus (1)

tālis tāle: such (6)

tam: so, so much (6)

tamen: nevertheless, still (19)

tamquam: so as, just as (2)

tangō tangere tetigī tactum: touch (8)

tantus -a -um: so great, so much (4)

tardus -a -um: slow, sluggish, lingering (2)

Tatius -iī m.: Tatius (1)

taurus -ī m.: bull (2)

tectum -ī n.: roof; building, house (2)

tegō tegere texī tectum: cover, conceal (5)

tēlum -ī n.: missile, weapon, spear (1)

temerārius -a -um: accidental; thoughtless, impetuous (1)

temere: (adv.) at random, casually (1)

temerō -āre: violate, desecrate, defile (1)

tempē: (indecl. noun, n. pl.) the Vale of Tempe in Thessaly; any pleasant valley (1)

temperō -āre: set bounds, control, regulate (1)

templum -ī n.: consecrated ground; temple (1)

temptō -āre: try, test; attack (2)

tempus -oris n.: time (8)

tempus -oris n.: the side of the forehead, temple (2)

tendō tendere tetendī tentum: stretch, extend, direct (one's steps or course) (2)

tenebrae -brārum f. pl.: darkness, the shadows (1)

Tenedos -ī f.: Tenedos (island) (1)

teneō -ēre -uī tentum: hold, keep (6)

tener -era -erum: tender (5)

tenuis -e: slender, thin (2)

tenuō -āre: make thin, make fine (1)

tepidus -a -um: warm, tepid (2)

ter: (adv.) three times, thrice (2)

tergum -ī n.: back, rear; **ā tergō**, from the rear (3)

terra -ae f.: land (3)

testificor -ārī: give proof of (1)

testis -is m.: witness (3)

thalamus -ī m.: marriage bed; bedchamber (2)

Thēseus -eī m.: Theseus (1)

Thrācius -a -um: Thracian (1)

Thrēicius -a -um: Thracian (1)

Tibullus -ī m.: Tibullus (1)

tigris tigris m.: tiger (1)

timeō -ēre -uī: fear, dread (9)

timidus -a -um: fearful, timid, shy (2)

timor -ōris m.: fear (2)

tingō tingere tinxī tinctum: wet, moisten; dye, color (1)

Tīthōnus -ī m.: Tithonus (1)

Tītyrus -ī m.: one of the shepherds in Virgil's *Eclogues* and the first word of *Eclogue* 1 (1)

tollō tollere sustulī sublātum: raise up, destroy (2)

torqueō torquēre torsī tortum: twist, wrench; torment, torture (3)

torrens -ntis m.: a rushing stream, torrent (1)

torus -ī m.: bed, couch, cushion (5)

tot: so many (1)

tōtus -a -um: whole, entire (10)

trabs -is f.: beam, tree (1)

tractō -āre: draw, drag, haul (1)

trādō -dere -didī -ditum: hand over, yield (1)

trahō trahere traxī tractum: drag, draw (1)

trāiciō -icere -iēcī -iectum: throw across; pierce, pass through (1)

trānseō -īre -iī -itum: go across (3)

tremō tremere tremuī: tremble, quake (2)

trēs tria: three (1)

tribūnal -ālis n.: tribunal (1)

tribuō tribuere tribuī tribūtum: grant, bestow, award (1)

tristis -e: sad, solemn, grim (3)

triumphō -āre: triumph, have a triumph (3)

triumphus -ī m.: triumph, triumphal procession (6)

trivium -ī n.: (often pl.) a crossroads, gutter (1)

Trōs Trōis m.: Trojan, man of Troy (1)

tū tuī tibi tē: you (sing.) (84)

tueor tuērī tūtus sum: protect, especially in a military sense (2)

tum or tunc: then (6)

tumeō tumēre tumuī: swell, puff up (1)

tumidus -a -um: swollen, tumid; enraged, violent (2)

tundō tundere tutudī tunsum: to pound, strike (1)

tunica -ae f.: tunic (4)

turba -ae f.: crowd, uproar (4)

turpis -e: ugly, unsightly; disgraceful (11)

tūtus -a -um: safe, protected (2)

tuus -a -um: your (40)

Tȳdīdēs -ae m.: the son of Tydeus, Diomedes (2)

— U —

ubi: where, when (2)

ūdus -a -um: wet, damp (2)

ullus -a -um: any, anyone (2)

ultimus -a -um: farthest, final, last, ultimate (1)

ultor -ōris m.: avenger, punisher (1)

umbra -ae f.: shade, shadow (6)

ūmeō -ēre: be wet, moist (1)

umerus -ī m.: shoulder (2)

umquam: ever (3)

unda -ae f.: wave, flowing water, water (1)

undēnī -ae -a: eleven each, eleven at a time (1)

unguis -is m.: fingernail; claw, talon (2)

ūnus -a -um: one (5)

urbs urbis f.: city (4)

urgeō urgēre ursī: press, drive on; urge, insist (1)

urna -ae f.: urn, pitcher (1)

ūrō ūrere ussī ustum: burn (5)

usque: up to; continuously (6)

ūsus -ūs m.: use, experience (6)

ut utī: as (+ indic.); so that, with the result that (+ subj.) (22)

uterque utraque utrumque: each of two (6)

ūtilis -e: useful (2)

ūtor ūtī ūsus sum: use, consume, employ (+ abl.) (1)

ūva -ae f.: grape (2)

uxor uxōris f.: wife (1)

— V —

vacca -ae f.: cow (1)

vacō vacāre: be empty, open, unoccupied (2)

vacuus -a -um: empty (3)

vadimōnium -ī n.: guarantee, contract (1)

valeō valēre valuī valītum: be strong, excel, be valid, prevail; **valē**, farewell! (11)

vallēs -is f.: vale, valley (1)

vallum -ī n.: palisade (1)

vānescō -ere: disappear, vanish (1)

vanus -a -um: empty; false, deceitful (1)

vapor -ōris m.: vapor, steam; heat (1)

variō -āre: vary, diversify; adorn with various colors (1)

Varrō -ōnis m.: Varro (1)

vārus -a -um: crooked, bent; diverse, different (1)

vātēs -is m.: poet, bard (4)

-ve: or (2)

vehō vehere vexī vectum: carry; **vehor vehī vectus sum**, travel, ride, carry, bring (2)

vel: or else, or; **vel ... vel**, either ... or (7)

vēlāmen -inis n.: covering, garment (1)

vēlō -āre: cover, clothe (1)

vēlum -ī n.: sail; fabric (2)

vēna -ae f.: vein (1)

vendō -dere -didī -ditum: sell, vend (3)

venēnum -ī n.: drug, venom; dye (2)

venia -ae f.: favor, indulgence; pardon, forgiveness (1)

veniō venīre vēnī ventum: come (15)

venter -ris m.: stomach, belly (1)

ventilō -āre: wave, fan; brandish (2)

ventus -ī m.: wind (4)

Venus -eris f.: Venus (14)

verber -eris n.: whip; a beating or blow with a whip (4)

verbōsus -a -um: wordy, verbose (1)

verbum -ī n.: word (9)

vērē: truly (1)

verēcundus -a -um: bashful, modest, shy (1)

verrō verrere verrī versum: sweep, sweep over, skim (1)

versō -āre: turn, spin; turn back and forth, twist; torment (4)

versus -ūs m.: line of writing, line of verse (3)

vertex -icis m.: a whirl, whirlwind; summit, top of the head (2)

vertō vertere vertī versum: transform (2)

vērus -a -um: true (3)

vēsānus -a -um: wild, frenzied, insane (2)

vester vestra vestrum: your (1)

vestīgium -ī n.: footstep, footprint, track (1)

vestis -is f.: garment, robe, clothing (5)

vetō -āre vetuī vetītum: forbid (1)

vetus veteris: old (2)

vexō -āre: attack constantly, harass, vex (1)

via -ae f.: way, street (2)

viātor -ōris m.: traveler, wayfarer (1)

vibrō -āre: vibrate, shake, move to and fro (1)

vīcīnus -a -um: neighboring, near (1)

vicis (gen.) f.: repayment of a good turn, requital (1)

victor -ōris m.: conqueror (2)

victrix -cis: victorious, triumphant (1)

videō vidēre vīdī vīsum: see (18)

vigil -ilis m.: sentry, guard (1)

vīlis -e: cheap, worthless; contemptible; of inferior rank (2)

vincō vincere vīcī victum: conquer (8)

vinculum -ī n.: bond, fetter, tie (4)

vindex -icis m.: champion, defender; avenger (1)

vindicta -ae f.: vengeance, punishment (1)

vīnum -ī n.: vine, wine (5)

violentus -a -um: violent, savage (1)

violō -āre: profane, dishonor, treat with violence, violate (1)

vir virī m.: man (16)

virgineus -a -um: maidenly, of a virgin (1)

virgō -inis f.: maiden, virgin, girl (2)

viridis -e: green (1)

vīrus -ī n.: bodily fluid, secretion (1)

vīs f.: force; (acc.) **vim**, (abl.) **vī**; (pl.) **vīrēs**, strength, force (4)

viscus -eris n.: internal organs; womb (1)

vīta -ae f.: life (1)

vītis -is f.: vine, grapevine (1)

vitium -ī n.: flaw, fault, crime (1)

vitreus -a -um: glassy (1)

vītricus -ī m.: stepfather (1)

vittātus -a -um: bound up by a fillet (a strip of fabric worn by women or in religious rituals) (1)

vīvō vīvere vixī victum: live (6)

vīvus -a -um: alive, living (2)

vix: scarcely (3)

vocō -āre: call (3)

volātilis -e: flying, fleeting (1)

volitō -āre: fly around (1)

volō velle voluī: wish, be willing (20)

volō -āre: fly (1)

voltur volturis m.: vulture (1)

voluptās -ātis f.: pleasure, enjoyment (3)

volvō volvere volvī volūtum: roll, wind, twist round (1)

vōs: you (pl.); (gen.) **vestrum/vestrī**, (dat./abl.) **vōbīs**, (acc.) **vōs** (7)

vōtum -ī n.: solemn promise, vow; hope (3)

vox vōcis f.: voice, utterance (6)

vulgus -ī n. and m.: the common people (3)

vulnus -eris n.: wound (2)

vultus -ūs m.: look, expression, face (10)

— Z —

Zephyrus -ī m.: a gentle west wind, the western breeze, zephyr (1)

zōna -ae f.: girdle (1)

This book need not end here…

At Open Book Publishers, we are changing the nature of the traditional academic book. The title you have just read will not be left on a library shelf, but will be accessed online by hundreds of readers each month across the globe. OBP publishes only the best academic work: each title passes through a rigorous peer-review process. We make all our books free to read online so that students, researchers and members of the public who can't afford a printed edition will have access to the same ideas.

This book and additional content is available at:
http://www.openbookpublishers.com/isbn/9781783741625

Customize

Personalize your copy of this book or design new books using OBP and third-party material. Take chapters or whole books from our published list and make a special edition, a new anthology or an illuminating coursepack. Each customized edition will be produced as a paperback and a downloadable PDF. Find out more at:

http://www.openbookpublishers.com/section/59/1

Donate

If you enjoyed this book, and feel that research like this should be available to all readers, regardless of their income, please think about donating to us. We do not operate for profit and all donations, as with all other revenue we generate, will be used to finance new Open Access publications.

http://www.openbookpublishers.com/section/13/1/support-us

You may also be interested in…

Cornelius Nepos, 'Life of Hannibal': Latin Text, Notes, Maps, Illustrations and Vocabulary
by Bret Mulligan

http://dx.doi.org/10.11647/OBP.0068
http://www.openbookpublishers.com/product/341

Cicero, On Pompey's Command (De Imperio), 27-49. Latin Text, Study Aids with Vocabulary, Commentary, and Translation
by Ingo Gildenhard, Louise Hodgson, et al.

http://dx.doi.org/10.11647/OBP.0045
http://www.openbookpublishers.com/product/284

Tacitus, Annals, 15.20-23, 33-45. Latin Text, Study Aids with Vocabulary, and Commentary
by Mathew Owen and Ingo Gildenhard

http://dx.doi.org/10.11647/OBP.0035
http://www.openbookpublishers.com/product/215

Virgil, Aeneid, 4.1-299. Latin Text, Study Questions, Commentary and Interpretative Essays
by Ingo Gildenhard

http://dx.doi.org/10.11647/OBP.0023
http://www.openbookpublishers.com/product/162